The Millionaire Mortgage Broker

The Millionaire Mortgage Broker

How to Start, Operate, and Manage a Successful Mortgage Company

Darrin J. Seppinni

McGraw-Hill

New York   Chicago   San Francisco
Lisbon   London   Madrid   Mexico City
Milan   New Delhi   San Juan   Seoul
Singapore   Sydney   Toronto

1 2 3 4 5 6 7 8 9 0   DOC/DOC   0 9 8 7 6

ISBN-13: 978-0-07-148156-4
ISBN-10:   0-07-148156-7

Silver Hill's Clear (Commercial Lending Easy as Residential) is a service mark of Silver Hill Financial, LLC.

Product or brand names used in this book may be trade names or trademarks. Where we believe that there may be proprietary claims to such trade names or trademarks, the name has been used with an initial capital or it has been capitalized in the style used by the name claimant. Regardless of the capitalization used, all such names have been used in an editorial manner without any intent to convey endorsement of or other affiliation with the name claimant. Neither the author nor the publisher intends to express any judgment as to the validity or legal status of any such proprietary claims.

This publication is designed to provide accurate and authoritative information in regard to the subject matter covered. It is sold with the understanding that neither the author nor the publisher is engaged in rendering legal, accounting, futures/securities trading, or other professional service. If legal advice or other expert assistance is required, the services of a competent professional person should be sought.

—From a Declaration of Principles jointly adopted by a Committee
of the American Bar Association and a Committee of Publishers

McGraw-Hill books are available at special quantity discounts to use as premiums and sales promotions, or for use in corporate training programs. For more information, please write to the Director of Special Sales, Professional Publishing, McGraw-Hill, Two Penn Plaza, New York, NY 10121-2298. Or contact your local bookstore.

*To my wife, Jayne, for teaching me the importance of love
and family*

CONTENTS

ACKNOWLEDGMENTS

It's often said that creating anything of value rarely is accomplished without the help of others. Such is the case with this book. I am deeply grateful to all who helped bring this project to life. A special thanks to Silver Hill Financial, LLC for their contribution on small balance commercial loans and to AllRegs for their contribution on regulations and compliance.

I want to take this opportunity to thank my family for their unwavering support throughout my life in both good times and bad. To my brothers, Kevin and Steven, both great successful salesmen who unselfishly contributed their suggestions and viewpoints on many topics that I covered in this book. My little sister, Leslie, who has grown into a beautiful and intelligent woman. As a recent Ph.D. graduate, she has a bright and successful career ahead with only the sky as her limit. I offer my very special thanks to my mother, Victoria, for all of her inspiration and remarkable strength. It was her strength that I thought of when times were rough, realizing that my challenges were dwarfed in comparison to what she has been through. She is my driving force and motivation. Finally I want to thank two very special women in my professional life: Meredith Bernstein, my literary agent, and Mary Glenn, my editorial director from McGraw-Hill, for all of their support on this project. I thank them both for believing in me.

INTRODUCTION

For years I have been assisting mortgage professionals with their efforts in becoming mortgage brokers. Lately, with the recent housing boom and all the media attention on the money that is being made in the mortgage industry, it seems that every other person I meet, from housewives to attorneys to accountants, wants to know how they too can start a mortgage business.

No Longer the Good Old Boys Club

The mortgage broker business has long been composed of small privately held businesses, firms founded by trailblazers and their protégés. It is not uncommon to find many husband-and-wife and father-and-son teams and, in some cases, an entire family can own and run a mortgage brokerage. In earlier years people would only enter the mortgage industry because of someone they knew—networking. It was always hard for outsiders to penetrate this industry because of the lack of training and information available.

I felt this was the right time to share the wealth of information that I have learned over the past two decades, from every important rule to every strategic move necessary to successfully run a mortgage brokerage. But that wasn't enough. I decided to gather information from hundreds of successful mortgage brokerages across the country to help me identify their successful formulas. As a result, this book has evolved after three years of research. In this book I reveal to you all the secrets, the most valuable information you will need. In that sense, I think of this book as your road map to success. Anyone with a burning desire to succeed can follow this step-by-step guide into one of the most financially rewarding businesses available today.

This book is more than a mere how-to book. As the founder of several mortgage brokerages, a mortgage bank, an escrow company, and the creator of Mortgage Smarts, I have interacted extensively with mortgage professionals. I have been extremely fortunate to be trained by the original pioneers of mortgage brokering, and throughout my career I have created alliances with some of the brightest minds in the business. Because of my time-tested experience, I know what works and what doesn't. By reading this book, you will learn proven success strategies that can help you avoid making costly mistakes as you start your own mortgage brokerage. Every possible topic is covered: from opening and managing an office, to creating business and strategizing for the future. With this book I will catapult you right to the top, saving you time and a bundle of money.

In the past people have thought of the mortgage business as being very complex, but with this easy-to-follow guide you learn how relatively simple the mortgage broker business can be. I have tried to demystify the mortgage broker business with this all-in-one resource book. Another misconception is that the business is boring. Well, let me tell you this: There is nothing boring about making a six-figure income in your first year. The mortgage industry gets in your blood. I love to help people achieve the American dream of homeownership by helping them with their financing needs. There is no more rewarding and satisfying business than the mortgage broker business.

The Opportunity

The mortgage industry is a billion-dollar business. There are countless success stories from individuals who have started a mortgage brokerage with no financial background and little money invested. Former mortgage brokers come from all walks of life, rich and poor, and from a variety of former professions, everything from dancers and restaurateurs to attorneys and newscasters.

We begin this book with a look at just a handful of success stories that will inspire anyone seeking a true business opportunity. If you have a burning desire to succeed, if you have determination, starting your own mortgage broker business is right for you. You may be the next Angelo Mozilo. Who is Angelo Mozilo? The biggest success story is that of Mr. Mozilo, who, along with his partner, started a mortgage company from an apartment in New York City that has become an industry giant, known as Countrywide Mortgage. *Forbes* magazine listed Mr. Mozilo as the ninth-highest-paid CEO in 2004 with personal compensation at $96.9 million along with a cash bonus of $17.3 million. This year his personal compensation is estimated to reach $100 million.

So who is this book for? Let me put it this way. A mortgage brokerage is unique in that an individual can choose to work from home and be a sole proprietor or open a full mortgage brokerage hiring several employees. This is a true equal opportunity business world; everyone is welcomed and has an equal opportunity at success. You don't need a college degree; you simply need a license and each state has its own licensing requirements. A few states have some educational course requirements. As an added bonus, Chapter 10 lists the educational and licensing requirements for a mortgage broker in all states from Alabama to Wyoming.

Whether you are a realtor, attorney, or accountant looking for an additional revenue stream; a loan originator looking to go to the next level and start his or her own mortgage brokerage; or just about anyone looking for a business opportunity, this is the book for you. So get ready for the opportunity of a lifetime, and welcome to the mortgage business!

The Millionaire Mortgage Broker

CHAPTER 1

INTRODUCTION TO THE MORTGAGE BROKERAGE BUSINESS

Success Stories

What Is a Mortgage Broker?

History of a Mortgage Broker

Success Stories

Opportunity + Determination = Success

Opportunity is an opening affording a possibility for success. You must make yourself available in order to spot the opening and take a chance. Determination is a firmness of purpose. It is the quality of being determined to do or achieve something. A person with purpose and much determination can achieve the impossible.

Mortgage brokering is undoubtedly the business of the future. A relatively new profession, mortgage brokers only evolved since the late 1970s, yet their success and growth rate have been truly phenomenal. Already 60 percent of mortgage brokers are in the top 25 percent income bracket in the United States. Mortgage brokering has created many a millionaire so it's easy to see why this industry has been dubbed "the new Wall Street."

In 1992 mortgage brokers accounted for a mere 25 percent of all mortgages processed in the United States. In 2004 mortgage brokers accounted for 68 percent of the $2.8 trillion in origination activity. The industry's fast growth rate is largely due to the lower-cost expense structure of a mortgage broker that allows him or her to offer lower rates and fees to consumers than a traditional mortgage lender. In fact, while the number of mortgage lenders continues to decline with mergers and consolidation, the number of mortgage brokers continues to grow.

However, nothing is more inspiring than to read the incredible success stories of literally thousands of individuals who began their careers with little money invested only to eventually become millionaires. Previously these stories were only shared within the mortgage industry, including the prestigious list of "Top 200" loan originators that is produced annually by the *Mortgage Originator Magazine* (*M.O.M.*). However, the mortgage industry is now mainstream and the general public is taking notice. I see more and more of these success stories featured in newspapers and media outlets across the country. I'd like to share just a handful of these inspiring stories to reveal the endless opportunities within the mortgage industry. You'll discover that with sheer determination, the possibilities are truly limitless.

Glenn Stearns

First Pacific Financial / Stearns Lending

Glenn Stearns grew up in a rough neighborhood in Maryland. He fathered a child in the eighth grade at age 14. Fueled by spirit and determined to overcome many obstacles, he managed to put himself through college.

As a college graduate Glenn Stearns drove out from Maryland to California with nothing more than a backpack to sleep on the floor of a friend's apartment. His story as it goes is that he was walking along the coast in Orange County marveling at the million-dollar estates and wondering how he could obtain this spectacular lifestyle. He decided to knock on the door of one beautiful home to ask what the owner did for a living. The answer was "real estate," and he says that is what decided his future right then and there.

After working as a loan officer for only 10 months, he decided to start his own business. That was in 1989. His business really took off when he negotiated a contract with the Department of

Housing and Urban Development (HUD) and became the largest HUD settlement company in the country. He also owned the largest Federal Housing Administration (FHA) auditing firm in the country.

Today Mr. Stearns heads a billion-dollar empire—Stearns Lending—which generates over $1.5 billion in sales with over $100 million in assets and credit lines of over $350 million. He was named Ernst & Young 2002 Entrepreneur of the Year.

Mr. Stearns began getting national attention when he appeared on *The Oprah Winfrey Show* in 2003, on a segment that featured how he and his wife (a former entertainment reporter) met in Las Vegas and later married. It included a view of their palatial estate in Newport Beach, California.

Now Mr. and Mrs. Stearns are getting a lot more attention after appearing on a reality show, "The Real Gilligan's Island." They beat out 14 contestants and won the cash prize of $250,000. They took the $250,000 and matched another $250,000 to donate to the Stearns Family Charitable Foundation, an organization dedicated to helping disadvantaged youth reach their full potential.

Source:
Daily Pilot: "Cast as Castaways, 2004."

Leif Thomsen

Mortgage Masters

Leif Thomsen is the 42-year-old founder of Mortgage Masters, a Massachusetts mortgage firm. He was born in Denmark and left school at age 14. A former restaurateur, he worked briefly as a mortgage broker before starting his own mortgage company.

In 1988, starting his business from a spare bedroom, in his first year he sold $50 million in loans earning him $500,000 in commissions. In 2002, Mortgage Masters, Inc., brokered 11,000 loans valued at $3 billion, earning Mr. Thomsen $10 million.

It's not just Mr. Thomsen making all the money. In 2002 five brokers working for his company earned more than $1 million, with his top salesperson, Tom Digan (a former electrical salesman), earning a whopping $1.7 million. In 2003 five of his loan originators were in the top 10 spots of the "200 List of Top Producers" by *Mortgage Originator Magazine*. They were:

#2 Tom Digan	$387 million originations
#3 Gerald McCarthy	$306 million originations
#5 Dave Gibbs	$250 million originations
#6 John Kalin	$220 million originations
#8 Luis Rodi	$203 million originations

Another employee of Mr. Thomsen, Mark Shippie was driving a Pepsi truck when a loan officer from Mortgage Masters driving a luxury car refinanced his home loan. Begging Mr. Thomsen for an opportunity as a mortgage originator, he quit his steady job to earn $480,000 in 2002, 10 times what he was paid as a Pepsi truck driver!

This business is for everyone. A young woman with absolutely no experience went to work for Mr. Thomsen and in her first year earned $750,000. He says, "I don't know of any business where you can do that." In fact the first woman to break the $100 million barrier was Bridgett Keator of Mortgage Masters, who ranked #24 nationwide in 2003 with $150 million originations.

In 2004 Mr. Thomsen was MortgageDaily.com's Mortgage Icon of the Year. He said, "This is a fantastic business for anybody out there who is a go-getter. . . . There's no other business you can come in without an education and make good money."

Sources:
Wall Street Journal Online: "Mortgage Brokers Benefit from Refinancing Boom," 2003.

MortgageDaily.com: "$10 Million Broker Is MortgageDaily.com Icon in 2003."

Mortgage Originator and Broker Magazine, Vol. 6, No. 4.

Angelo Mozilo

Countrywide Financial Corp.

Of course there is no bigger story and no bigger accomplishment than that of Mr. Angelo Mozilo who along with his partner,

David Loeb, started a mortgage company out of a New York City apartment in 1969, only to grow it into the nation's No. 1 mortgage lender.

Mr. Mozilo has a humble background as the son of a butcher, who grew up in the Bronx, worked as a messenger boy at age 14 for a mortgage company, and worked himself through Fordham University. As chairman and CEO of Countrywide Financial, Mr. Mozilo's personal compensation in 2005 alone will reach $100 million, the *New York Times* reports. Last year his cash bonus of $17.3 million, was the largest among chief executives of all companies in the Standard & Poor's 500-stock index, according to Paul Hodgson of the Corporate Library, a corporate governance organization.

Countrywide Financial is listed on the New York Stock Exchange. *Fortune Magazine* reports that over the last 20 years, Countrywide had the best stock market performance of any financial services company, delivering a staggering 23,000 percent return to investors.

With 50,000 employees, Countrywide's success partly can be attributed to its heavy penetration of local real estate and builder offices—795 offices in total.

Mr. Mozilo was quoted as saying that he felt underestimated and was bothered by the snobbish attitude of the people on Wall Street who came from Ivy League schools. He went on to say that in his younger years when he was asked what business he was in and he replied "the mortgage business," people would say, "Second mortgages? Sub-prime?" He thought people said this because of his appearance. He says today when he meets a stranger he no longer says he is a mortgage guy. "Now I say I run a financial services business....I don't know why. It makes me feel better, I guess—status."

Sources:
New York Times: "The Mortgage Maker vs. the World," Oct. 2005.

MortgageDaily.com: "Top 5 Personalities in Mortgage Lending during 2003," Dec. 2003.

Judy Dunham

AME Financial

Judy Dunham had an interesting background working as a librarian, teacher, a women's counselor, waitress, and even a casino 21 card dealer before entering the mortgage business. She began her mortgage career as a girl Friday for a mortgage brokerage where she was paid $1,000 a month. After only two years she got her broker's license and formed AME Financial with two other loan officers. That was in 1984. In 1986 Ms. Dunham became the sole owner of AME Financial, and today it is one of the largest privately owned lenders in the country, funding $3 billion in loans in 2004.

Ms. Dunham received the 2005 Mortgage Sales Excellence Award at the Third Annual Top Women Producers and Managers Conference.

This is an incredible accomplishment. Anyone who can withstand the ups and downs of the mortgage market after 20 years deserves recognition and respect.

Ms. Dunham says the following about being a woman in the mortgage industry: "If I've encountered discrimination over the years in the mortgage industry, it really has only been reverse discrimination in my favor. There are a lot of women in the mortgage industry, and they tend to bend over backwards to help a female owner."

She goes on to say, "I wanted to find something where I could make money and have fun.... It gets in your blood."

Source:
Broker Magazine: "An Event for Top Women Producers Honors Judy Dunham with Its Sales Excellence Award," Vol. 7, No. 7.

Joseph Aldeguer

Mortgage Exchange

Joseph Aldeguer is the 38-year-old founder of The Mortgage Exchange—a Chicago mortgage firm. A college dropout, his previous profession was a commodities salesman. He and his then girlfriend started the business with $12,000 that he put on his credit card.

His girlfriend became his wife, and Jill Moore is a 50–50 partner and the company's chief financial officer. Jill, a high school graduate, grew up on a farm outside of Peoria. Her former jobs included receptionist, a fill-in aerobics instructor at a health club, and a manager at a leather clothing shop. Her previous salary was $35,000 a year.

Mr. Aldeguer has an hour-long radio show with topics on real estate investment that generates leads for his 200 employees. In 2004 his company generated a total revenue of approximately $12.5 million, earning Joseph and Jill between $6.25 million and $12 million.

Joseph and Jill weren't the only ones making money in their new careers. Galvin Beal a loan officer working for the Aldeguers was a former accountant who had been laid off three times before he was hired at The Mortgage Exchange in 2001. Gavin is now earning more than $100,000 a year, more than double his previous $40,000 a year accounting jobs.

Source:
New York Times: "With Mortgages, Instant Wealth for Middlemen," Oct. 2005.

Jon Volpe

Nova Home Loans

Jon Volpe is CEO of Nova Home Loans, an Arizona mortgage firm. He has a very interesting background starting off as an abandoned teen living in a garage with his drug-abusing brother. It was entirely possible that he would end up following in his brother's footsteps.

Overcoming many obstacles, including physical—at a slightly below average height of 5′7′′—he became a three-sport star in high school and eventually made it to Stanford University, where he was leading rusher in the Pac-10 conference. His lifetime goal was to play football for the Pittsburgh Steelers but after suffering a career-ending injury with the Canadian Football League he returned to his hometown of Tucson, Arizona, to rehab his shoulder. That is where he met his now partner, Ray Desmond, who at the time owned a company called Nova Financial & Investments, Inc.

After only six months in the mortgage business, Mr. Volpe decided he wanted to become the top producer at Nova. He immediately set goals for himself and then exceeded them, just as he had done in his sports career. After achieving the number 1 spot as loan originator for Nova for seven consecutive years, he decided to reach higher at a spot in the top 1,000 in the country. He landed in the top 100, then top 10, and eventually landed the top number 1 spot in 2001 and again in 2003. In 2003 Mr. Volpe was the number 1 national top producer of the prestigious Mortgage Originator award by originating a total of $411 million.

Now a millionaire, Mr. Volpe has a reputation as a charitable man who donates six figures to groups such as The Boys & Girls Club of Tucson, Toys for Tots, and his own charity, Miracle on 16th Avenue. He says, "I remember how Jim Click (a local car dealer) would pay so that I could attend football camps in high school. I always said that someday I wanted to be in a position to do the same for others."

Source:
Tucson Weekly: "Like Trying to Catch a Cannonball," Feb. 2004.

Doug Bui, President

J. C. Jimenez, Vice President

East West Mortgage

Doug Bui, 57, is a native of Vietnam and founder of East West Mortgage, a Virginia mortgage firm. In 1986 Mr. Bui started East West Mortgage with a staff of three, including himself, his sister, and a part-time employee. Today the company employs more than 400 employees and is licensed in 44 states. East West Mortgage closed $1.5 billion in mortgage loans in 2005.

When Mr. Bui first started East West Mortgage, he took risks with different marketing approaches. Early on he employed the use of the Internet even though it was not yet a proven business model. As one of the first in the industry to use the Internet as a marketing tool, he was well ahead of the pack when this form of marketing became mainstream.

In 1996 J. C. Jimenez and his family came to the United States from Colombia. A civil engineer he went to work for East West Mortgage and learned the business from the ground up. Today he is vice president of sales, helping round out a multiethnic company, dominating the "emerging market" of first-time buyers.

East West offers 24/7 services via the Internet or phone with loan services in 10 different languages and a strong focus on the Hispanic community. *Broker Magazine* estimates East West to be the seventh largest lender to Hispanics in the country.

In April 2005 East West Mortgage became the first company to form an advertising partnership with Washington, D.C.'s new Hispanic radio station, El Zol 99.1 FM. El Zol is focusing on the Hispanic community as its next major market nationwide and is working hard to promote the new D.C. station.

Jimenez said, "If you are foreign, and nothing else connects you to the environment, certainly owning a home gives you a sense of stability. It is the very first real step into the American dream. That is the only way not to live from paycheck to paycheck, especially for low-income buyers. The only thing that allows you to leverage any kind of money is your home. It is ensuring a much better quality of life."

Sources:

Timescommunity.com: "Cutting-edge Strategy, Hard Work Help East West Mortgage Grow," July 2005.

Hispanic PR Wire: "East West Mortgage Joins New FM Radio Station to Continue Outreach to D.C.'s Growing Hispanic Market," April 2005.

Arthur Aranda

Garden State Mortgage

Arthur Aranda started Garden State Mortgage, a New Jersey mortgage firm, in 1991, as a sole proprietor/mortgage broker with no investors. A Mexican-American farmer from Wisconsin, he began his mortgage career as a loan processor and then a loan officer. He says, "As different as it was from anything I had done, I found it to be satisfying and fascinating. I decided I wanted to succeed in the mortgage business."

Today his company has five locations in the New Jersey area, is licensed in four states as a direct lender, and funds more than $250 million a year. In April 2003, Mr. Aranda was named as one of the top 100 Latino entrepreneurs in *Hispanic Magazine*.

According to the U.S. Census Bureau 2000, New Jersey has the sixth-largest Hispanic population in the country. Estimated to have the fifth-largest concentration of Latino businesses, Latinos represent over 14 percent of New Jersey's population.

In 1997 Garden State Mortgage began a program directed at helping more area Hispanics own homes by encouraging and educating Spanish-speaking home buyers. Mr. Aranda says, "Even though Hispanics have become the largest ethnic minority in the country, they lag behind in home-buying statistics.... One of our goals is to help reverse that trend, and we have seen an increase in Hispanic homeownership since we started this program."

Garden State provides brochures, application forms, and loan documents and conducts $2\frac{1}{2}$-hour First Time Homebuyer Seminars in Spanish. In addition, Mr. Aranda has a Spanish-language Web site at www.casadehipotecas.com. His targeted niche awards him with a 90 percent referral-based business.

In 2003, Garden State Mortgage became the first employee-owned mortgage company in New Jersey, and the first mortgage company in the United States to implement an Employee Stock Option/Ownership Plan (ESOP). An ESOP, an IRS-qualified benefit plan, enables employees to invest in employee stock, resulting in an employee-owned company. Mr. Aranda says, "For people who work their whole lives there is nothing better than to have an ownership interest in the company they help to build.... I hope that Garden State Mortgage Corp. becomes an example for other New Jersey businesses to follow."

Hispanic purchasing power continues to energize the nation's consumer market. According to projections of the Selig Center study, Hispanics controlled about $736 billion in spending power in 2005 and is expected to grow 8.8 percent up to $1 trillion by 2008. Other consumer spending is expected to grow by 4.9 percent.

Carol Johnson

Johnson Mortgage Corporation

Carol Johnson founded Johnson Mortgage Corporation (JMC) in 1993, a Louisiana mortgage firm.

Ms. Johnson began her mortgage-banking career at age 25, as an entry-level loan processor. Her hard work and determination quickly led to her managerial position after only one year. In 1985 United Federal Savings and Loan Association recruited Ms. Johnson to launch the first minority-owned mortgage-banking operation in Louisiana. In 1990 she served as Executive Director of the New Orleans Home Mortgage Authority and restructured the agency to efficiently provide assistance grants to needy first-time home buyers.

Her expertise in agency-assisted grants enabled her to offer those same loan programs when she formed her own company. To assist families who earn less than 80 percent of the median income in the area, JMC provides financing for many local non-profit agencies such as:

- Desire Community Housing Corporation
- Concerned Citizens for a Better Algiers
- The City of New Orleans

In addition, JMC works with a community down payment assistance program, referred to as the Soft 2nd Mortgage Program, which issues $25,000 to eligible home buyers.

Ms. Johnson and JMC have received the following awards:

- Ms. Johnson has been awarded the Golden Hammer Award for being voted #1 Lender in New Orleans, 1997, 2001
- The Federal Housing Commissioner recognized JMC as one of the top five FHA-approved lenders in the United

States for providing FHA-insured mortgages to African-American first-time home buyers, 1997

- The Women's League of New Orleans acknowledged Ms. Johnson for outstanding service in helping single mothers achieve homeownership, 1997–2004

Ms. Johnson founded JMC with a vision that she could end the inconsistencies and inattention placed on female and minority home buyers. Today Ms. Johnson takes pride in her part in helping more than 7,000 Metropolitan New Orleans families finance their homes.

Vance Leudtke

Alpine Affiliates

One of the youngest owners of a mortgage brokerage may well be Vance Leudtke, founder of Alpine Affiliates, an Arizona mortgage firm. After six years in the Marine Corps and three years in Reserve Officer Training Corps (ROTC), Mr. Leudtke at the ripe age of 28, along with his wife, Casey, founded Alpine Affiliates in 1997.

Alpine Affiliates was originally founded in Brooklyn Center, Minnesota, where Mr. Leudtke began his career as a partner with another mortgage firm. In 1999 the Leudtkes relocated to Arizona, prompted by the exploding real estate growth that the state was experiencing.

Driven to start a different type of mortgage company, he wanted to combine mortgage lending and title and appraisal services to offer home buyers a "one-stop-shopping experience." Since then the business has evolved to several different profit centers: Alpine Lending, Equity Management, Inc., American Home Realty, and Metro Title.

With more than 500 employees and eight branch locations in four states, it's no surprise that the company gained the 30th national spot in *Broker Magazine*'s "Top Brokers in 2001."

Since then Alpine continues to grow at a substantial rate. In 2003 the company was said to generate more than $38 million in revenue by processing nearly $500 million in residential real estate loans.

Mr. Leudtke says the key to his success is "assembling a team of the best executives, and offering world-class customer service across the board."

Source:
BizAz Magazine: "Young Entrepreneurs," 2003.

What Is a Mortgage Broker?

The proper definition of a mortgage broker is a licensed professional who solicits borrowers and negotiates, finds, and places mortgage loans for a fee. The job of a mortgage broker is to originate and shop the loan on behalf of the borrower in order to find the loan program with the lowest rate and cost. A mortgage broker arranges a mortgage with the intention of brokering that loan to a lender and/or bank. Typically a mortgage broker has established relationships with several lenders or banks, thus having an extensive choice of loan programs. A professional mortgage broker has a wide knowledge of loan products (from A paper loans to sub-prime loans). This enables a mortgage broker to provide a loan for almost *any* customer with almost *any* financial situation. The mortgage broker serves both the borrower and the lender and will work as the middleman throughout the loan process.

However, mortgage brokers are not simply "middlemen." They provide an invaluable service in our communities by educating and guiding consumers through the complicated process of residential mortgage lending. Because mortgage brokers are typically small business owners, they are able to save the consumers substantial amounts of money. A recent study conducted by Georgetown University reveals that mortgage broker customers pay lower costs and a lower annual percentage rate (APR) than those provided by creditors within the same lending arena. Consumers who go through a mortgage broker are more likely to be better informed about loan costs, loan programs, and options. J.D. Powers & Associates reported, "Mortgage Brokers provide a valuable service for home loan customers, and they may be more in tune with customer satisfaction and advocacy."

Mortgage brokers do not actually lend the money in a residential mortgage transaction. The broker is paid a commission for finding

1. A loan from the consumer and/or

2. A percentage of the loan (in a yield-spread premium) from the lender for bringing them the loan

The mortgage broker is an independent contractor, and the loan is simply "brokered" to the lender/bank; thus the loan is closed under the lender/bank's name. There are some circumstances when a broker will act as a bank and fund the loan under their own name, but in most cases a mortgage broker performs origination services up to the point of funding.

What Does a Mortgage Broker Do?

A mortgage broker does the following:

- Determines the consumer's financial goals and circumstances.

- Prequalifies the borrower for a loan by running a credit report and taking an initial loan application, referred to in the industry as a 1003.

- Shops the loan with various lenders to find the loan that best suits the consumer's needs with the best rate and terms available.

- Provides the borrower with required predisclosures (predisclosing estimated fees, rate, and terms of the proposed loan).

- Obtains a preapproval from the lender and/or bank.

- Collects all the necessary documentation requested by the lender or bank for final approval.

- Orders an appraisal (that is paid for by the borrower).

- Orders a title policy and exam (a report used to verify the legal owner of the property along with a public records search for any court judgments or liens against the property. This report is paid for by the borrower at the closing of the loan.)

- Submits the loan package to the lender for final approval. Once the lender approves the loan (reviews all documentation including the appraisal of the property and title examination), the loan documents are ready for signing. The mortgage broker will arrange the signing of the loan documents. This is done between the settlement/ escrow company and the lender or bank that prepares the loan documents.

- Follows up with the settlement or closing company to ensure that the loan documents are returned to the lender for funding.

- Follows up with the lender to make sure that all funding conditions are met and the loan is ready to fund.

How Is the Mortgage Broker Paid?

Once the loan is funded, the settlement/escrow company releases loan funds to all parties involved. Mortgage brokers typically charge an origination fee to the borrower for their services. This fee is reflected in the predisclosures and in the final closing statement. In addition a mortgage broker may earn a yield spread premium. A yield spread premium (YSP, also referred to as a rebate) is a percentage of the loan amount (typically 1, 2, or 3 percent) that the broker is paid for bringing the loan to the lender. This fee is included in the rate. It is not an additional cost to the borrower. However, it is RESPA law to reflect this premium on the Good Faith Estimate in order to disclose to the borrower that the interest rate obtained is higher than par pricing and, therefore, provides a rebate to the broker. The yield spread premium is reflected again at closing on the settlement statement form HUD1. The closing statement identifies the amount to be paid and the payee. The mortgage broker receives his or her pay directly from the escrow company.

How Much Can a Mortgage Broker Earn?

High volume is the driving force in the mortgage industry. A mortgage broker is paid a percentage (usually 1 to 3 percent) of the loan amount as compensation for their services. Therefore, on a loan amount of $250,000 a broker's compensation can be anywhere from $2,500 to $7,500. The more loans you close, the more you are paid. For example, if you close 10 loans in a month, your compensation could range between a low of $25,000 to $75,000 for that month. Compensations like these have made mortgage brokers some of the most profitable small businesses in this country.

Can a Mortgage Broker Work from Home?

In most cases a mortgage broker is allowed to work from home. However, each state has its own regulations for licensing of a home-based mortgage brokerage. Chapter 10 contains detailed educational and licensing requirements for mortgage brokers in all 50 states.

What Does It Take to Become a Mortgage Broker?

Many people would say that salesmanship would be the most important skill of a mortgage broker. I happen to disagree. You can develop sales skills but if you are not comfortable selling, you certainly can hire top salespeople for your organization. It is more important to be a great marketer rather than a great salesperson. You have to *get* the business first in order to sell anything. If you want to develop or enhance any skill, pick marketing. This is surely what you will need to become successful.

Fundamental skills required to properly conduct business would include basic knowledge of mathematics to at least high school level, integrity, and honesty. Strong interpersonal skills to help you build a quick rapport with clients, financial institutions, and other real estate professionals are essential.

Lastly, you must qualify for licensing. In Chapter 10 you will find a detailed list of all requirements necessary to become a licensed mortgage broker in your particular state.

History of a Mortgage Broker

Before there were any mortgage bankers or brokers, consumers had to rely on traditional bank financing for a home loan. A consumer who needed a home loan would go down to his or her local bank and accept the interest rate, terms, and fee offered by the bank agent. At the time, banks serviced their own loans so in many cases consumers would pay their mortgage payment at their bank. Consumers had limited resources when shopping for a home loan and even fewer options in mortgage products. The norm was 80 percent loan-to-value loans with a rare option for a 90 or 95 percent loan-to-value, always requiring private mortgage insurance. There was no 100 percent financing.

In the early 1980s conventional loans were handled by banks and savings-and-loan associations (S&Ls), and mortgage bankers handled government loans. The mortgage broker profession evolved from the old thrift-based business typically handling equity loans and loans that were turned down by banks. The deregulation of the lending industry created a more competitive marketplace. Ultimately S&Ls were replaced by mortgage bankers, and mortgage brokers continued to evolve.

These days, lenders do not keep mortgages. They sell them in bundles in the secondary market, to three of the main purchasers of loans: Fannie Mae, Freddie Mac, and Ginnie Mae. These mortgages are then sold as "mortgage-backed securities" on Wall Street. Mortgage lenders and banks realized that it was not cost-effective to open a branch in every little town across America so they began relying more and more on the services of mortgage brokers. This process allowed the brokers to compete with the banks, thereby driving down the cost of credit to the consumer.

The mortgage financing system has come a long way in 20 years. Today, a consumer has access to an unlimited selection of mortgage products and options.

Why Do Lenders Use the Services of a Mortgage Broker?

Some mortgage lenders and banks have their own *retail* division, where the lender has a loan origination department for the purpose of origination loans directly to the consumer. However, to maintain a large overhead for receptionists, loan officers, processors, underwriters, closers, and shippers, lenders have to mark up their rates twice as high as the rate offered to the mortgage broker in its *wholesale* department. Wholesale is when a mortgage lender or bank offers its loan products to mortgage brokers, allowing the mortgage broker to originate the loan and offer its loan products to the consumer. Again, because the mortgage broker typically has a lower overhead than the mortgage lender or bank, it can afford to offer a lower rate than if the consumer had gone directly to the lender or bank.

Mortgage brokers are entrepreneurs who have been able to find a niche in the market and provide very valuable and important services to both the lender and consumer. The purchase of a home is the largest transaction most consumers will encounter. That in itself is a terrifying experience. A mortgage broker guides the consumer through the tedious lending process. A broker will work as a liaison between the borrower, real estate agency, processor, lender/underwriter, appraiser, title company, and settlement or closing attorney.

As our unemployment claims rise across the country, the jobs in the mortgage industry continue to grow, with a 10 percent increase from 2004. The Bureau of Statistics reports that approximately 500,000 people were working in the mortgage industry in 2005.

Why Do Consumers Use a Mortgage Broker?

There are three main reasons why consumers seek out a mortgage broker for their real estate financing needs.

1. The mortgage broker is well entrenched in our neighborhoods, easily attracting the consumer.

2. A mortgage broker deals with a vast number of mortgage lenders increasing the variety of loans that can be offered to the consumer. This enables the mortgage broker to find the ideal loan for the consumer's needs.

3. The broker is usually a small business owner, who has a lower overhead than a lender or bank and thus is capable of offering a lower cost for the loan.

National Association of Mortgage Brokers

Code of Ethics

Honesty & Integrity NAMB members shall conduct business in a manner reflecting honesty, honor, and integrity.

Professional Conduct NAMB members shall conduct their business activities in a professional manner.

Honesty in Advertising NAMB members shall endeavor to be accurate in all advertisements and solicitations.

Compliance with Law NAMB members shall conduct their business in compliance with all applicable laws and regulations.

Confidentiality NAMB members shall avoid unauthorized disclosure of confidential information.

Disclosure of Financial Interests NAMB members shall disclose any equity or financial interest they may have in the collateral being offered to secure a loan.

CHAPTER 2

HOW TO GET STARTED

Forming Your Mortgage Company

Preparing for State Licensure

State Licensing Terms and Definitions

Forming Your Mortgage Company

Knowledge + Preparation = Money

Knowledge is the understanding gained through information, learning, or study. Information is a collection of facts and data. A person with knowledge is ahead of the game. Preparation is the measure to be ready for a particular purpose. Success cannot be achieved before knowledge and preparation have been attained.

It was 1987 when my partner and I decided to open up our own mortgage company.

I had had a successful five-year career as a loan originator by developing relationships with new home builders and servicing their developments. My partner had established relationships with real estate brokers and their agents. When the mortgage company we worked for decided to close its doors, my partner and I decided to go for it and open up our own company. Neither of us had ever been self-employed, but we were young go-getters who were willing to learn.

At the beginning we did not yet have an office. We actually began in the living room of our processor's home. The second month in business we were profitable. We were so busy that the money just started rolling in. It was truly remarkable. I remember taking our deposits to the bank and the teller asking me, "What business are you in?"

In those days a mortgage broker was a fresh new face in the mortgage industry. There were no training materials and no information available for a young entrepreneur like myself. In fact, there was no Web access, no computer, actually no fax machine yet. We hand carried verifications and personally delivered and picked up loan documents. When computers came into the picture, our mortgage company was one of the first to use a network system for our loan originators. We were pioneers leading the way for a brand-new industry that has grown by leaps and bounds in just 20 years.

Don't get me wrong. There were many challenges that we encountered, but we persevered, sharing all the rewards that come with a successful and growing mortgage company. My partner and I eventually parted, both accomplishing separate successful careers. Becoming self-employed and owning my own mortgage company brought me more satisfaction than I could have ever dreamed. It was the best decision I ever made, and I never looked back.

These days, there are still many challenges a new business owner faces, and there are specific challenges for the mortgage broker. The financial rewards for a successful mortgage broker are boundless. However, every mortgage broker starting out always wants to know: What does it take to be successful? I always say the same thing: *knowledge and preparation.*

How Do I Get Started?

One of the first decisions you will make as an entrepreneur will be to determine which type of business structure to use in your company formation, be it a sole proprietorship, corporation, partnership, LLC, or LLP. The type of business structure you choose will determine your personal liability and tax implications.

Mortgage brokers are not allowed to apply for state licensure as individuals.

I suggest that you review very carefully the benefits and disadvantages of each business structure, and, if necessary, consult with a professional. I will begin by providing a review of the characteristics for each business structure.

Sole Proprietorship

A sole proprietorship is the most common and simplest form of business structure. A sole proprietorship has no legal entity. The business is owned and managed by one person. A sole proprietor has complete control over the business and its operations and is financially and legally responsible for all debts and legal actions against the business.

To get started as a sole proprietor, you can simply walk into your county clerk's office and apply for a business permit. There are no formal or legal organizational arrangements to be made as with the other types of business structures. One exception is when a business is conducted under a name that does not show the owner's surname. In that case, some states (like California) require that the owner file a fictitious business name statement (or trade name) and post notice. Check with your state for trade name requirements.

Check with your secretary of state and county clerk's office to determine whether the business name you have chosen is available. For trademark registrations, you may check online at: www.uspto.gov.

Because a sole proprietorship is not a separate legal entity, it does not require that taxes be filed separately. All profits and losses of the business are reported and filed with the owner's personal income tax return. These figures are found in Schedule C of an individual's federal income tax return.

Corporation

A corporation is a separate and distinct entity from the people who control, manage, and own it. A corporation can open a bank account, own property, and do business, all under its own corporate name. A corporation is owned by its stockholders (also known as shareholders) who are *not* personally liable for the debts and liabilities of the corporation. One key reason for forming a corporation is the limited liability protection provided to its owners.

Stockholders are the owners who elect a board of directors, who in turn elect the officers. The board of directors is responsible for making major business decisions and overseeing the general affairs of the corporation. The officers of a corporation under the supervision of the board of directors are responsible for the day-to-day management of the corporation. A corporation generally must have three officers: a president, a treasurer, and a secretary. A person may hold more than one office, and in fact the same person may hold all three offices.

In general there are two types of corporate structures. One type is a *closely* held corporation, where there is a small number of stockholders who own the corporation's shares who are also the officers and board members who work for the corporation. The *publicly* held company is the opposite. The stockholders may be part of the public, and thus the stockholders are not exclusively board members or officers of the corporation.

The main difference between a C corporation and an S corporation is the consideration of federal tax laws. A C corporation is the traditional corporation that pays its corporate tax returns (first time taxed) and then distributes its profits to its stockholders. When the stockholders pay income tax on those dividends (second time taxed), they encounter what is referred to as double taxation.

In order to avoid double taxation, a corporation may elect to be taxed as a pass-through with a Form 2553. Filing this form with the IRS converts a C corporation to an S corporation. Sole proprietorships, partnerships, an LLC, and S corporations are pass-through entities. This means that these entities are not subject to income tax. Instead the owners are taxed individually on the income, taking into consideration their share of the profits and losses.

The disadvantage of a corporation is the huge aspect of corporate formalities that must be followed in order to receive the benefits of being a corporation. A corporation is ruled by its articles of incorporation and bylaws, which must be filed with the commissioner or secretary of state. Once you receive the filed articles of incorporation, which signifies the formation of a corporation in your state, your corporation will need to hold an organizational meeting of the initial stockholders and directors. At this meeting the directors will typically adopt corporate bylaws, distribute corporation stock to its stockholders, and appoint corporate officers. In most states, directors must meet at least once a year, as directors typically must be elected (or reelected) each year. These formalities and corporate minutes are required to maintain corporation status and, therefore, must be properly documented. A certified copy of the resolution of the board of directors will be required when filing for state licensure.

Partnership

The legal definition of a partnership is "an association of two or more persons to carry on as co-owners of a business for profit." There are two forms of partnership: general partnership and limited partnership.

A general partnership is when there is no registration with the state and there is no written agreement. In a general partnership, each of the partners shares in the profits of the partnership based on their percentage of ownership.

In a general partnership, each partner is liable for the acts of the others, the financial losses of the partnership, and there is no protection of personal property as with a corporation. Under a general partnership, assets of any of the partners can be used to cover the business's liabilities regardless of which partner incurred the liability.

With regard to taxes, the partnership is *not* a separate taxable entity; instead the profits are passed through to the partners. The individual partners are taxed on the income they receive from the partnership.

Similar to a sole proprietorship, a general partnership registers a business name with the county or city clerk's office in which the business is located.

A limited partnership is when an agreement has been established to include both a general partner and limited partners. A general partner will have more control of the partnership; for example, the general partner is the only one who can dissolve the partnership. A general partner has no limitations on the dividends from the profits that he or she can receive, and has no limitations on the liability he or she may incur. Limited partners, on the other hand, will have a prorated amount of ownership based on their investment, which will determine their share of profits and share of limited liability.

Limited Liability Company (LLC)

An LLC can be described as a cross between a corporation and a partnership (or sole proprietorship). It is similar to a corporation as it is a legal entity separate and distinct from its owners, thus protecting the owners from personal liability. One of the main advantages of an LLC over a partnership or sole proprietorship is the liability protection of the owners.

An LLC also allows for a more flexible setup and operating structure than a corporation while providing the pass-through taxation of a partnership (if a multimember LLC) or a sole proprietorship (if a single-member LLC).

The advantage of an LLC over a corporation is the management. All owners of an LLC are typically referred to as members who have full control and voting interest, referred to as member-managed. Thus, an LLC does not require a board of directors or officers, or formal meetings in order to maintain an LLC status. The management arrangements are specified in the articles of organization, which must be filed with the secretary of state. In addition, there is an operating agreement, which helps define the company profit sharing, ownership, responsibilities, and any ownership changes.

For tax considerations, a single-member LLC is taxed through his or her personal tax returns (typically found on Schedule C). A multimember LLC is taxed the same as a partnership; a partnership return is filed with a Schedule K-1 provided to each partner/member reflecting each partner's proportion of profit and loss.

Each state has different rules governing the formation of an LLC, so check your state regulations, and consult with a professional if necessary.

Limited Liability Partnership (LLP)

An LLP is similar to an LLC as it is organized under state law and offers a degree of liability protection for individual partners. An LLP is essentially a form of general partnership with one significant difference. In a general partnership, individual partners are liable for the partnership's debts and obligations whereas the partners in an LLP have a varying degree of liability protection. The laws differ from state to state.

For federal tax purposes, both an LLC and LLP are treated as partnerships, unless they elect to be treated as a corporation by filing a Form 8832.

What Other Decisions Do I Have to Make?

If you have decided to form a corporation, LLC, or LLP, you will now have to decide where to incorporate. You are entitled to incorporate in any state in the United States, not just the state where the principal place of business will be. The reason you might consider incorporating in another state is that another state may have more flexible governing laws and/or offer better tax treatment.

When you file a business organization in the state of its principal place of business and you will be conducting business in that state, this is referred to as a *domestic organization*. A business organization filed in a state other than its principal place of business is considered a *foreign corporation*.

As a mortgage broker, you will be requesting licensure in the state(s) in which you want to conduct business. Many brokers decide to conduct business in several states, and in this case you would need to file for a Certificate of Authority, or Certificate for Foreign Authority with the secretary of state. For more details on these requirements, refer to Chapter 10, "Educational and Licensing Requirements for the Mortgage Broker."

Preparing for State Licensure

How Do I Prepare for a Mortgage Broker's License?

After you have formed your business structure, your next step is to get your company licensed. Each state has specific requirements for licensure before any business can be conducted in that state. In other words, if your company is in Alabama, and you become licensed in Alabama, you cannot conduct business in Georgia, unless you *also* become licensed in Georgia. All but two states, Alaska and Colorado, require a mortgage firm to be licensed in order to conduct mortgage activities in their specific state.

The loan process involves the placement of a lien on a residential property. In order to ensure and protect their citizens, each state has in place a department in charge of regulating mortgage service providers. Each department is responsible for supervising anyone who is licensed (or seeking licensure) and develops state-specific rules and regulations in order to maintain well-managed and properly operated mortgage service providers.

To begin the application for state licensure you must be prepared to provide a credit and background check (in some cases, a criminal background check), a financial profile, and a copy of your business organizational documents (such as articles of incorporation, certified copy of the resolution of the board of directors, or trade name registration) along with your application.

As we just mentioned, a credit check will be conducted, so be prepared by checking your credit report. Bad credit will make your application *very* difficult to approve. The regulating departments require licensees to demonstrate reasonable financial responsibility and the ability to operate in a manner that will protect the property rights of their citizens. At the very least you must settle all collection accounts, charge offs, judgments, outstanding tax liens, or child support payments.

In most states a criminal background check is required. Therefore, if you have been involved in criminal activity, it is unlikely that your application will be approved. While minor traffic offenses will not affect your chances for a license, convicted felons in most cases cannot be licensed.

In all cases, once you have established your business structure, you will need to register your company with the secretary of state. You will find all the necessary contact information in Chapter 10.

Company Registration

The secretary of state in each state has its own requirements for registering your company for the purpose of conducting mortgage activities. In most cases you are required to be registered with the secretary of state *prior* to submitting a license application to become a mortgage broker.

As a sole proprietor you will need to file a trade name or fictitious name with the secretary of state. If a corporation, most states will require you to provide a Certificate of Good Standing and/or a Foreign Corporation Certificate from the state of incorporation.

In most states, a mortgage broker is not allowed to conduct business with more than one fictitious name or "doing business as (DBA)." However, you are allowed to apply for multiple licenses, each with its own fictitious name (or DBA).

Registered Agent

Corporate laws in nearly every state require a registered agent and a registered office. If you are forming a mortgage company in the state where your business is located, most states allow an officer, director, or the company itself to act as the registered agent. However, due to a potentially awkward situation of being served on the business premises or the documents falling into uninformed hands, most businesses choose the services of a professional registered agent.

A registered agent acts on a mortgage company's behalf in the state of corporation and/or qualification. The primary duties include providing a registered office address, receiving service of process, and acting as a local mailing contact with the secretary of state and other regulatory agencies. The registered agent also forwards any tax notices and state reports, when and where applicable. For example, if your company were named in a lawsuit, notice would be served upon the registered agent, who would immediately notify the designated company contact.

REGISTERED AGENT COMPANY SPOTLIGHT

Parasec/Paracorp

640 Bercut Dr., Suite A   318 N Carson St.

Sacramento, Ca. 95814   Las Vegas, NV 89701

Tel: (800) 533-7272

www.parasec.com

Services include forwarding all correspondence via first-class mail. Service of Process will initiate a same-day contact, for a nominal fee of $125 per state.

Parasec provides entity formation services.

What Type of Questions Will I Need to Answer on a Mortgage Broker License?

Be prepared to identify what type of business organization is applying for licensure. If a corporation, then a biographical report (name, address, social security numbers, driver's licenses, etc.) is typically required, identifying each individual who has 5 to 25 percent or more ownership in the business.

In addition, most regulating departments will want the applicant to provide the following information:

- Report other states that the applicant's business is licensed in.

- Report if any other type of business is conducted or will be conducted from the applicant's office location.

- Disclose if business is a parent or subsidiary of any other company.

- Document whether the applicant's office will be a place of business or residence. (Not all states allow mortgage brokers to conduct business from a residence. Refer to Chapter 10 to find out which states allow this practice.)

What Other Responsibilities Will I Have as a Mortgage Broker?

Maintain Well-Documented Employee Records

If the state you are requesting licensure in requires loan originators to also be licensed, then you are responsible to ensure that loan originators in your employment properly meet these requirements. I recommend reading *The Mortgage Originator Success Kit*, published by McGraw-Hill, which is my first book. It provides the education and licensing requirements for loan officers in all states from Alabama to Wyoming.

Some states, in addition to requiring that a loan originator be licensed, require the employing mortgage broker to conduct a background check on all employees prior to their hire. If your state requires an employee background check, then you will want to keep these records in your employee file.

Disclosures

Each state has its own state-specific disclosures. As you are aware, you are *always* required to disclose a borrower with a Good Faith Estimate and Truth-in-Lending Disclosure three business days from initial application. Mortgage brokers are required to provide additional disclosures in most states, which include, but are not limited to:

- A Mortgage Broker Agreement (discloses the broker's nature of involvement in the loan transaction. Each state may require specific terminology which must be included in a Mortgage Broker Agreement Disclosure form. Check your state's requirements.)

- A Loan Origination Agreement (similar to the Mortgage Broker Agreement)

- An Application Disclosure (disclosure of any upfront costs)

- Anti-coercion Disclosure (discloses the borrower's right to take insurance through any insurance agent they choose)

- Right to Receive a Copy of the Appraisal form

- Adjustable Rate Disclosures (if loan is an adjustable rate mortgage)

If you are acting in a dual capacity as a mortgage broker and real estate broker, sales agent, or attorney in a transaction, you must disclose in accordance with your state.

Audits

As a licensee/mortgage broker you are required to maintain books, accounts, and records of all transactions available for examination by a supervisor or representatives of the regulating epartment in your state. These audits can be conducted at anytime, but typically are annually or at least every 24 months.

Annual Reports

An annual report is usually required by each state. The annual report contains the licensee's business and operations information during the preceding calendar year.

What About Assets?

A mortgage broker seeking licensure must prove that he or she has financial responsibility to operate a well-managed mortgage business. Therefore, you will need to have a certain amount of net assets, also known as net worth requirement. In addition some states may have bond requirements. Below we have provided a brief definition of a surety bond and fidelity bond, along with a list of surety bond companies.

Surety Bond

A surety bond is required in some states. A surety bond is a contract with an insurance underwriter, which ensures that the licensing department can collect any unpaid fees from the licensee. A list of surety bond companies is provided for reference in Chapter 9, "The Mortgage Broker Resource Directory."

Fidelity Bond

A fidelity bond is a contract with an insurance underwriter that covers dishonesty, errors, and omissions of the employees of a licensee that funds, purchases, and/or services loans.

For detailed licensing requirements in your state and any other states you want to conduct business in, please refer to Chapter 10, "Educational and Licensing Requirements for the Mortgage Broker." There is a state-by-state guide with licensing details for all 50 states.

State Licensing Terms and Definitions

To assist you with the broker licensing application process, we have compiled a list of frequently encountered vocabulary words and their definitions.

Attestation
Each application typically has an attestation to certify that all information was provided in a truthful and correct manner, with a signature of the applicant and proper notarization.

Audited Financial Statement
Business financial statements audited by a Certified Public Accountant to establish the financial condition of a business and express an opinion as to the accuracy of the statements in accordance with Generally Accepted Accounting Principles (GAAP).

Branch Location/Office
When a business organization has more than one office. When applying for state licensure you must identify a main location and disclose any additional locations or offices. Typically, a separate license and licensing fee will be needed for each branch location.

Brick and Mortar
This term is referred to when a state requires a mortgage broker to maintain a physical office location in the state in which it seeks to conduct business. We have identified which states have this requirement in Chapter 10, "Educational and Licensing Requirements for the Mortgage Broker."

Certificate of Good Standing (or Certificate of Authority)
A certificate issued by the secretary of state's office allowing a foreign corporation (or entity) to conduct business in its state.

Commitment
A written statement by a lender that sets forth the terms and conditions upon which the lender is willing to make a particular mortgage loan to a particular borrower.

Compensation

Anything of value or any benefit including points, commissions, bonuses, referral fees, loan origination fees, and other similar fees but excluding periodic interest resulting from the application of the note rate of interest to the outstanding principal balance remaining from time to time.

Continuing Education

Some states with educational requirements for licensees require that loan originators and/or mortgage brokers continue with some educational classes in order to maintain their licensure. Typically specific classes and hours are required. In addition, continuing education must be met through an *approved* continuing education provider.

Domestic Corporation

A business organization conducting business in the same state in which their principal office is located.

Dual Agency

When a real estate (agent or) broker also conducts the mortgage transaction. A dual agency disclosure is required.

Executive Officer

The chief executive officer, the president, the principal financial officer, the principal operating officer, each vice president with responsibility involving policy-making functions for a significant aspect of a person's business, the secretary, the treasurer, or any person performing similar managerial or supervisory functions with respect to any organization whether incorporated or unincorporated.

Finds a Loan

Means to assist a loan applicant in locating a lender for the purpose of obtaining a loan for the applicant and to make arrangements for a loan applicant to obtain a loan.

Foreign Corporation

A business organization conducting business in a state other than where its principal office is located.

Investor

A person who lends or invests in mortgage loans.

Junior Lien

Also referred to as a second mortgage; this is a lien placed after a first lien has been recorded on a property.

Letter of Intent

A surety bond provider will provide a letter of intent stating that the applicant has met all criteria required and the company will issue a bond upon direction.

Licensee

A person licensed under the rules and regulations of state legislature.

Mortgage Banker

A mortgage banker makes loans secured by mortgages or deeds of trust on residential properties and funds the loan with their own warehouse line.

Mortgage Broker

A corporation, partnership, limited liability company (LLC or LLP), or sole proprietor who, on behalf of a loan applicant and for commission or money, finds a loan or negotiates a land contract, loan, or commitment for a loan, or engages in table funding.

Mortgage Loan Closing

The day by which all documents relating to the mortgage loan have been executed and recorded and all monies have been accounted for under the terms of the escrow instructions.

Negotiates

Means to discuss, explain, or present the terms and conditions of a loan or land contract with or to a loan applicant.

Originates

Means to make an underwriting decision on a loan and close a loan.

Principal

A natural person who, directly or indirectly, owns or controls an ownership interest of 25 percent or more in a corporation or any other form of business organization, regardless of whether the natural person owns or controls the ownership interest through one or more natural persons or one or more proxies, power of attorney, nominees, or other entities or devices, or any combination thereof.

Record Retention

Each state has specific requirements in regard to where the records of all mortgage transactions may be kept. Record retention is necessary to ensure that the mortgage broker is capable of providing records in a timely manner for any audits or complaints received by the regulatory agency.

Registration

In some states, licensing is not required for loan originators or mortgage brokers, but rather registration is required. Registration allows the state to keep track of mortgage professionals, such as loan originators, mortgage brokers, and mortgage bankers and their activities.

Regulatory Agency

The agency that regulates the licensing and activities of a mortgage broker. The regulatory agency for each state is identified in Chapter 10.

Service a Mortgage Loan

The collection or remittance for another, or the right to collect or remit for another, of payments of principal, interest, trust items such as insurance and taxes, and other payments pursuant to a mortgage loan.

Statutes and Regulations

Each state has its own statutes and regulations pertaining to mortgage lending or mortgage brokering.

Table Funding

A transaction in which a person conducts a loan closing in the person's name with funds provided by a third party, and the person assigns the loan to the third party within 24 hours of the loan closing.

Trust Account

A mortgage broker receiving monies from a borrower for payment of third-party provider services must maintain these funds in a federally insured financial institution in the form of a trust account. Monies maintained in the trust account need to be exempt from attachment or garnishment. A mortgage broker shall not in any way commingle any other operating funds with trust account funds. Withdrawals from the trust account shall be only for the payment of bona fide services rendered by a third-party provider or for refunds to borrowers.

Usury Law

Consumer credit regulation depends on the state's civil usury law. Certain states have statutory limits (ceilings) on consumer loan interest rates.

Wet Funding

There are certain states that are referred to as "wet funding" states which require that actual cash be at the closing table. In other words, disbursement of funds must be at closing, which would require any and all outstanding conditions to be met with the lender *prior* to closing.

CHAPTER 3

OPENING YOUR OFFICE

10 Things You Should Know Before Opening Your Office

Getting Started Checklist

Mortgage Technology Terms and Definitions

10 Things You Should Know Before Opening Your Office

Purpose + Action = Results

Purpose is the object toward which one strives in order to achieve something. It is said that a person with a purpose will always accomplish results. Action is the process of accomplishing an objective. It is the exertion of power. Action springs as a willingness to reach for the stars.

Preparing to open up a business can be a daunting experience.
There are numerous decisions to make, and the right choices will not always be obvious. Making the right decisions when first starting out can be crucial to the success of your mortgage brokerage. Take the time to do plenty of research, enlist the help of professionals when necessary, and *plan* your business strategy.
Anyone can start a business, but how well you prepare yourself for this endeavor will determine your success. So how do you prepare for a successful mortgage brokerage? The first step is to build your business fundamentals.

In this chapter we will provide you with some of the most important aspects to consider when setting up your mortgage brokerage company. My goal is to provide you with my "blueprint for success," a clear outline to ensure a solid foundation toward a successful career as a mortgage broker.

1. Establish an Office Space

As a sole proprietor/mortgage broker starting out, you may choose to work from home. Home-based businesses have increasingly become more acceptable in the eyes of both state licensing officials and mortgage lenders. However, not all states allow mortgage brokers to conduct business from their homes, so you will need to check your state license regulations (see Chapter 10 in this book). Also check with the lenders you plan to work with, as not all lenders approve of a home office–based mortgage brokerage.

The following steps are aimed at the mortgage broker who plans to open an office and hire employees. Your first step to starting your mortgage company will be to establish an office space. There are a few options to choose from: rent an executive office, lease an office space, or purchase an office space.

Renting an executive office space is a great choice for the mortgage broker who does not want to work from home but is not yet prepared to take on the challenges of leasing an office and hiring employees. Nowadays, there are executive suites available in most areas of the country.

What Is an Executive Suite?

An executive suite is a small office space(s) that is available for temporary or short-term use. These offices come fully furnished and provide a variety of amenities and services, such as a professional telephone answering service, high-speed Internet access, mail services, conference room access, and clerical support (for faxing and photocopying). The main advantage is that there is no minimum lease term. In some cases there is no lease to sign, just a license agreement.

In addition, some of the larger providers of executive office space typically have several locations across the country, allowing renters to also have access to these locations. This extended use can be of particular benefit to the mortgage broker who services more than one area or state.

The advantage of using an executive suite is the flexibility of expanding or contracting your business as necessary without the need to sign a long-term commitment. An additional benefit is the financial ease of obtaining an office space that brings a professional image. This can be a great benefit for the mortgage broker seeking lender approval in a state that does not allow a home-based business.

The disadvantage comes when the additional charges are tacked on. When you rent an executive suite, typically you just rent the use of the office space itself. You are charged extra for all calls that come in and out, the use of any clerical support, and, of course, the use of the conference room. Some renters curtail their expenses by bringing their own fax and small copiers into their office space. Even with these additional charges, an executive suite is an excellent choice for those mortgage brokers who are just starting out without an existing clientele and limited financial resources.

Types of Lease Agreements

Straight or Flat Lease:
When the same monthly payment is made throughout the entire lease term.

Net Lease:
A lease that requires the tenant to pay maintenance, taxes, insurance, etc., along with the fixed rent. Also known as "triple net."

Percentage Lease:
Uses a percentage of the net or gross sales to determine the monthly rent. Typically not applicable to mortgage brokers but rather retail operations.

Leasing an Office Space

Leasing an office space can be one of the largest expenses a new business owner will encounter when first starting out. Commercial real estate has its own terminology and implications. Therefore,

I suggest that you work with a professional real estate broker who has your best interests in mind when negotiating an office lease term.

First you must determine how much office space you need. This will depend on your business model. Will you have in-house loan agents and processors? If so, then typically you want to seek out an *open space* plan where you can set up workstations. Most experts recommend you allocate approximately 150 to 175 square feet per employee. Your real estate broker will help you determine how many employees you can house when looking at office space. Remember that office space is typically leased for a 3- to 5-year period, so if finances allow, I suggest that you plan ahead by obtaining a small amount of additional space allowing you to grow into it as your business grows.

Other factors when considering the amount of office space to take is to allow enough space for such things as large copiers, several fax machines, a production area, storage space for your loan files, a storage area to house office supplies, and a conference room or meeting room. Be prepared by designing your ideal office layout. This will help you when looking at various office spaces.

A mortgage brokerage relies heavily on computers and telephones, so I recommend that you review the office floor plan specifications for telephone, computer, and printer outlets. You may have your IT and phone systems people actually visit your prospective office location to suggest any improvements or modifications for wiring. If need be, your negotiations can include the installation of proper wiring to accommodate your specified needs.

Be familiar with the following lease terms:

Build to Suit

This is when the landlord will make improvements based on your specifications. The cost of construction is factored into the lease terms. Most build-to-suit provisions apply to long-term leases (5 to 10 years).

Escalation Clause

This is a clause in the lease that allows the landlord to increase the rent in the future. This allows the renter to ease into a higher rent in the future, as the renter builds up his or her business.

Concessions

These are benefits or discounts that are given to the "lessee" by the landlord to motivate the closing of the lease. These concessions can include remodeling or upgrades (referred to as "build-outs") and reduced rent for the initial term of the lease.

HVAC (Heating, Ventilation, Air-conditioning)

The landlord is generally responsible for maintaining the HVAC; however, be sure to check for extra charges for these services to be provided after hours or on weekends. Most mortgage brokers when starting out or when business is robust spend many hours working after hours and on weekends.

Option to Renew

It is wise to seek an option to renew your rent at a fixed predetermined price at the negotiation table. It can save you money down the road should the price for office space escalate.

Right of First Offer for Additional Space

When an office space becomes available in your building, right of first offer will require your landlord to offer you this space first before it is put on the market.

Sublease

The most common method of getting out of a lease obligation is to sublease the space to another tenant. Your lease must include a clause that allows for a sublease agreement. Keep in mind that a sublease does not relieve you (the original tenant) of obligation in the event of default by the subtenant.

When Should You Buy Office Space?

Most small business owners do not purchase office space when they are first starting out. However, low interest rates can entice many well-positioned entrepreneurs to buy a building rather than lease an office space. One reason is that in some cases, the monthly mortgage payment, insurance, and taxes can be roughly the same as a lease payment. The owner's equity can certainly boost his or her financial worth. A healthy financial statement can be a great benefit for the new mortgage broker seeking lender approval.

Purchasing an office space, however, is not for everyone, and it is not typically recommended for business owners who are just starting out. Many times a start-up company or even a fast-growing mortgage brokerage will need as much capital as possible to fund the growth of their business. When deciding whether to purchase an office building, I suggest that you seek out the advice of a professional financial planner.

2. Office Equipment and the Use of Technology

What kind of equipment will you need?

The amount of office equipment a new mortgage broker will need to start a business will obviously depend on several factors, such as the amount of investment and the type of business plan, model, or strategy. However, a mortgage broker can start a business as a sole proprietor, with the minimum equipment investment: a telephone, a multiuse fax machine (to include a copier), a computer, and a printer.

For the mortgage broker leasing an office space and hiring a staff, with in-house loan originators and loan processors, the amount of equipment will increase. A list of necessary equipment includes (but is not limited to) the following:

- *Telecommunications.* A mortgage brokerage will have heavy phone traffic, so a good phone system is essential. Phone systems can be costly, so make sure you shop around with several vendors for the best price and for the system that best suits your needs. When shopping, make sure that you know how many lines and extensions you will need. If you want to include an automated attendant, you will need a PBX system. The basic features you are looking for in a phone system are voice mail, speakerphone, music on hold, speed dial, and transfer. Make sure that you invest in a modular system that will grow with your business. I recommend buying a major brand, e.g., Nortel, Lucent, and Avaya.

- *Copier.* A heavy-duty copier is a must for a mortgage brokerage company because an enormous amount of paperwork will need to be copied. Loan processors are required to copy a full loan package before sending a loan to the lender, and loan officers will copy conditions received from their borrowers. These heavy-duty machines require constant maintenance, so I suggest an extended warranty and a reputable brand.

- *Fax machines.* The number of fax machines will vary with the amount of business you are conducting. However, most small mortgage brokerages begin with a minimum of two fax machines, one for incoming and one for outgoing faxes. In addition, you can incorporate e-fax service so you can accept faxes by e-mail. This is a great addition for loan originators. Conditions from borrowers can be received directly to their computer, avoiding the risk of lost or missing documents.

- *Paper shredder.* A mortgage broker handles personal financial and confidential information on a daily basis. It is your responsibility to require your staff to dispose of this confidential information in a secure manner. Provide either an in-house paper shredder or hire a paper shredding service, which will shred documents on-site.

What About the Use of Technology?

The use of technology has played an integral role in the evolution of the mortgage broker and mortgage lender. The use of computers and the Internet has changed how many industries conduct their business and none more than within the mortgage industry. The use of technology has lowered the cost of obtaining information and thus has lowered the cost of conducting business.

Mortgage lenders can now obtain and analyze information on potential borrowers more quickly, which has lowered transaction costs and increased the housing market, allowing more families to qualify for mortgage loans. In addition, lower costs allow mortgage brokers and mortgage lenders more flexibility with their operational costs in order to better withstand market changes.

What About Hardware?

When first starting a mortgage brokerage, I recommend that you purchase your hardware and office equipment. Purchasing your equipment keeps your monthly overhead costs down. However, as your business grows and you want to add more computers, fax machines, and furniture, an alternative is to lease your equipment. By leasing your equipment you improve your cash flow by keeping your cash intact instead making small monthly payments on a lease agreement.

An excellent resource when shopping for computers is *PC Magazine* online. Visit www.PCMAG.com and CNET.com for comparison shopping and reviews.

A single-user computer is referred to as a desktop. A local area network (LAN) is when you have several computers in close proximity that are directly connected to each other, enabling them to share and exchange a variety of information and resources. There are benefits to having a network.

- A network allows your employees to share files. For example, your loan originators and loan processors can access and view the same loan application at the same time.

- Several computers can share the same printer. One example may be to have all loan processors sharing one printer and all loan originators sharing another printer.

- Communication exchange allows all employees to send, receive, and store e-mails.

- A LAN makes it easy to back up your company's data. (Make sure you implement a backup system policy for your business.)

When first starting out and you have fewer than five employees, you can keep your costs down with a *peer-to-peer network*. This is the most basic type of network, connecting each computer directly to each other, without the need for a server. As your business grows, you can incorporate a *client-server network*, where all computers are directly connected to a server and the server manages the network. A client-server network allows your client computers (workstations) to run faster and leaner. As a mortgage broker you must be able to conduct your business in a fast and efficient manner. For that reason, I strongly recommend the incorporation of a client-server network as soon as your finances allow.

What About Telephone Technology to Keep Costs Down?

The use of automation and technology is a good example of sources available to keep your operational costs at a minimum. You can eliminate the use of a receptionist by using an automated answering system with a prerecorded message to greet your callers. With this system, your customers would simply press the extension of the party they are trying to reach.

If you choose an automated answering system, I recommend that you include your fax number and e-mail address in your prerecorded greeting, to minimize the use of a live person for general questions. Since most companies that have automated services also include voice mail, this has become a popular and mainstream use of communication.

There are many phone systems available for the small business owner. Establish what features you need (such as auto attendant, voice mail, etc.) and evaluate the cost to determine which phone system best suits your communication requirements.

What Software Will You Need?

Mortgage brokers rely heavily on efficient loan origination system (LOS) software. Your first step in setting up your company automation needs is to choose which software system best suits your business model. Your loan origination software program should have the following capabilities:*

- Allow loan agents to provide marketing material to potential borrowers

- Prequalify borrowers and produce the loan application and disclosures

- Have access to automatic underwriting

- Have the capability to send an electronic loan file to the lender

- Have processing capabilities and the ability to process appropriate form, and interface with closing document service providers

One of the most widely used loan origination software program is Ellie Mae's Encompass. Encompass provides brokers, loan officers, and processors a unified platform to efficiently originate loans, from prospecting and marketing, to loan processing, pipeline management, and loan submission.

One of the software's many features is the anytime access to up-to-the-minute company-wide loan pipeline data. On this loan origination software program authorized users can access a centrally stored electronic loan file, make changes that are automatically visible to all users keeping appropriate staff apprised of up-to-date loan information without having to route paper files from one person to the next. Other key features include the automatic loan compliance check, electronic document management, and secure electronic document delivery. I am particularly impressed with the automation of manual processes such as ordering settlement services (title, credit, flood, insurance, etc.) and submitting loans to lenders without ever having to reenter

---

*For a list of loan origination software providers, please refer to Chapter 9, "The Mortgage Broker Resource Directory."

data or leave the origination system to visit another site. Adding to all these features is the marketing and lead generation tool that is built into this software program that allows for mortgage originators to generate more business. It's no wonder that Encompass is used by an estimated 120,000 mortgage originators nationwide.

Chief Executive Officer of Ellie Mae, Sig Anderman, says "Sixty eight percent of Encompass users report that they are processing loans up to 50 percent faster thanks to Encompass. That's a major feat in this industry. By using Encompass, loan officers can spend less time processing their loans and more time generating new business."

Broker Perspective

"Your success as a mortgage originator can depend greatly on the technology at your disposal," said Jeremy Thacker, president of Dallas Lending. "A high quality loan origination system is critical. I'm a strong believer in Ellie Mae's Encompass which, unlike most loan origination software on the market, does a lot more than simply help you fill out loan forms. It helps significantly reduce paperwork, speed up the origination process, lower operational costs, and keep compliant.

"With Encompass, I can process loans electronically without relying on paper. At the point of sale, I enter the borrower's information straight into the system and my processor can simultaneously review the loan file from where it's posted without having to physically route the file. The system also integrates to over 2,000 third parties such as credit bureaus and title companies plus over 45 lenders, so there is no need to ever leave the system and reenter loan data to order required documents and services, nor to submit loan documents to lenders. I also get great peace of mind from Encompass since it makes sure I'm complying with laws and regulations—and steering clear of fines. Encompass even includes extensive marketing tools, document management capabilities to handle electronic documents, a lead center, and much more. It's an amazing software program that I would recommend to any mortgage originator," says Thacker.

Ellie Mae offers four editions of Encompass; including a personal edition for the company of one, a multiple-user edition, and a Web-based edition. For more information visit their Web site at: www.EllieMae.com or call (888) 955-9100.

3. Hiring Employees

Before you begin hiring employees you will need to apply for an Employer Identification Number (EIN). An EIN is an identification number assigned to businesses for taxpaying purposes by the IRS or state taxing authorities. An EIN is required for corporations and partnerships, and it is required for a sole proprietorship if you intend to hire employees.

For more information on whether you are required to obtain an EIN number, you can go to the following Web site: www.irs.gov/businesses/small/.

How Do You Staff Your Start-Up Mortgage Brokerage?

There are various resources available for employers seeking employees:

- Job Web sites
- Your own Web site
- Referral program
- Develop your own training program
- Team agencies
- Employment agencies
- Want ads

Job Web sites

Nationalmortgagenews.com
Lenderscareer.com
Mortgageboard.net
Mortgagejobs.com
Mortgagejobstore.com
Mortgagerecruiters.com
Mortgagedaily.com
Careerbuilder.com
Hotjobs.yahoo.com

Your Own Web Site

You will always be seeking good loan originators; they are critical to your success. The better the loan originator, the more-loans you close, and the more successful your business will be. Therefore, I recommend that you keep some form of ongoing recruitment effort in place. Consider it a continuous talent search. For instance, you can place an ongoing advertisement for loan originators on your Web site (should your business model include one). Also, if you run out of in-house space for loan originators, make sure you set up your loan origination software system so that you can incorporate the use of outside and/or home-based loan originators. This way you don't miss out on an opportunity when a good loan originator comes your way.

Referral Program

When it comes to hiring loan agents, it is a smart idea to put a referral program in place. Loan agents partake in quite a bit of networking; consequently, when one loan agent finds a good mortgage brokerage, he or she usually tells their network of other loan agents. You can set up a referral program that pays a flat fee for referrals. For example, the referring loan agent receives a flat fee of $500 after the new loan agent is employed a minimum of three months (a typical probation period). Another option is to offer the referring loan agent an override of the new loan agent's production for a fixed period of time (e.g., a 6-month period). In this case the referring loan agent would receive 5 percent override on the total commissions earned by the new loan agent.

Develop a Training Program

Many mortgage companies attract inexperienced but talented sales people with an in-house training program. My book *The Mortgage Originator Success Kit* is an excellent training tool. It provides all the mortgage fundamentals necessary for anyone interested in starting a career as a loan originator. In fact, many experienced loan agents have found this book to be an excellent resource tool that they can refer to time and time again.

Employment and/or Temp Agencies

Even though I don't recommend the use of recruiters because of the high recruiting fees, temporary personnel agencies are a good source for your clerical needs. This allows you to check out the employees' performance prior to hiring them on a permanent basis.

One advantage of using a temporary agency is that the agency takes care of all the temporary workers' employment paperwork. It's simple: all you do is sign a slip of paper verifying the temporary worker's dates of employment and hours worked. The temporary worker returns this slip of paper to the agency and the agency pays the worker. You don't have to worry about payroll taxes or employee benefits.

Want Ads

The most economical way to find employees is by placing a want ad in your local newspaper. This is the best way to get your message to the greatest number of applicants in your area.

What About the Interview Process?

The best way to begin your selection process for a prospective employee is to ensure that you know exactly what tasks your new hire will be expected to perform. Make sure that you have a job description for each position you intend to fill. You can eliminate many misunderstandings and frustrations down the road, by simply covering your expectations up front to your new employee. Be prepared and have answers to simple questions like what hours you want them to work, what type of compensation you will be paying, what type of benefits you provide, etc.

Even though a resume provides an employee's history, a personal face-to-face interview is necessary to get a feeling for the comfort and character of the person sitting across from you. Make sure you go over the resume with questions like the following.

Questions You Should Ask a Prospective Employee

- What were your specific tasks or functions at your last employer?

- What made you decide to leave your last (or current) employer?

- What type of production did you have at your last employer? (Obviously you are looking for high-producing loan originators and processors.)

- What are your long-term goals?

- Are you familiar with our specific loan software program? Make sure they know the specific tasks they will be responsible for.

Most important is covering the compensation topic. You will obviously ask what their compensation was at their previous job. However, if you are limited to a certain salary or hourly wage, you may want to provide an opportunity for advancement to compensate for more pay. For example, you might offer a receptionist the ability to move into a loan processor's assistant position (by providing some assistance to your processor while he conducts his receptionist duties). This will enable him to learn how to process a loan and eventually have an opportunity for advancement as a loan processor.

Even though you are the one placing the ad, a prospective employee will also have his or her own questions to ask. Any successful loan originator or loan processor will want to know whether your company is capable of providing him or her with the necessary tools to ensure his or her continued success. When conducting your interview, don't just jump in and demand answers to all of your questions. Make sure you talk about your company, any opportunities for advancement, and the future of the business. Outline the benefits the prospective employee will have by joining your company.

Questions from a Prospective Employee

- Is this a salaried position? (The loan originator or loan processor will want to know whether a salary is paid or does the position have a commission-only structure.)

- What lenders do you use?

- What loan programs do you offer your customers?

I have interviewed many prospective employees. When I felt that I had a strong contender, I always finished my interview with a tour of my office and introduced them to a few key people. This gives the prospective employee a chance to take a look at your operation. Experienced loan originators can determine the amount of your business based on the amount of activity in your office. A busy mortgage brokerage will have several phone lines ringing, people will look actively busy, and there is a fast-paced energy among all employees.

Once you are ready to extend an offer, get excited. When you telephone the prospective employee, begin the conversation with congratulations. This will make your potential employee feel like he or she is the chosen one. This is a good way to solidify your prospective employee's choice of selecting your company to work for.

What Type of Staff Is Needed for a Mortgage Brokerage?

This will vary depending on your business model and the degree and amount of business you are producing or want to produce. Below you will find a brief list of required employees and their primary duties in no particular order:

- *Receptionist*. A person whose primary duties include answering phones, greeting customers, inputting preliminary information into your origination software program, picking up mail, signing for loan packages, and any other clerical duties as needed.

- *Loan processor assistant*. If a significant amount of business is carried out, a loan processor assistant would be needed. The loan processor assistant's main duties include performing verifications, inputting loan applicant's basic information into your software system, copying the loan file, and stacking the loan file for the lender.

- *Loan processor*. A loan processor's duties include evaluating the credit and income for prequalification purposes. Performing verification of employment, deposits, and rental or mortgage history. Ensuring that the loan package fits the lender's program guidelines. Will prepare and submit the loan package to the lender. If necessary collects any additional information required by the lender from the borrower (in some cases, the processor is required to have the loan originator collect this information from the borrower). Orders title and escrow, and any other services such as appraisal, pest inspections, or surveys. Orders the loan documents from the lender. Coordinates the closing with the lender, borrower, and closing agent.

- *Loan originator*. This person's primary task is to take a loan application, prequalify a borrower for a loan program that best suits the applicant's situation, sell the loan program rate and fees to the borrower, collect the necessary documentation in order to submit the loan package for processing, follow up with the processor and borrower throughout the loan process until the loan is closed.

- *Junior loan originator*. This position can be offered to a very good salesperson who does not have a lot of mortgage background, but is willing to take small pay for a limited/agreed-upon period of time in order to train under one of the more experienced loan originators. When your business is robust, the services of a Junior Loan Originator (also known as a loan originator assistant) will be very helpful.

- *Bookkeeper*. Bookkeeping services keep track of the company's accounts receivable and payable. A bookkeeper will also prepare your P&L statement and balance sheet, which you will always need for lender approval. For state licensure, you will need to have a current P&L statement and in some cases an audited financial statement from a Certified Public Accountant.

- *Payroll*. A payroll person determines the salaries, commissions, and payroll deductions for employees.

- *Personnel*. Maintains employee records and attendance. May handle benefits package information.

- *Office manager*. An office manager oversees all functions of the mortgage brokerage, including hiring and terminating employees, provides training, fills in when employees are absent, etc.

Outsourcing

A start-up mortgage brokerage can benefit from outsourcing many functions. One way to keep costs down when first starting out is to outsource your loan processing. In this case, the loan processor is paid as an independent contractor, and is paid only and when the loan is funded, and as specified on the final closing statement.

Other functions that can be outsourced are payroll and personnel, which can be outsourced to a payroll service, and bookkeeping services, which can be outsourced to an independent contractor.

Take a look at the sample Employment Application form provided at the end of this chapter.

4. Checking for References and Maintaining Employee Records

No matter how perfect the person you just interviewed seems for the job, I strongly urge that you ask for references. Take the time to contact past employers to verify dates employed and position held. The time you take to check out references is minimal compared to the time you waste by hiring the wrong employee.

Your services as a mortgage brokerage include the handling and processing of an individual's personal and financial information. The United States has very specific confidentiality laws. Therefore, it is your responsibility as the employing broker to enforce a policy for checking references as part of your hiring process.

When hiring loan originators, you actually need to take one step further and conduct a full background check. In fact, certain states mandate this process as a license requirement.

I recommend that you develop a release form for an applicant to sign allowing you to conduct a background check as part of your company hiring policy. Then you can let the prospective employee know about this policy during the interview process. If they are interested in the position, they can sign the release form at that time.

A wide selection of online service providers will provide a background check and criminal check on a prospective employee for a small fee.*

What About Maintaining Employee Records?

As an employer, your first responsibility when hiring employees is to verify that each new employee is legally eligible to work in the United States. You are legally required to have the new employee complete a Form I-9, Employment Eligibility Verification, and Form W-4, Employee's Withholding Allowance Certificate. In addition, the new employee must provide you with a copy of two pieces of identification. These documents should be maintained in the employee file.

Maintaining proper employee records is *critical* for a mortgage brokerage. A properly documented employee record can save you a lot of money and headaches in the future. Should you unknowingly hire a dishonest loan originator who causes you problems, you can minimize any future liabilities by providing a well-documented employee record indicating that you properly performed due diligence prior to hiring.

Your employee record should include (but not be limited to):

- Application for employment (signed by you and your employee)

- Copy of employment agreement

- A statement that includes who performed the employee's reference check (include date and signature of person conducting the reference check and list who or which employers and/or supervisors gave the reference)

- Signed release form for a background check

- Copy of background check

*For a list of background check providers, please refer to Chapter 9, "The Mortgage Broker Resource Directory."

- Copy of loan originator license (if required)
- Form I-9 and Form W-4
- Copy of driver's license and/or proof of legal residency
- Copy of Social Security card

5. Salaries

The mortgage industry is driven by volume; therefore, loan originators are normally paid on some type of commission structure. An outside loan originator, who generates his or her own business and pays for his or her own expenses, generally receives a higher compensation than a loan originator who sits in your office, is provided with leads, and has no expenses.

The loan originator is paid a percentage (industry standards vary between 10 to 50 percent for in-house loan originators to 50 to 100 percent for outside loan originators) of the total compensation received on a loan transaction.

For example:
On a loan transaction of: $100,000
Total charges to the borrower (1% of loan amount): $1,000
*Yield spread premium (1% of loan amount): $1,000
Total compensation on the loan: $2,000

---

*Yield spread premium (YSP) is what the lender pays the mortgage broker for bringing them the loan. The amount of yield spread premium paid by the lender is posted on the lender's rate sheet. In this case, the loan originator sold the loan at a rate that pays 1% YSP.

Commonly, an outside loan originator is paid on a commission-only pay structure. Therefore, if your commissioned pay structure for an outside loan originator is 50 percent and your loan originator funded five loans that generated a total compensation of $20,000, then his or her pay is $10,000.

An in-house loan originator is paid either a small salary plus a small commission, or can be paid no salary and a higher commission.

Obviously, the main advantage for you as the employing mortgage broker that has a commission-only structure plan for loan originators is that *you* only pay when *you* are paid. A loan originator is well compensated, but he or she is only paid for the amount of business produced and *not* until the loan funds.

Hot Topic *When does an outside loan originator become an independent contractor?*

You will need to do some research to determine when you can pay a loan originator as an independent contractor. There are several variables that need to be taken into consideration. First, there are the state requirements. Does your state require a loan originator to be licensed? Does your state allow for loan originators to be compensated as independent contractors? Some states such as Arizona, Arkansas, Delaware, Florida, Kentucky, Maryland, Minnesota, New Mexico, North Carolina, and Texas require that loan originators be paid as an employee (W-2).

The IRS defines an employer-employee relationship as one that depends on whether the employee is subject to the will and control of the employer, based on the 20-Factor Test, provided below. Be familiar with these rules. I recommend that you review IRS revenue ruling 87-41 and obtain professional advice.

IRS 20 Factor Test

1. *Instructions.* If a worker is subject to comply with employer instructions, as to when, where, and how work is to be performed, it is most likely classified as an employee status.

2. *Training.* Requiring or providing training suggests an employee status.

3. *Integration.* The greater the degree of integration of the services performed by the worker into the business, the more likely an employee relationship is established.

4. *Services rendered personally.* If services must be performed personally by the worker, this can constitute an employee relationship.

5. *Control of assistants.* Who is responsible for hiring, supervising, and paying assistants? If the employer, rather than the worker, has control of the assistants, then this constitutes an employee-employer relationship.

6. *Ongoing relationship.* A continuing relationship suggests an employee-employer relationship.

7. *Set hours of work.* Designating set hours of work classifies an employee relationship.

8. *Full-time work.* A worker who must devote full working time to an employer is being controlled and constitutes an employee status.

9. *Work on employer's premises.* On-premises work indicates employer has control and constitutes an employee status.

10. *Order of sequence.* Work that must be performed in a specific order or sequence established by the employer constitutes an employee status.

11. *Oral or written reports.* A requirement that the worker provide regular progress reports demonstrates control and thus constitutes employee status.

12. *Payment method.* If payment is on a fixed periodic basis, e.g., hourly, weekly, or monthly, rather than upon completion of work, that is a good indicator of an employee status.

13. *Payment of expenses.* Payment of the worker's business and/or travel expenses indicates regulation of business activities and thus an employee status.

14. *Furnishing tools and materials.* Independent contractors typically provide their own tools and materials.

15. *Significant investment.* If the worker invests in the facilities used for work, this would constitute an independent contractor status.

16. *Realization of profit or loss.* The ability to realize either a profit or loss in performing the work is a characteristic of an independent contractor.

17. *Serving more than one firm.* A worker who provides services to several customers simultaneously is considered an independent contractor.

18. *Serving the public.* A worker whose services are regularly available to the general public is an independent contractor.

19. *Right to discharge.* The right to discharge at will indicates an employer-employee relationship. An independent contractor is usually only discharged if he or she failed to meet contract requirements.

20. *Right to quit.* An employee may resign at will, but an independent contractor may be contractually obligated to perform a task or service.

What About Salaried Workers?

Determining the salary scale for a new hire will obviously depend on the employee's capability to perform the job and prior experience. In addition, the pay scale will depend on what part of the region your mortgage brokerage is located in. I suggest that you do a little research by checking with neighboring mortgage brokerages to measure their pay scale for the same position you are attempting to fill.

How Often Should You Pay Your Employees?

State governments have some rules on this matter, but in general you must pay your employees regularly and you must establish a pay period. The most common pay period is semimonthly, that is, to pay on the 1st and 15th of every month.

Should You Pay Your Employee a Salary or at an Hourly Rate?

You will need to establish the difference between an exempt and nonexempt employee. An exempt employee is one that is "exempt" from overtime regulations. The U.S. Department of Labor specifies certain classes of workers as exempt. These would include your administrative personnel (i.e., office manager), outside salespeople, licensed professionals (i.e., loan originators), and highly skilled professionals (i.e., loan processors, bookkeeper).

An hourly wage earner is a "nonexempt" employee and thus must be paid for every hour of overtime that he or she works. Keep in mind when hiring a receptionist that just because you offer him a salary does not make him an exempt employee. A receptionist would not fall into the specified classes as described above by the U.S. Department of Labor. In general, the more responsibility and independence or discretion an employee has, the more likely the employee is to be considered exempt.

What About an Incentive Bonus?

Again, because the mortgage industry is driven by volume, many mortgage brokers pay their loan processors a salary plus a bonus after a certain amount of loan production has been reached. The clerical staff is generally not compensated with an incentive bonus, unless those people also provide assistance in the production.

6. Employee Contracts and HR Manuals

How Important Is an Employee Contract?

An employee contract is an agreement between an employee and employer and specifies the terms and conditions of the employment.

Employee contracts are imperative when it comes to hiring loan agents and in some states it is a requirement (e.g., California). An employee contract clearly defines the employer's policy and procedures by which the employee must abide. An employee contract defines:

- The employment (position to be held)
- Term of employment
- Compensation
- Employee benefits
- Expenses

- Noncompete clause

- Confidential information

- Terms of termination

- Dispute resolution

- Entirety of agreement

- Liability for fraud

- General provisions

If you employ loan agents as independent contractors, then you should have a separate contract, identified as an "Independent Contractor Agreement."

Take a look at the sample Employment Agreement and Independent Contractor Agreement provided at the end of this chapter.

Remember, as a mortgage broker you are responsible for the actions of any loan originator conducting business under your license. A fully executed employment contract and proper due diligence are the best forms of protection to minimize any future liabilities.

What Is an HR Manual?

An employee handbook, or human resources (HR) manual, provides the principles by which your company governs its employee relations in a fair and consistent manner. It is a way to ensure that all employees understand the policies, procedures, and rules of your company.

When a new employee is hired, he or she should be provided with an HR manual. My advice is that you require that new employees sign an acknowledgment stating they have read the manual and have received a copy of the manual.

It is very important, however, to make sure that you have a properly worded handbook. The danger of creating an HR manual is that it can be misconstrued and interpreted as an employment contract. Your best defense against this danger is to include a written disclaimer indicating that the manual is not and should not be considered an employment contract.

When creating your HR manual, you want to lower the risk of any potential legal hassles, so you want to be clear, concise, and comprehensive. Don't leave explanations of the results and consequences of actions open to interpretation.

A proper HR manual requires regular updating. Develop a handbook that meets your initial needs and design it so you can expand it over time. My suggestion is that you have an attorney or legal service create and maintain your HR compliance manual.

7. A Payroll Service

Any small business owner will tell you that payroll processing can be a difficult and time-consuming task. What does payroll processing entail? It is the calculation of employee wage earnings and deductions, calculating and paying payroll taxes in a timely manner, keeping track of employee attendance (includes updating vacation and sick pay), and deducting the employee-contributed payments for any employee benefits that you may provide.

There are many complicated federal and state laws governing employee compensation. Even if you only have a few employees, it is a smart idea to take advantage of a payroll service. Taking care of your own payroll needs opens up the possibility for human error, putting you and your company in harm's way. Some of the biggest problems businesses face with regard to their accounting is the improper application of payroll taxes. The fee for a payroll service is so minimal that it generally tends to cost half of what it would to do it in-house.

How Does a Payroll Service Work?

The convenience and ease of a payroll service are big considerations when deciding on outsourcing this function. Basically you just report how many hours each employee worked, and the payroll service calculates the payroll, deductions, and withholdings.

Then you receive professionally printed checks, pay vouchers, and reports at your door, ready for payday.*

I suggest that you look for a payroll service that guarantees their services (calculations). With this guarantee, the payroll service will pay for any penalties if an error is made.

Additional functions that a payroll service provides:

- Direct deposit

- Online services with individual employee pay history

- New hire reporting. Reports new hires to proper agencies to keep you in compliance

- Flexible compensation plans to provide for pretax benefits

- Management of state unemployment insurance

- Management of employee retirement benefits

- Management of worker compensation benefits

What About Providing Employee Benefits?

Providing some form of benefits package is a way for business owners to attract and retain their employees. As a small business owner you actually are not legally required to provide any benefits other than mandatory worker's compensation insurance. However, even small business owners will provide the very basic benefits: health insurance coverage, paid vacation or sick days, and possibly a 401(k) plan.

A small business owner typically pays for the employee's health insurance coverage but not for dependents. If employees want insurance coverage for their dependents, they generally pay for that coverage themselves. If you want to provide vacation and sick day pay, you simply adopt that policy by deciding how many sick days and vacation days you want to give your employees and put it in writing. For example, this would be a policy that would be found in your HR manual. The norm for a small

---

*For a list of payroll service providers, please refer to Chapter 9, "The Mortgage Broker Resource Directory."

mortgage brokerage is to provide one week of paid vacation time after the employee has been employed for a full year with your company. In regard to providing a 401(k) plan, you can find more information on the IRS Web site: ww.IRS.gov/retirement.

As your mortgage brokerage grows and as finances allow you to attract choice employees, you may want to offer a more comprehensive employee benefit package. A comprehensive plan can include health insurance, disability insurance, life insurance, vision and dental coverage, cafeteria plans, and paid time off (vacation or sick pay).

Which Taxes Does the Employer Pay?

As an employer with employees, you must pay taxes. There are some taxes that are paid just by the employee, and then there are taxes that must be shared by you and your employee. You will be responsible for timely payment or deposit of employment taxes withheld from employees, and your matching share. Employment taxes are

- *Federal income taxes.* These are paid by the employee and withheld from the employee's pay.

- *Social Security and Medicare Taxes (FICA).* As an employer you pay half of the FICA taxes and withhold the other half from the employee's pay.

- *Federal Unemployment Tax (FUTA).* Federal unemployment taxes fund state unemployment benefits and administrative costs. The employer is responsible for paying this tax. An employer must pay federal unemployment tax on the first $7,000 earned by each employee during a calendar year.

- *State Unemployment Tax.* Again, the employer pays the state unemployment tax. Rates are based on a business's location, size, and number of employees, and vary state by state. In addition, some states also require employers to pay a disability tax every quarter to cover the state's disability program. You will need to check with your state's requirements.

8. Employee Laws

There are certain laws you should become familiar with as an employer. Let's begin with the federal wage law, Fair Labor Standards Act (FLSA). The FLSA establishes minimum wage, overtime pay, record keeping, and child labor laws. For more information, please refer to the Department of Labor's Employment Law Guide.

What Is the Rule on New Hire Reporting?

Federal and state-mandated regulations require employers to report information on newly hired employees shortly after their hire date. Penalties can be incurred due to late filings or mistakes. If you outsource to a payroll service, your payroll processing company can provide this service.

Are There Poster Requirements?

There are agencies within the Department of Labor (DOL) that enforce some statutes and regulations requiring that notices be posted within the workplace. For more information, refer to the DOL Web site at: http://www.dol.gov/osbp/sbrefa/poster/matrix.htm.

What Is Worker's Compensation?

Worker's Compensation Insurance is intended to benefit both the worker (employee) and the employer. Worker's compensation benefits provide coverage for medical expenses and compensation for lost wages for an employee as a result of an accident, injury, or illness caused on the job. It is intended to protect workers and their dependents against hardship from injury or death arising out of the work environment. The employee receives fixed monetary awards (usually on a weekly or biweekly basis), eliminating the need for any lawsuits. Worker's compensation benefits are paid without regard to who was at fault or questions of negligence.

Each state has different laws regarding how much coverage a company must buy, what percentage of an injured employee's wages a company must pay if he or she is unable to work, and how long a company must cover an injured employee. Every state except Texas requires employers to purchase worker's compensation insurance that covers an injured employee's medical expenses and lost wages.

Worker's compensation premiums will depend on your payroll amount and employer classification. Base rates will vary slightly from state to state. In addition, a few states require employers to purchase insurance through a single state agency (e.g., California), whereas others allow private insurers to offer worker's compensation policies. Worker's compensation insurance is mandated by state law and has its own worker's compensation statutes, so check with your state insurance commissioner's office or your insurance agent for more information.

To find out more information on your state's worker's compensation regulations, you can check this Web site: http://www.dol.gov/esa/regs/compliance/owcp/wc.htm.

What About Terminating an Employee?

One of the unpleasant tasks of running a small business is the occasional necessity of terminating an employee. The cause for termination can be any number of reasons; however, it should be a legitimate business reason in order to avoid being sued for wrongful termination. Obviously, you are at greater risk firing an employee who has made prior complaints, for example, for sexual harassment or complained about illegal conduct by your company. But did you know that you may also be at risk by firing an individual over 40, or if the employee is a member of a protected group (based on race, sex, disability, religion, or national origin), or where inconsistent promises have been made to the employee? Some reasons for terminating an employee would be

- Violation of company policy
- Repeated unexcused absenteeism or tardiness
- Consistent incompetence
- Physical violence on the job

- Use of drugs or alcohol on the job

- Commission of illegal acts

- Falsification of any information

The best protection against a wrongful termination suit is to have an "at-will employment" relationship. That means that either the employer or employee can terminate the relationship at any time for any reason, or for no reason. If you provide an employee contract, an at-will clause is usually included. If you have employees who are not under contract, make sure they sign a document upon hiring that indicates they are "at-will employees."

What if the employee has done nothing wrong but is underperforming? You will want to create a warning policy, whether oral or in writing, and make sure the warning is clearly documented in the employee's file. Your HR manual should include clear policies about types of conduct that constitute termination. Remember, you want to let your employees know in writing what is expected of them and what the consequences are should they not meet those expectations.

Here are some helpful hints when it becomes necessary to terminate an employee:

- Check your employment agreement to make sure you have included an at-will employment clause. If not, you may need to provide a warning, allowing the employee an opportunity to improve prior to termination.

- Make sure you have properly documented your employee's file if any warnings have been given.

- Explain the reasons for termination.

- Prepare a final paycheck for salaried employee, and for commissioned employees make sure to arrange for final payments as agreed upon on the employee (or independent contractor) agreement.

- Explain any conditions with the termination. For example, the amount of time for continuation of any benefits.

- Let the employee know how long they have to gather their belongings and leave the premises.

- Prepare to collect anything the company provided the employee, for example, office keys, access cards, etc.

- Change computer passwords and, if necessary, change door locks and security access codes.

The task of terminating an employee is an uncomfortable one for both parties. I suggest that when allowed, you end your meeting with a handshake and on a positive note.

9. Bookkeeping and Accounting

Setting up a proper bookkeeping and accounting system is an essential part of operating a mortgage brokerage business. To begin this process, the IRS requires that you figure taxable income on an annual accounting period called a *tax year*. A tax year can be a calendar year, fiscal year, or short tax year.

A calendar year is the most common tax year used by individuals. A calendar year is 12 consecutive months beginning January 1 and ending December 31. This means that if you adopt the calendar year as your tax year, then you must maintain your books and records and report your income and expenses incurred from January 1 through December 31 of each year.

If you file your first tax return using a calendar tax year and you later begin business as a sole proprietor, become a partner in a partnership, or become a shareholder in an S corporation, you must continue to use the calendar year unless you get IRS approval to change it.

A fiscal year is 12 consecutive months ending on the last day of any month except December. A 52–53 tax year is a fiscal year that varies from 52 to 53 weeks but may not end on the last day of the month. To obtain more information on accounting periods, check the IRS Web site at: www.irs.gov/businesses/ index.html.

The IRS also requires that each taxpayer use a consistent accounting method, which is basically a set of rules, used to determine when income and expenses are reported. The IRS determines that the regular use of an accounting method is the only way to clearly reflect your gross income and expenses; therefore, you must use the same accounting method from year to year. The most commonly used accounting methods include the cash method and the accrual method.

What Is the Cash Method?

The cash method of accounting is when you report income in the tax year you receive it and deduct expenses in the tax year you actually pay them. For example, a calendar year cash method taxpayer received $100,000 of gross income in 2006 and $50,000 of expenses (or bills) were incurred to generate the $100,000 of income but did not pay those bills until 2007. The expenses paid on 2006 income would not be reflected until the 2007 tax year.

What Is the Accrual Method?

Under the accrual method of accounting, you report income in the tax year earned and deduct expenses in the year incurred. The purpose of an accrual method of accounting is to match income and expenses in the correct year.

To determine which accounting method is best suited for your business model, I suggest that you consult with your accountant or CPA. You can obtain more information on this topic at the IRS Web site: www.irs.gov/businesses/index.html.

How Should You Select a Desktop Accounting Software Program?

Establishing an accounting system can be significantly simplified by using one of the basic accounting software packages available to businesses today. The most widely used accounting software programs are QuickBooks (www.QuickBooks.com) and Quicken (www.quicken.com).

When seeking an accounting software program for your business, you are looking for basic features. Does it do the following?

- Track money in and out

- Write checks, pay bills, and record expenses

- Run a profit and loss (PL) statement and balance sheet

Which Financial Reports Should You Be Very Familiar With?

As a small business owner your challenge will be handling multiple tasks in your day-to-day operations. However, in order to properly manage and control your business operation, you must keep track of your cash flow. Therefore, it is extremely important to become familiar with and regularly review your financial statements.

A profit and loss statement, also known as a P&L or income statement, is a periodic summary of your business activity during a specific time, be it a month, quarter, or year.

The basic formula is simple:

Revenue (gross profits) − operating expenses
= earnings before taxes − income taxes = net income

By regularly reviewing your P&L statement, you are basically answering a very simple question: "Am I making any money?" A P&L statement is an important decision-making tool because it can help you monitor your operating expenses. You can use your P&L statement to assist you in making decisions on when to make necessary adjustments to increase or decrease expenses. Keeping accurate financials not only provides a clear picture of your company's financial health but it also shows that you are capable of properly managing the finances of your business.

Along with a P&L statement comes a balance sheet (also referred to as a statement of financial condition). The balance sheet lists everything the company owns and everything the company owes to creditors and provides the company's net worth.

Again, the formula is simple:

Company assets − company liabilities = company's net worth

The balance sheet provides a snapshot of the company's financial position at a point in time.

Balance Sheet Definitions

Assets

Anything the company owns, to include cash. Assets can include office equipment (computers, fax machines, phone systems, etc.), cash in checking or savings accounts, opening or owner's capital, and any investments (to include real estate) in the company's name.

Assets include (1) current assets: these are the amounts that constantly change, e.g., cash amounts in checking and savings accounts, and (2) fixed assets: office equipment, vehicles, or any investments owned by the company. Other assets may include opening capital.

Liabilities

Anything the company owes. Liabilities also consist of two types: (1) current liabilities; any bills owed to vendors, employee payroll, and any short-term loans. A liability to be considered current is a bill that needs to be paid within one year. (2) Long-term liabilities are obviously any debts or bills that are over a one-year term.

Equity

Usually consists of the owner's equity. Also referred to as owner's capital, equity is any debt that is owed to the owner. Most small business owners will invest money into the business (opening capital).

What's the Difference Between a Bookkeeper and an Accountant?

The Bookkeeper

As you begin your services as a mortgage brokerage, you will not need a full-time bookkeeper. Begin by employing an independent contractor, to come in a few hours once a week and increase his or her hours as warranted. As we discussed earlier, it is important to maintain accurate and proper books, specifically in a financial field such as the mortgage business.

A bookkeeper's functions include (but are not limited to):

- Making all journal entries
- Writing checks to pay company debts
- Preparing financial statements
- Reconciling books with bank statements

The Accountant

Selecting an accountant should require a bit more due diligence on your part. You will be seeking an individual that you can trust explicitly not just for tax advice but financial guidance for your future growth. I highly recommend that you find an accountant who is familiar with the mortgage industry. Seeking a good accountant is like seeking a good doctor; you must have a good comfort level and a large amount of trust. It may take meeting and interviewing with several accountants before you find the one that you feel the most rapport with.

An accountant in addition to preparing your taxes can provide an *audited financial statement*. A Certified Public Accountant (CPA) will audit your business's financial statements to establish the financial condition of your business and express an opinion as to the accuracy of the statements in accordance with Generally Accepted Accounting Principles (GAAP).

An updated P&L statement and balance sheet (or, in some cases, audited financial statements) will regularly be requested when you seek state licensure and lender approval.

What Is "Paper Trail"?

Documentation is key, so make sure you maintain a good record keeping system, by organizing important company records in one designated area. For example, file your financial records accordingly, in either your office, or with a trusted managing principal. When you begin seeking state license and lender approval, you should have easy access to vital financial and company information.

Your record keeping system should include a file for each of the following:

- Current financial statements.

- Reconciled bank records.

- Current tax records.

- Corporate records (whether articles of incorporation, partnership agreements, or trade name filings).

- Licenses (to include any business license and state licenses). Keep a copy of licenses in your files. An original copy of any licenses should hang in your office lobby.

- Contracts (keep records of office lease agreements, any equipment lease agreements, and any work-for-hire agreements).

- Intellectual property (such as trademarks or copyright filings).

10. Your Mission Statement

You may believe that creating a mission statement when you are first starting a mortgage brokerage is just not important. I must disagree. Every organization should have its mission, values, and vision. As you begin developing your business, you are creating your company culture, the manner by which you want to be perceived by your clients and business associates. You are identifying your company's core values. Remember, as a mortgage broker, you are holding a highly important financial position. You have certain responsibilities and standards of practice that must be observed.

A mission statement should be an attainable, clear motivational point of focus. It is your vision to focus your efforts and hopes in an attempt to achieve your goals in the future. It's important for a company to identify its values and vision and have it in writing, but that's only the beginning. Make sure that you incorporate this mission in everything you do. A well-written mission statement should inspire commitment from both your employees and your clients.

What Should Your Mission Statement Include?

You might want to begin by identifying why your organization was created (what opportunities or needs there are to fill) and explain how your business will address these needs. Next, identify by what values your company will conduct its business. Your employees will be conducting business every day as representatives of your company. You want them to make the right decisions and set their priorities in a manner that best represents your company image.

Here are just a few examples of a mission statement:

RBC Mortgage

Our mission is to be the lender of choice for America's consumers. We are committed to providing the broadest selection of products, most competitive pricing and superior service for borrowers through our exceptional mortgage consultants. In this way, we will continue to deliver outstanding long-term growth and financial and operating performance for the benefit of our customers, teammates and business partners.

We believe that the dream of home ownership should be attainable and affordable. We are committed to making the process of obtaining a mortgage as simple and convenient as possible and to forming lasting relationships with our customer and business partners.

We will continue to expand to new markets and to add new products and services, so that eventually for anyone who wants to own a home—all across the nation and around the globe—we will be there.

New Century Financial Corporation

Our mission is to be a world-class mortgage company, a great company to do business with and a great place to work. We will strive to continuously meet and exceed the expectations of each of our customers and business partners by: providing loan originators and borrowers with competitive rates, a variety of loan programs and service that is prompt, courteous and responsive to the unique characteristics of every customer; delivering what we promise to investors in our loans; providing our associates with a work environment characterized by communication, teamwork, opportunities for growth and rewards for performance; and delivering superior returns on the investments of our stockholders.

What Is Purpose Statement?

While you are creating your mission statement, you can consider developing a purpose statement for your company. A purpose statement is a brief statement of what your company will strive to achieve. A purpose statement can be extracted from your mission statement. For example:

Sample purpose statement (from PHH Mortgage mission statement):

"We promise to treat our customers like family while providing financing for the American dream."

Create one powerful sentence that everyone in your office can memorize and put into practice every day! You can use your purpose statement in all of your marketing material, business cards, letterhead, and on your Web site. It is an excellent marketing tool and excellent way to instill your company's values.

Getting Started Checklist

- **Have you determined the type of business structure your organization will assume?** You may need to seek professional advice to help you determine which business structure is best suited for your needs.

- **Have you followed the appropriate procedures to register your business name?** Typically sole proprietorship and partnerships register with the county clerk's office. Corporations, LLC, and LLP register with the secretary of state corporation division.

- **Have you determined if your state has any additional license or permit requirements?** To check on mortgage broker licensing requirements, refer to Chapter 10, "Educational and Licensing Requirements for the Mortgage Broker."

- **Have you determined if your state has any specific educational and licensing requirements for a mortgage broker?** You can check in Chapter 10 for a state-by-state guide, including the contact information for your state regulating division.

- **Have you registered for a federal employer identification number (EIN)?** Generally you will need to register for an EIN number if you hire employees, operate as a corporation or partnership, or have a Keogh plan. Check the IRS Web site at: http://www.irs.gov/businesses/small.

- **Have you chosen a tax year for payment of federal taxes?** Refer to the IRS Web site at: http://www.irs.gov/businesses/small.

- **Have you registered with your state for payment of state taxes?** Check with your state Department of Treasury.

- **Have you chosen an accounting method?** Refer to the IRS Web site at: http://www.irs.gov/businesses/small.

- **Will you be hiring employees?** Check for state and federal government responsibilities.

- **Will you be hiring loan agents?** Check to see if your state has any licensing or registration requirements for your loan agents.

- **Have you checked with your state for any business location requirements?** Refer to Chapter 10.

- **Have you checked with your state for net worth requirements for a mortgage broker?** Refer to Chapter 10.

- **Have you obtained a surety bond or fidelity bond?** Refer to Chapter 10.

Mortgage Technology Terms and Definitions

A

Algorithm

The art of calculating with any species of notation. A formula for solving a particular problem. An algorithm has a clear-cut set of rules and a clear stopping point. Algorithmic formulas are components of mortgage software systems such as pricing engines and AVMs.

Application

For technology purposes, application is a program or group of programs designed for end users. Software can be divided into two general classes: systems software and applications software.

Architecture

Architecture refers to the planning phase of the software development process, much like architecture refers to the same phase in the process of building a house. This planning phase serves as a road map for current and future development for the product. An open architecture allows the system to connect easily to devices and programs made by other manufacturers.

AUS

Automated underwriting system, also referred to as AU, is a software system such as Fannie Mae's Desktop Underwriter, Freddie Mac's Loan Prospector, Countrywide's CLUES and pmiAURA. AU contains underwriting logic and mortgage loan purchase rules used to approve a loan and convey approval conditions.

Auto-populate

Fill in automatically. In mortgage lending, an operation in which a Java applet or other means is used to take information from a database and transfer it to predetermined fields in an online mortgage loan application or other form, saving costly repetitive steps and preventing errors.

AVM

Automated valuation model. Software tool that employs computer analytics, real estate sales data, and other elements to arrive at an estimate of value independent of on-site human appraisal.

B

Bandwidth

The transmission capacity of an electronic pathway such as a communications line, computer bus, or computer channel. In a digital line, it is measured in bits per second. The bandwidth of optical fiber is in the gigabit (billion-bits-per-second) range, while Ethernet coaxial cable is in the megabit (million-bits-per-second) range.

Bit

Short for *binary digit*, the smallest unit of information on a machine. A single bit can hold only one of two values: 0 or 1. More meaningful information is obtained by combining consecutive bits into larger units. For example, a byte is composed of 8 consecutive bits.

Broadband

Broadband refers to the ability of the user to view content across the Internet that includes large files, such as video, audio, and 3D. Broadband refers to an increased ability to do so, whereas the term *narrowband* can refer to the inability to do so. Broadband capability typically is speeds greater than 56 kbps.

Byte

One character of information, usually 8 bits wide.

C

Configuration

(1) The way a system is set up, or the assortment of components that make up the system. Configuration can refer to either hardware or software, or the combination of both. (2) The physical arrangement of those components (what's placed and where). (3) The software settings that enable two computer components to talk to each other (as in configuring communications software to work with a modem).

CTI

Computer telephony integration refers to systems that enable computers to act as call centers, accepting and routing incoming communications such as phone calls, faxes, and Internet-based messages.

D

Data

In general, data is information. In computer usage, data is distinct pieces of information usually formatted in a special way (for example, XML).

Data can exist as numbers, text, bits, bytes, and other forms. The term *data* is often used to distinguish binary machine-readable information from textual human-readable information. In computer usage, data files (files that contain binary data) are usually distinguished from text files (files that contain ASCII data). In database management systems, data files are the files that store the database information, whereas other files, such as index files and data dictionaries, store administrative information, known as metadata.

Database

A collection of information organized into records, each of which contains labeled categories (fields), making it easy for a computer program to select its desired pieces of data—in other words, an electronic filing system.

DES

Data encryption standard, a standard for encrypting data, developed at IBM in 1976. Using a 56-bit key, DES encryption is a method to encrypt data files prior to sending through the Internet.

Desktop

A personal computer (PC) or professional workstation that's designed to fit on a desk. This term also describes what you see on your computer screen when no applications are running.

Digital Signature

Refers to electronic signatures that are created in a more rigorous technology that captures the signed document in a formula that is embedded in the electronic document. Digital signatures can be validated to determine whether a document has been tampered with in any way.

DNS

Domain name system helps users to find their way around the Internet. Its principal use is the lookup of host IP addresses based on host names. The host names are also known as domain names. Some important domains are .com (commercial), .edu (educational), .net (network operations), .gov (U.S. government), and .mil (U.S. military).

Document

In the PC world, the term *document* is used to describe any file produced by an application (program).

DOS

Disk operating system. Most often used as a shorthand for MS-DOS (Microsoft disk operating system), which was originally developed by Microsoft for IBM and is the standard operating system for IBM-compatible personal computers. Precursor to Microsoft Windows NT and OS/2 Warp.

Download

To copy a file or files from a main source, such as a Web site, to a CD or to one's own computer. Downloading can also refer to copying a file from a network file server to a computer on the network.

E

Encryption

The process of protecting information as it moves from one computer to another. The information is encoded before it is sent and decoded with a secret key when it is received. *Unencrypted data* is called plain text; *encrypted data* is referred to as cipher text.

Ethernet

A local-area network (LAN) architecture originally developed by Xerox PARC and further developed by DEC and Intel. Ethernet can operate over several different media including fiber optic, coaxial cable, and twisted-pair cable. This 10 Mbps networking scheme is widely used because it can network a wide variety of computers, it is not proprietary (as in the case of intranet), and components are widely available from many commercial sources.

F

Fiber Optics

A method of transmitting light beams along optical fibers (which are actually bundles of glass). A light beam can be modulated to carry data (information) resulting in high-speed transmission. Fiber-optic cables have several advantages over traditional metal cables.

Frames

An HTML technique for combining two or more separate HTML documents within a single Web browser screen. Some Web sites offer a "frames" version and a "no frames" version. Search engines will often index only the part of a framed site within the <NOFRAMES> section.

FTP

File transfer protocol is the standard method for downloading and uploading files over the Internet.

G

Gateway

In computer networking, a combination of hardware and software that links two different types of networks, so that information can be exchanged, for example, between different e-mail systems.

H

Homepage or Home Page

The front page or first page of a Web site, also commonly used to refer to the first document you come to in a collection of documents on a Web site.

Host

(1) Commonly thought of as the place where your Web site resides. An Internet host has a unique Internet address (IP address) and a unique domain name or host name. (2) A computer system that is accessed by a user working at a remote location. Typically, the term is used when there are two computer systems connected by modems and telephone lines. The system that contains the data is called the host, while the computer at which the user sits is called the remote terminal.

Hostname

Name which officially identifies each computer attached to the Internet.

HTML

Hypertext Markup Language; the authoring language used to create documents on the Web. HTML is a mark-up language that uses tags to structure text into headings, paragraphs, lists, and links. It tells a Web browser how to display text and images. You can see a Web page's HTML code if you select "view source" from the View menu in your Web browser.

HTTP

Hypertext Transfer Protocol; the standard Internet protocol for the exchange of information used on the World Wide Web. HTTP defines how messages are formatted and transmitted, and what actions Web servers and browsers should take in response to various commands. Entering a URL into a browser sends an HTTP command to the Web server directing it to find and transmit the requested Web page.

Hypertext

A text-linking system that allows jumping between related information in a document by clicking on a button or highlighted word. The icon that you select to view (the associated object) is referred to as a hypertext link or button.

I

Icon

A small picture that represents an object or program. For example, the graphic symbols located on your desktop activate a program.

Interface

(1) The way a computer communicates with a user or application, referred to as a user interface. (2) The actual connection between two applications or two hardware devices that facilitates the exchange of data. "To interface" is to make an appropriate physical connection between two pieces of hardware so that the equipment can communicate or work together effectively.

Internet

A global network connecting millions of computers that facilitates data transfer and communication services, such as remote login, file transfer protocol (FTP), electronic mail (e-mail), newsgroups, and the World Wide Web. Originally developed as ARPANet by the U.S. Department of Defense in order to provide a "fail-safe" communications system in the event of nuclear attack. In 1995 the World Wide Web, the portion of the Internet accessed by browsers, received U.S. government approval for commercial use.

Internet Protocols

Protocols such as Transmission Control Protocol–Internet Protocol (TCP/IP), Domain Name Services (DNS), Simple Mail Transfer Protocol (SMTP), Lightweight Directory Access Protocol (LDAP), Extensible Markup Language (XML), Hypertext Markup Language (HTML), Secured Hyper-Text Transport Protocol (HTTPS), and Secured Socket Layer (SSL).

Internet Telephony

A category of hardware and software that empowers people to use the Internet to transmit telephone calls, enabling inexpensive phone-based communications anywhere in the world. Internet telephony products may also be referred to as IP telephony, voice-over-the-Internet (VOI), or voice-over-IP (VoIP).

Intranet

A private network based on TCP/IP protocols belonging to a company or organization intended for internal use only. An intranet's Web sites look and act just like any others, but the firewall surrounding an intranet fends off unauthorized access.

IP Address

A numeric address that identifies a computer on a TCP/IP network. The format of an IP address is a 32-bit numeric address written as four numbers separated by periods.

IT

Information technology; a broad term that refers to the managing and processing of information and their devices, especially within a large organization or company. An IT department is the technical group within a company, responsible for overseeing, managing, evaluating, and upgrading the various forms of technology the company is using.

J

Javascript

A scripting language developed by Netscape to enable Web authors to design interactive sites. Although it shares many of the features and structures of the full Java language, it was developed independently. JavaScript can interact with HTML source code, enabling Web authors to spice up their sites with dynamic content.

L

LAN

Local area network; a network (located in close proximity, restricted by distances of up to one mile) connecting personal computers and workstations (each called a node) providing high-speed communication over dedicated private communication links (such as fiber optics, coaxial cable, or twisted-pair wiring).

LOS

Loan origination software; used by mortgage brokers and mortgage lenders to manage the origination and processing of mortgage loans.

M

MERS

Mortgage Electronic Registration System. Using technology developed by EDS, MERS (http://www.mersinc.org) acts as a national clearinghouse for mortgage information by tracking mortgage ownership and servicing rights electronically.

Mirror Sites

A Web site(s) that is a copy of an existing Web site that is often on different servers. Usually, mirror sites use larger and faster systems than the original, so it's easier to obtain material from the mirror. Mirror sites are useful when the original site generates too much traffic for a single server to support.

Module

(1) In software, a module is a part of a program. Programs are composed of one or more independently developed modules that are not combined until the program is linked. A single module can contain one or several routines. (2) In hardware, a module is a self-contained component.

N

Narrowband

Low-speed access to the Internet using dial-up modems running at 56 kbps or less.

.net

In Web services, .net (dot net) is the Microsoft platform that incorporates applications and services and depends on four Internet standards: HTTP, XML, SOAP, and UDDI. .net eliminates boundaries between applications and the Internet. Software is rented as a hosted service, using the Internet to house all of a user's applications and data.

Node

A device that is connected to a network, such as a computer/workstation or a printer. Every node has a unique network address, sometimes called a Data Link Control (DLC) address or Media Access Control (MAC) address.

O

Open Source

Any program whose source code is made available for use or modification by users or developers. As opposed to proprietary systems, a system with open specifications allows software to be used in a variety of computing environments and with various other software programs.

P

Packet

The unit of data sent across a network. Information is sent over the Internet (and other networks) in packets.

P2P

Peer-to-peer. A network in which you have more than one computer, sharing files from each other's hard drives. Opposite of client-server network, in which each computer shares resources with a server.

PDF

Portable document format; a PDF file is an electronic facsimile of a printed document.

Plug-in

A hardware or software module that adds a specific feature or service to a larger system.

Portal

A generic term for any site such as AOL; provides an entry point or gateway to the Internet for a significant number of users and provides services such as e-mail, forums, search engines, etc.

Protocol

Agreed-upon format and rules that computers must follow in order to exchange messages.

R

RAM

Random-access memory; the most common type of computer memory. RAM retains memory on a short-term basis and stores information *while you work* and is one of the things that makes your computer run faster.

RDBMS

Relational Database Management System; a type of database management system that stores data in the form of related tables.

ROM

Read-only memory; computer memory on which data have been prerecorded. Once data have been written onto a ROM chip, they cannot be removed and can only be read. Unlike a computer's random access memory (RAM), ROM does not lose its data when the computer power is turned off. It is sustained by a small long-life battery.

Router

An electronic device that connects two or more networks and forwards data packets from one network to the other. Routers are located at gateways, the places where two or more networks connect.

S

S/key

The purpose of S/key is to eliminate the need for the same password to be conveyed over a network each time a password is needed for access. A series of passwords are created at once, and each password is used only one time to prevent access by unauthorized persons.

Scaleable

A term that refers to how well a hardware or software system can adapt to increased demands. For example, a scalable network system would be one that can start with just a few nodes but can easily expand to hundreds of nodes.

Server

A computer that shares its resources, such as printers and files, with other computers on the network. An example of this is a Novell NetWare Server that shares its disk space with a workstation that does not have a disk drive of its own.

Sniffer

A program or device that monitors data traveling over a network. Sniffers can be used both for legitimate network management functions and for stealing information off a network. Unauthorized sniffers can be extremely dangerous to a network's security because they are virtually impossible to detect and can be inserted almost anywhere. This makes them a favorite weapon in the hacker's arsenal. On TCP/IP networks, where they sniff packets, they're often called packet sniffers.

Solution

A computer software term that implies a product or service provides a reliable means of addressing a problem or performing an operation.

Splash Page

The page of a Web site that the user sees first before being given the option to continue to the main content of the site. A splash page is an initial display that must be viewed before a visitor reaches the main page.

SSL

Secure socket layer encryption; a protocol developed by Netscape for transmitting private documents via the Internet. SSL works by using a private key to encrypt data that are transferred over the SSL connection. Both Netscape Navigator and Internet Explorer support SSL, and many Web sites use the protocol to obtain confidential user information, such as credit card numbers. Typically, Web pages that require an SSL connection start with https: instead of http:.

Switch

(1) In networks, a device that filters and forwards packets between LAN segments. LANs that use switches to join segments are called switched LANs. (2) In telecommunications, a switch is a network device that selects a path or circuit for sending a unit of data to its next destination. A switch may also include the function of the router, a device or program that can determine the route and specifically what adjacent network point the data should be sent to.

T

T1

A dedicated phone connection capable of carrying data at a very high speed (as in 1.544 Mbps).

T3

An extremely fast phone connection supporting data rates of 43 Mbps. This is more than enough speed to provide full-screen, full-motion video. T3 lines are most commonly used by ISPs and large networks.

TCP

Transmission control protocol; one of the main protocols in TCP/IP networks. Whereas the IP protocol deals only with packets, TCP enables two hosts to establish a connection and exchange streams of data. TCP guarantees delivery of data and also guarantees that packets will be delivered in the same order in which they were sent.

TCP/IP

Transmission control protocol/Internet protocol; the set of protocols that make services like remote login (TELNET), file transfer (FTP), and e-mail (SMTP) possible among computers that don't belong in the same network.

U

Unix

A multiuser, multitasking operating system, Unix (pronounced YOO-niks) was developed in the early 1970s. It was designed to be highly portable, enabling it to be installed on any computer with a compiler for the high-level programming language C.

URI

Uniform resource identifier; the generic term for all types of names and addresses that refer to objects on the World Wide Web. The most common form of URI is a URL such as http://mortgage-smarts.com.

URL

Uniform resource locator; the global address of documents and other resources on the Internet. World Wide Web pages are assigned a unique URL.

V

Virus

A destructive program or piece of code loaded onto your computer without your knowledge. Most viruses replicate themselves; the most common virus is transmitted through e-mail, while a more dangerous type of virus can transmit itself across networks and bypass security systems. Antivirus programs can periodically check a computer system for known types of viruses.

W

Web Site

A site (location) on the World Wide Web. Each Web site contains a home page, which is the first document users see. The site might also contain additional documents and files.

WWW

World Wide Web; a global system of Internet servers that support specially formatted documents that can be read and interacted with by computer. The documents are formatted in a language called HTML that supports links to other documents, as well as graphics, audio, and video files. Not all Internet servers are part of the World Wide Web. The Web is a subsystem of the Internet.

X

XML

Extensible Markup Language; Internet programming language offering more efficient data delivery over the Web. It enables Web authors and Web developers to create their own customized tags to provide functionality not available with HTML. XML must be implemented using "parser" software or XSL.

XSL

Extensible Scripting Language; a specification for separating style from content when creating HTML or XML pages.

Z

Zip

A popular data compression format. Files that have been compressed with the Zip format are called Zip files and usually end with a .zip extension. A special kind of zipped file is a self-extracting file, which ends with a .exe extension. You can unzip a self-extracting file by simply executing it.

SAMPLE EMPLOYMENT APPLICATION

> **Please be aware that as part of {Your Mortgage Brokerage Name} hiring process, it is necessary to undergo a reference check and if applying for a Loan Originator position, a background check will also be conducted.**
>
> **General Consent to Background Investigation**
>
> As a condition of Company's consideration of my employment application, I give permission to: {Your Mortgage Brokerage Name} to investigate my personal and employment history. I understand this background investigation will include, but not be limited to, verification of all information on my employment application.
>
> In addition, my signature on this document can be used as a release of information for any past employers, to release any information to {Your Mortgage Brokerage Name} as deemed necessary to complete a background check for employment purposes.
>
> Applicant's Signature: Date:

Personal Contact Information

Name : (Last Name First)	Social Security Number: _____
	Driver's License Number: _____
Physical Home Address: (No PO Boxes Accepted)	Physical Business Address:
Home Telephone:	Business Telephone:
Home Fax:	Business Fax:
Home E-mail:	Business E-mail:

This information must remain accurate throughout your employment with {Your Mortgage Brokerage Name}. If any of the above information changes at anytime, please submit updated and current information to:

Previous Employment

Please provide your employment history for the past five years:

Name of Present or Last Employer:			
Address	City	State	Zip
Starting Date	Leaving Date	Job Title	
May we contact your Supervisor? ☐Yes ☐No			
Name of Supervisor	Title	Phone	
Duties			
Reason for leaving			

Name of Previous Employer:			
Address	City	State	Zip
Starting Date	Leaving Date	Job Title	
May we contact your Supervisor? ☐Yes ☐No			
Name of Supervisor	Title	Phone	
Duties			
Reason for leaving			

Education

SCHOOL LEVEL	NAME AND LOCATION OF SCHOOL	NO OF YRS. ATTENDED	DID YOU GRADUATE?	AREA OF STUDY OR DEGREE
Grammar School				
High School				
College				
Trade, Business or Correspondence School				

References

Below give three names of persons you are not related to that you have known for at least one year. At least one of these must be a business reference.

NAME		ADDRESS	BUSINESS	YEARS KNOWN
	1			
	2			
	3			

Below please provide at least one bank reference.

NAME		ADDRESS	BUSINESS	YEARS KNOWN
	1			
	2			

Service Record

Have you been convicted of a felony within the last five years?	☐ YES ☐ NO
If yes, please explain. (This will not necessarily exclude you from consideration. Reminder: a background check is conducted on all applicants for loan agent/loan officer/loan originator position.)	

Sample Employment Agreement

This employment agreement is made effective for all purposes and in all respects as of this _____ day of ____, 20____, by and between {Your Mortgage Brokerage Name} hereinafter known as ("Employer") and _____ hereinafter known as ("Employee") who shall collectively be known herein as the "Parties."

Recitals

WHEREAS, Employer is engaged in the business of brokering mortgage loans.

WHEREAS, Employer wishes to employ Employee and Employee wishes to accept such employment on the terms and conditions recited below;

The premises have been considered and with acknowledgment of the mutual promises and of other good and valuable consideration herein contained, the Parties, intending to be legally bound, hereby agree as follows;

A. Capacity of Employment. The duties to be performed by Employee for Employer are generally described as follows: generate and process loans in accordance with Broker's general plans and policies and in compliance with Broker's guidelines.

1. Employee shall have the following title: Loan Agent

B. Term of Employment—*At-Will Employee*. Employer shall employ Employee in the capacity set forth above commencing on (agreed-upon date) or such other date as the Parties may agree to, and continuing with no fixed termination date, until either Party shall give proper notice of termination of this employment agreement to the other.

1. No Fixed Contract Period. There shall be no fixed date for termination of this employment agreement and it shall continue indefinitely until either Party gives proper notice to the other as required in this paragraph. Furthermore, Employee specifically waives any rights he or she may or may not have under state law (such as the Model Employment Termination

Act or like legislation) requiring that any and all termination of employment be "for good cause." <u>This is an at-will employment arrangement and, as such, no cause is required by either party for termination hereof.</u>

2. Notice Period. Any Party wishing to give notice of termination of this agreement, or of any intention not to renew at the end of a contract period, shall give the other Party ten (10) days advance notice. The notice period does not commence until actually received by the other Party. Should state or federal law require a longer notice period, the longer notice period so required under the law shall be applicable to this contract.

3. Method of Notice. Notice of termination or an intention not to renew this contract shall be given in writing by any method.

4. Notice to Employer. All notices under this contract to be given to Employer shall be communicated to: {Name Appropriate Person of Contact, Brokerage Name and Address}.

C. Termination for Cause. Employer may terminate this employment contract at any time "for cause," the grounds for which are defined below. In the case of termination for cause, Employer shall have no obligation to Employee for salary, bonus, or other compensation, or any other form of benefits under this agreement <u>except</u> for: (a) compensation earned prior to termination, (b) vested benefits Employee has accrued under any retirement compensation plan sponsored by Employer, or (c) other benefits mandated under federal or state law for departed employees (such as COBRA benefits). Also Employer will pay Employee compensation for commissions earned as per this employment contract, for any loans originated by Employee that fund no later than _____ days after termination. The "notice period" and "notice method," if any, contained in Paragraph B above do not apply to termination for cause. Employer must give actual notice to Employee of termination for cause but may deliver said notice by any manner, orally or in writing. Employer may make termination for cause effective immediately. Should state or federal law require a notice period, the notice period so required under the law shall be applicable to this contract. <u>This is an "at-will" employment contract</u> wherein no cause is required for termination. This paragraph concerning "for cause" termination, if triggered through commission of the below acts by the Employee, merely allows the Employer to terminate without complying with the notice provisions contained in the preceding paragraph.

<u>Grounds for cause termination.</u> Commission of any of the following acts by Employee constitute grounds for the Employer to terminate the Employee "for cause" under this paragraph:

1. Employee is charged with a felony crime,

2. Employee commits a crime of moral turpitude such as an act of fraud or other crime involving dishonesty,

3. Employee uses illegal drugs,

4. Employee fails to perform his or her duties in a competent manner,

5. Employee violates his or her duties of confidentiality and/or noncompetition under this agreement,

6. Employee sends loans to another mortgage broker,

7. Employee participates in providing any borrower information to any other mortgage broker, loan agent, or any other individual outside of {Your Mortgage Brokerage Name},

8. Employee commits any act or acts that harm the Company or Company's reputation, standing, or credibility within its operation or with its customers, mortgage lenders, or third-party providers.

9. Employee fails to perform his or her duties assigned to him or her for any reason,

10. Employee loses his or her license (if required).

D. Compliance. During the course of this agreement Loan Agent will comply and/or incur compliance with any and all state or federal statutes, laws, rules or regulations applicable to Broker, including, but without limitation, the following:

Truth-in-Lending Act

Equal Credit Opportunity Act

Real Estate Settlement Procedures Act

Fair Lending

Consumer Protection Act

Fair Credit Reporting Act

Patriot Act

Federal & State Usury Laws

All applicable regulations of the Mortgage Lending Division

Nevada Business & Professions Code

Lender's own lending guidelines

E. Limitations on Authority. Loan Agent shall have no authority to bind Broker to contract or otherwise, or to make any representation or warranty on behalf of Broker, unless authorized in writing by the President.

F. Required Confidentiality. For so long as the Employee shall remain employed by Employer and for a period of one (1) year after termination of employment with Employer for any reason, Employee shall not disclose or communicate any "Confidential Information" of Employer to any person or entity other than Employer nor use said "Confidential Information" for any purpose or reason other than the benefit of Employer. For purposes of the preceding sentence, "Confidential Information" means (but is not limited to) any information regarding Employer's business methods, business policies, procedures, techniques, development projects or results, sales information, or sales materials, financial information of any kind, trade secrets, or other knowledge possessed by Employer which is not generally known by individuals outside of the Employer (including Employer's employees, consultants, and advisors). Also,

"Confidential Information" shall additionally include, but not be limited to, the following information of the Employer:

1. Borrower's lists or borrower's information,

2. Sales strategy, techniques, or methods,

3. Information pertaining to products or services belonging to Employer,

4. Internal company reports of any kind,

5. All marketing strategies.

G. Noncompete Agreement. For as long as employee shall remain employed by Employer and for a period of one (1) year after termination of employment with Employer for any reason (to be known as "noncompete period"). Employee shall not directly or indirectly solicit business from borrowers or potential borrowers of Employer nor engage in (as an employee, principal, shareholder, partner, consultant, or any other capacity) any enterprise conducting business activities that are the same or similar to those of the Employer within the "Noncompete geographic area" (defined below). Finally, during the Noncompete Period, Employee shall not directly or indirectly solicit any employee of Employer for employment elsewhere (i.e., employment with any person or entity other than Employer).

1. Employee's bar from soliciting business from "customers, borrowers or potential borrowers of Employer" applies to all individuals or entities who were or are "borrowers or customers" of Employer at any time during the Noncompete Period.

2. The brief description of Employer's business activities contained in the recitals to this agreement shall not be considered an exclusive and exhaustive list of the business activities of Employer.

3. The term "Noncompete Geographic Area" for purpose of this agreement shall be defined as competing within the USA.

H. Employee Compensation. For all services rendered by Employee under this agreement, Employee shall be entitled to the compensation as follows:

Additional Benefits. Employer further agrees to pay for and provide Employee during the period of employment, the following benefits in addition to the compensation as mentioned in the preceding paragraph:

Vacation

Health Insurance

Parking

For all above-listed benefits subject to written Employer plan, the Employee's eligibility to receive said benefit shall be governed by the eligibility requirements contained in the Employer plan. Employer shall make all plan documents, or accurate summaries thereof, available for inspection by Employee.

I. Reimbursement. If reimbursement is required from a lender pertaining to a loan that the Loan Agent was paid a commission for, or the Loan Agent was the loan officer for as per the third page of the loan application, the Loan Agent will be required to reimburse Broker immediately for those costs.

J. Licensing. Loan Agent agrees to apply for licensure with the {Your State Licensing Division} under said Broker and is to maintain that license in good standing throughout the term of this Agreement.

K. Advertising. Your broker prior to distribution must approve all marketing material.

L. Conflict of Interest. Loan Agent acknowledges that the obligations of the Loan Agent are special and unique. Loan Agent agrees that he or she will not at any time during the term of this Agreement serve as an officer, director, employee, or otherwise have an interest in any entity that engages in business similar to that of Broker. This provision does not apply to stock ownership in a publicly traded company.

M. Automobile. Loan Agent will, at his/her own expense, procure an automobile for any use in traveling and making calls on clients and prospective clients. Loan Agent agrees to indemnify and hold Broker harmless from any claims arising out of or relating in any way to the operation or use of that automobile by Loan Agent. Furthermore, Loan Agent will at all times during the term of this Agreement keep in full force and effect, at his/her sole expense, a policy of automobile insurance on each automobile used by him/her at any time to carry out any of the duties under this Agreement.

N. Loan Processing. The corporate processing team must perform all processing.

O. Dispute Resolution. In the event of a disagreement or dispute between Broker and Loan Agent or with other people within the organization, arising out of or connected with this agreement, which cannot be resolved by and between the parties concerned, the disputed agreement shall be submitted to the American Arbitration Association.

P. Indemnification. Loan Agent shall be solely responsible for his/her conduct hereunder and Loan Agent hereby agrees to indemnify and hold Broker harmless from all costs, liability and expenses, including attorney's fees and legal costs, which Broker incurs by reason of any act or omission of Loan Agent contrary to the terms and conditions hereof, for any reason including negligent acts, errors or omissions, and false or fraudulent acts or statements or any act or omission contrary to the laws of the State of {Your State} or any other law or regulation to which Broker is subject.

Q. Liability for Fraud. Loan Agent's commissions will be denied or charged back (if previously paid) to the Loan Agent against future Commissions and/or Commissions on any loan determined by Broker to be fraudulent, whether the fraud is committed by the Loan Agent or by the borrower, where Loan Agent knew or should have known of the borrower's fraud. Broker further reserves the right to deny or charge back all or any part of any Commission on a loan that has pre or post closing deficiencies which, in the opinion of the Broker, based upon its policies and procedures, qualifies as a "Charge Back Item" to Loan Agent.

R. General Provisions.

R.1 <u>Continuing Obligations.</u> The termination of this Agreement shall not affect any rights or obligations accruing prior thereto or any continuing obligations of the parties hereunder.

R.2 <u>Notice.</u> Any notice, request, instruction or other document to be given hereunder shall be in writing and shall be deemed to have been given when delivered personally, or when mailed, postage prepaid, addressed to the party to be given notice as follows:

To Broker: _____

_____

To Loan Agent: _____

R.3 <u>Entire Agreement.</u> This Agreement supersedes any and all other agreements, either oral or in writing or implied in fact, between the parties hereto with respect to the performance by Loan Agent and Broker, and contains all of the covenants and agreements between the parties with respect to that performance. Each party to this Agreement acknowledges that, with respect to the Agreement, no representations, inducements, promises or agreements, orally or otherwise, have been made by any party, or anyone acting on behalf of any party, which are not embodied herein, and that no other agreement, statement or promise not contained in this Agreement shall be valid or binding.

R.4 <u>Modifications.</u> Any modification of this Agreement will be effective only if it is in a writing that (i) is signed by both parties; (ii) specifically references this Agreement and (iii) specifically expresses intent by both parties to modify this Agreement.

R.5 <u>Effect of Waiver.</u> The failure of either party to insist on strict compliance with any of the terms, covenants or conditions of this Agreement by the other party shall not be deemed a waiver of that term, covenant or condition, nor shall any waiver or relinquishment of any right or power at any one time or times be deemed a waiver or relinquishment of that right or power for all or any other times.

R.6 <u>Partial Invalidity.</u> If any provision in this Agreement is held by a court of competent jurisdiction to be invalid, void, or unenforceable, the remaining provisions shall nevertheless continue in full force without being impaired or invalidated in any way.

R.7 <u>Law Governing Agreement.</u> This Agreement shall be governed by and construed in accordance with the laws of the State of {Your State}.

S. Acknowledgment. Loan Agent acknowledges that he/she has had the opportunity to consult with independent counsel of his/her own choice concerning this Agreement, and that he/she has taken advantage of that opportunity to the extent that he/she desires. Loan Agent further acknowledges that he/she has read and understands this Agreement, is fully aware of its legal effect, and has entered into it voluntarily based on his/her own judgment.

_____

Please print your name   Date

X_____

Please sign your name

Address _____

Res: (   ) _____-_____   Cellular:(   ) _____-_____

Fax: (   ) _____-_____   E-mail: _____

Social security number _____ - _____ - _____

Please attach copy of:

[ ] original signed W9

_____

President,

_____

Mortgage Broker Company

_____

Sample Independent Contractor Agreement

This Agreement made and entered into this _____ day of
_____, 20___, by and between {Your Mortgage Brokerage},
herein referred to as Broker and

_____ herein
referred to as Loan Agent.

Recital

A. Broker is a {Your State} corporation who provides loan
brokerage services.

B. Broker and Loan Agent desire to enter into this Agreement
to establish the terms and conditions of Loan Agent performance as a loan officer as set forth below.

Agreement

Now, therefore, in consideration of the foregoing premise, as
well as the promises, covenants and conditions set forth herein,
the parties agree as follows:

1. <u>Performance.</u> Loan Agent's duties under this agreement,
to be performed with the approval and concurrence of the
President of Broker are as follows:

Generate and process loans in accordance with Broker's
general plans and policies and in compliance with Broker's
guidelines.

Such duties may be curtailed, augmented or modified from
time to time as deemed mutually agreeable to Broker and Loan
Agent. Loan Agent will at all times perform in an honest and
ethical manner. Loan Agent acknowledges and agrees that he/she
will devote his/her utmost knowledge and best skills to the performance under this Agreement and will devote his/her full business time to the rendition of such services. Loan Agent will
conduct business exclusively on behalf of Broker and will not
engage in any other gainful occupation, as per HUD Handbook
4060.1 REV-1, paragraph 2-14, including but not limited to,

marketing, distribution or development of any products related to the real estate loan industry which requires his/her personal attention without prior written consent of the President of Broker ("President").

2. <u>Compliance.</u> During the course of this agreement Loan Agent will comply and/or incur compliance with any and all state or federal statutes, laws, rules or regulations applicable to Broker, including, but without limitation, the following:

> Truth-in-Lending Act
>
> Equal Credit Opportunity Act
>
> Real Estate Settlement Procedures Act
>
> Fair Lending
>
> Consumer Protection Act
>
> Fair Credit Reporting Act
>
> Patriot Act
>
> Federal State Usury Laws
>
> All applicable regulations of the Mortgage Lending Division
>
> Lenders' own lending guidelines

3. <u>Broker's Policies and Regulations.</u> Loan Agent agrees to comply with Broker's policies and regulations, including those set forth in Broker's policies and procedures manual, if any, and any subsequent amendments or additions thereto. In the event of any conflict between those policies and regulations and this Agreement, the terms of this Agreement govern.

4. <u>Independent Contractor Relationship.</u> This agreement does not constitute a hiring by either party. It is the intention, that so far as shall conform to the law, that Loan Agent is an independent contractor and not the Broker's employee and will be treated as an Independent contractor for State Tax purposes. This agreement shall not be construed as a joint venture or partnership and neither party shall be held liable for the obligations incurred by the other.

5. <u>Limitations on Authority.</u> Loan Agent shall have no authority to bind Broker to contract or otherwise, or to make any representation or warranty on behalf of Broker, unless authorized in writing by the President.

6. <u>Compensation.</u> As compensation for the services to be rendered by Loan Agent hereunder, Broker will pay Loan Agent pursuant to the schedule attached hereto as Exhibit "1." Fees shall be due and payable to Loan Agent only after Broker has collected payment to which Loan Agent is entitled for the related transaction.

6.1 <u>Timing of Payment.</u> Fees shall be paid to Loan Agent for each transaction only after Broker has received copies of all documentation in connection with that transaction.

6.2 <u>Liability for Loan Expenses.</u> In the event that a transaction is canceled or not completed for any reason, Loan Agent is liable to pay any outstanding fees incurred by them on behalf of their borrower. This includes but is not limited to appraisals, credit reports, lender cancellation fees or mandatory lock penalty.

6.3 <u>Nonliability for Uncollected Commissions.</u> In no event will Broker be liable to Loan Agent for Loan Agent's share of commissions not collected, nor is Loan Agent entitled to any advance or payment from Broker upon future commissions.

7. <u>Dispute Resolution.</u> In the event of a disagreement or dispute between Broker and Loan Agent or with other people within the organization, arising out of or connected with this agreement, which cannot be resolved by and between the parties concerned, the disputed agreement shall be submitted to the American Arbitration Association.

8. <u>Indemnification.</u> Loan Agent shall be solely responsible for his/her conduct hereunder and Loan Agent hereby agrees to indemnify and hold Broker harmless from all costs, liability and expenses, including attorney's fees and legal costs, which Broker incurs by reason of any act or omission of Loan Agent contrary to the terms and conditions hereof, for any reason including negligent acts, errors or omissions, and false or fraudulent acts or

statements or any act or omission contrary to the laws of the State of {Your State} or any other law or regulation to which Broker is subject.

9. <u>Liability for Fraud.</u> Loan Agent's commissions will be denied or charged back (if previously paid) to the Loan Agent against future Commissions and/or Commissions on any loan determined by Broker to be fraudulent, whether the fraud is committed by the Loan Agent or by the borrower, where Loan Agent knew or should have known of the borrower's fraud. Broker further reserves the right to deny or charge back all or any part of any Commission on a loan that has pre or post closing deficiencies which, in the opinion of the Broker, based upon its policies and procedures, qualifies as a "Charge Back Item" to Loan Agent.

10. <u>Reimbursement.</u> If reimbursement is required from a lender pertaining to a loan that the Loan Agent was paid a commission for, or the Loan Agent was the loan officer for as per the third page of the loan application, the Loan Agent will be required to reimburse Broker immediately for those costs.

11. <u>Licensing.</u> Loan Agent agrees to apply for licensure with the {Your State Licensing Division} under said Broker and is to maintain that license in good standing throughout the term of this Agreement.

12. <u>Advertising.</u> Your broker prior to distribution must approve all marketing material.

13. <u>Termination.</u> Either party may terminate this agreement, with or without cause, with written notice. Notice is to be delivered to: {Your Mortgage Brokerage Name and Address}.

14. <u>Solicitation of Employees or Customers.</u>

14.1 <u>Information about Other Employees and Independent Contractors.</u> Loan Agent will be called upon to work closely with employees and independent contractors of Broker in performing services under this Agreement. All information about such employees and/or independent contractors which becomes known to Loan Agent during the course of his/her performance under this Agreement, and which is not otherwise known to the public, including compensation or commission structure, is a Trade Secret of Broker, as defined below, and will not be used by Loan Agent in soliciting employees and/or independent contractors of Broker at any time during or after termination of his/her employment with Employer.

14.2 <u>Solicitation of Employees and Independent Contractors Prohibited.</u> During the term of this Agreement and for two (2) years following its termination, Loan Agent will not, directly or indirectly, ask or encourage any employee(s) and/or independent contractor(s) of Broker to leave their employment or to terminate their contract with Broker, solicit any employee(s) and/or independent contractor(s) of Broker for employment, make any offer to compensate any employee or independent contractor of Broker as an employee, independent contractor or otherwise, or retain any employee or independent contractor of Broker as an employee, independent contractor or otherwise.

14.3 <u>Solicitation of Customers Prohibited.</u> For a period of two (2) years following the termination of this Agreement, Loan Agent will not, directly or indirectly, solicit the business of any of Broker's customers, other than those borrowers whose loans were closed by Loan Agent.

15. <u>Trade Secrets.</u> During the course of this Agreement, Loan Agent will have access to various trade secrets of Broker. A "Trade Secret" is information, which is not generally known to the public and, as a result, is of economic benefit to Broker in the conduct of its business. Loan Agent and Broker agree that Trade Secrets include, but are not limited to, all information developed or obtained by Broker and comprising the following items, whether or not such items have been reduced to tangible form (e.g., physical writing): all methods, techniques, processes, ideas, research and development, trade names, service marks, slogans, forms, customer lists, pricing structures, menus, business forms, marketing programs and plans, layouts and designs, financial structures, operational methods and tactics, cost information, the identity of or contractual arrangements with suppliers, the identity or buying habits of customers, accounting

procedures, and any document, record or other information of Broker relating to the above. Trade Secrets include not only information belonging to Broker which existed before the date of this Agreement, but also information developed by Loan Agent for Broker or its employees during the term of this Agreement and thereafter.

15.1 <u>Restriction on Use of Trade Secrets.</u> Loan Agent agrees that his/her use of Trade Secrets is subject to the following restrictions during the term of the Agreement and for an indefinite period thereafter so long as the Trade Secrets have not become generally known to the public:

15.1.1 <u>Nondisclosure.</u> Loan Agent will not publish or disclose, or allow to be published or disclosed Trade Secrets to any person who is not an employee of Broker unless such disclosure is necessary for the performance of Loan Agent's obligations under this Agreement. The President must first authorize disclosure to someone who is not an employee of Broker in writing.

15.1.2 <u>Use Restriction.</u> Loan Agent will use Trade Secrets only for the limited purpose for which they were disclosed. Loan Agent will not disclose any Trade Secrets to any third party (including subcontractors) without first obtaining Broker's written consent and will disclose Trade Secrets only to Broker's own employees having a need to know. Loan Agent will promptly notify Broker of any Trade Secrets improperly or prematurely disclosed.

15.1.3 <u>Nonremoval.</u> Loan Agent will not remove any Trade Secrets from the offices of Broker or the premises of any facility in which Broker is performing services, or allow such removal, unless permitted in writing by the President.

15.1.4 <u>Surrender Upon Termination.</u> Upon termination of this Agreement for any reason, Loan Agent will surrender to Broker all documents and materials in his/her possession or control, which contain Trade Secrets.

16. <u>Unfair Competition, Misappropriation of Trade Secrets and Violation of Solicitation Clauses.</u> Loan Agent and Broker

acknowledge that unfair competition, misappropriation of Trade Secrets or violation of any of the provisions contained in this Agreement would cause irreparable injury, that the remedy at law for any violation or threatened violation thereof would be inadequate, and that Broker will be entitled to temporary and permanent injunctive or other equitable relief without the necessity of proving actual damages. Loan Agent and Broker agree that such relief will be available in a court of law regardless of the arbitration provision set forth in this Agreement.

17. <u>Conflict of Interest.</u> Loan Agent acknowledges that the obligations of the Loan Agent are special and unique. Loan Agent agrees that he/she will not at any time during the term of this Agreement serve as an officer, director, employee, or otherwise have an interest in any entity that engages in business similar to that of Broker. This provision does not apply to stock owner-ship in a publicly traded company.

18. <u>Automobile.</u> Loan Agent will, at his/her own expense, pro-cure an automobile for any use in traveling and making calls on clients and prospective clients. Loan Agent agrees to indemnify and hold Broker harmless from any claims arising out of or relat-ing in any way to the operation or use of that automobile by Loan Agent. Furthermore, Loan Agent will at all times during the term of this Agreement keep in full force and effect, at his/her sole expense, a policy of automobile insurance on each automo-bile used by him/her at any time to carry out any of the duties under this Agreement.

19. <u>Loan Processing.</u> The corporate processing team must perform all processing.

20. <u>Accounts.</u> No savings, checking, investment or other accounts may be established by Loan Agent in the name of Broker or in any name similar to that of Broker. The determi-nation as to similarity of names is within the sole discretion of Broker.

21. <u>General Provisions.</u>

21.1 <u>Continuing Obligations.</u> The termination of this Agreement shall not affect any rights or obligations accruing prior thereto or any continuing obligations of the parties hereunder.

21.2 <u>Notice.</u> Any notice, request, instruction or other document to be given hereunder shall be in writing and shall be deemed to have been given when delivered personally, or when mailed, postage prepaid, addressed to the party to be given notice as follows:

To Broker: _____

_____

_____

To Loan Agent:

21.3 <u>Entire Agreement.</u> This Agreement supersedes any and all other agreements, either oral or in writing or implied in fact, between the parties hereto with respect to the performance by Loan Agent and Broker, and contains all of the covenants and agreements between the parties with respect to that performance. Each party to this Agreement acknowledges that, with respect to the Agreement, no representations, inducements, promises or agreements, orally or otherwise, have been made by any party, or anyone acting on behalf of any party, which are not embodied herein, and that no other agreement, statement or promise not contained in this Agreement shall be valid or binding.

21.4 <u>Modifications.</u> Any modification of this Agreement will be effective only if it is in a writing that (i) is signed by both parties; (ii) specifically references this Agreement and (iii) specifically expresses intent by both parties to modify this Agreement.

21.5 <u>Effect of Waiver.</u> The failure of either party to insist on strict compliance with any of the terms, covenants or conditions of this Agreement by the other party shall not be deemed a waiver of that term, covenant or condition, nor shall any waiver or relinquishment of any right or power at any one time or times be deemed a waiver or relinquishment of that right or power for all or any other times.

21.6 <u>Partial Invalidity.</u> If any provision in this Agreement is held by a court of competent jurisdiction to be invalid, void, or unenforceable, the remaining provisions shall nevertheless continue in full force without being impaired or invalidated in any way.

21.7 <u>Law Governing Agreement.</u> This Agreement shall be governed by and construed in accordance with the laws of the State of {Your State}.

22. <u>Acknowledgment.</u> Loan Agent acknowledges that he/she has had the opportunity to consult with independent counsel of his/her own choice concerning this Agreement, and that he/she has taken advantage of that opportunity to the extent that he/she desires. Loan Agent further acknowledges that he/she has read and understands this Agreement, is fully aware of its legal effect, and has entered into it voluntarily based on his/her own judgment.

_____   _____
Please print your name   Date
X_____
Please sign your name
Address _____
Res: (   ) _____-_____   Cellular:(   ) _____-_____
Fax: (   ) _____- _____   E-mail: _____
Social security number _____ - _____ - _____
Please attach copy of:
[ ] original signed W9

_____

President,

_____

Witness

Exhibit 1

Commission

　　For all loans closed, Loan Agent will be compensated according to the following schedule:

Commission Structure:

_____

Print Name

_____

Sign and Date

CHAPTER 4

SALES AND MARKETING FOR THE MORTGAGE BROKER

A Lesson in Cold Calling

Blockbuster Selling Techniques

High-Powered Marketing Strategies

A Lesson in Cold Calling

Ambition + Perseverance = The Act of Overcoming Failure

Ambition is a strong desire to achieve a goal. A person who aims at nothing has nowhere to go.
Perseverance is the persistence to stick to a course of action. Failure is the path of least persistence.

Early on in my career I learned the significance of persistence when it comes to sales. I grew up in New York City and my first sales job at 17 was for a wholesale office furniture company. My job as a solicitor was to pass out color-coded flyers and give a short pitch on our low prices and quality furniture. My assigned territory was from midtown to Wall Street. I was given strict criteria: walk into an office, ask for the person in charge of ordering supplies, and hand him or her a flyer. If security or anyone else tried to stop me from soliciting in the building, I was to leave immediately but return as soon as they left. Under no circumstances was I to leave any building until all my flyers were distributed.

The color-coded flyers were used to determine which solicitor brought in the customer, and a small commission was paid on each sale. As an athlete I knew the benefits of speed, efficiency, and a competitive spirit. Armed with my flyers I realized that I could make more money if I doubled my required sales calls. My determined persistence and efficient time management quickly made me the top solicitor in just three months.

No Fear

Of course I encountered a lot of opposition. In fact one day I found myself at the New York Time-Life Building where I was approached by a security officer who informed me of their "no solicitation" policy and asked me to leave the building. Following my employer's orders, I left the building but after a short while I returned. Unfortunately, I was spotted by the same security officer who escorted me to his office and was about to call the police. I urged him to call my employer instead, which he reluctantly agreed to do. My employer came to my aid, signed a release form, and I was allowed to go. Upon leaving the premises, my employer congratulated me on my determination, paid me a bonus, and told all the other solicitors they should have half of my tenacity. Shortly thereafter he changed his criteria accepting certain "no solicitation policies." However, my lesson had been learned; as a "good soldier" I had not only been rewarded but also praised!

Unknowingly I was developing cold calling skills that have remained with me to this day. I learned how to be assertive by believing I had an important message to deliver, and I was not accepting any resistance. I learned "no" never means "no"—it means "not now."

When selling yourself, first and foremost you must *believe* in yourself and your services in order to properly convey your message. Condition your mind over and over again with positive thoughts. By picturing in your mind the outcome that you want, you are strengthening your mind to overcome rejection. "See it, believe it, become it." I call this my mental rehearsal. By the time I walk into an office I have built up my belief system so much that my sales pitch sounds easy and natural.

Analyzing Fear

Fear is only the anticipation of rejection. What's the worst that can happen anyway? You can walk into an office and be told that your services are not needed. That's not so bad. By realizing this, you can turn these preconceived notions into optimistic thoughts. What if you walk into that same office just at the time they *are* in need of your product or service? Think of all the business you will be generating with this new positive outlook.

Identifying Your Market

Of course you want to target a respective market. The key to cold calling is to identify the appropriate person to buy your product or service. I began my mortgage career as a loan originator and developed my career soliciting real estate agents. That meant I had to cold call many a real estate office seeking out referrals. First I knew that real estate agents would be working with potential home buyers and these home buyers would be seeking out financing for their homes. I began by putting together a schedule. Each week I would walk into a certain real estate office on the *same* day and at the *same* time. Even though I was told they had no referrals for me, they soon began to expect me. They realized that if I was this determined to come week after week after several rejections, I would be equally as determined when working on their clients' loans. Eventually I gained the confidence of these realtors and began to get loan referrals.

Cold Call Tip
When conducting a cold call in person *always:*

- Act as if you belong; approach your destination with authority.

- Look into your prospect's eyes.

- Have a smile on your face.

- Give a strong, confident handshake.

Additional suggested reading material on cold calling:
Cold Calling Techniques That Really Work by Stephen Shiffman, September 2003.
Red Hot Cold Call Selling: Prospecting Techniques That Pay Off by Paul S. Goldner, October 1995.

Telephone Cold Calling Techniques

I hadn't realized but my real training on cold calling had not yet started. The "gold rush" was on and my father decided to move my family from New York to California, where we landed in Beverly Hills. My father was the best salesperson I've ever met. He was an effective communicator with an uncanny ability to effortlessly make a sale. He had what is known as "natural charisma." He decided it was time I began training under his strict supervision. I was about to sell office products over the phone by cold-calling clients off a marketing list.

Prepare a Script

Most experts will agree that selling over the phone is much more difficult than selling face to face. The key to a phone sale is to *be prepared*. My training began with a carefully drafted script. I rehearsed my sales pitch with my father—this was a painstaking task. As we role-played, my father would barrage me with all the obstacles possible. As grueling as this may sound, it was extremely helpful as I faced my first live call. Knowing that I was well prepared for any obstacles helped me relax and be more natural.

You don't need to follow a script word for word. Use a script as a tool to remind yourself of what questions to ask. This will give you confidence and let you concentrate on delivering your message. I suggest that you rehearse your script with a friend and have him or her ask you some tough questions. Be the best you can be by evaluating and critiquing yourself so you can continually improve your habits.

Have a Solid Opening

You only have a few seconds to catch the attention of your prospect. Your opening statement is critical and should contain the principal benefits for your prospective client.

For example: "Hello, my name is Jane from The Mortgage Shoppe. The reason for my call today is to inform you of a special loan program we have where you may be able to save hundreds of dollars off of your current mortgage payment. Is this something you may be interested in?"

The objective during the first few minutes of your call is to continue phrasing your questions so that your prospective client delivers a YES answer. After your opening statement, your next question may go like this:

For example: "I am offering a free analysis right over the phone and it only takes a few minutes. Are you interested?"

As you continue to develop a YES attitude, your prospective client becomes more receptive and open to your call. This allows you to proceed with your call, take a loan application, and give your borrower a loan quote.

Become a Great Listener

Now just because you have given a potential borrower a quote on a loan program doesn't mean you have a loan commitment. Mortgage originators are not paid on loan applications *taken*; they are paid on loans *closed*. It's important to truly listen to your borrowers' needs. What are their objectives with the loan? Are they refinancing to simply lower their interest rate or are they interested in taking cash out of their equity for some particular reason? Ask relevant questions. Your questions should be posed in a manner that encourages your potential clients to reveal their true needs and desires.

The biggest mistake many mortgage originators make during a sales call is to talk too much. I am not sure if this is due to nervous energy or just the fact that some people like to hear themselves talk. Whatever the case, it is an awful mistake to make.

Make sure you allow your clients plenty of time to speak. Do not interrupt their thoughts and concerns. Make sure you clarify and acknowledge what they are saying.

Set a Goal

By setting a daily goal you develop mental determination. If you don't achieve your day's goal, make double the calls the following day. Setting goals allows you to measure your progress; in the beginning it will be day-by-day, then month-by-month, and eventually year-by-year.

Overcoming Objections

When you are given an objection, don't easily accept it and hang up. Think about it for a minute; put yourself in their shoes.

People are busy and they receive many solicitations. Be considerate of their feelings. You can try an answer like the following:

For example: "I understand you are busy, but we've been able to save so many homeowners hundreds of dollars off their mortgage and thought you might want to do the same."

This will give them an opportunity to really think before turning away an opportunity on a real savings.

Be Passionate About Your Services

If you believe in your product or service, it's going to come across to your client. As a mortgage broker, you are providing a true service to your community. You may be helping a family achieve the American Dream of buying their first home or maybe an existing homeowner is in a pinch and needs to cash out some equity from his home for an emergency. In either case you are performing a great service to your community, and it is something to be proud of and take seriously. You are not simply selling a loan; you are assisting people with an important financial transaction. Remind yourself of this fact on each loan transaction and treat it as if it were your first.

Treat each borrower with respect, courtesy, and pay attention to the details.

Follow up, follow up, follow up! Remember your client is evaluating and judging you not only by what you say but by what you do. *Trust is earned.*

Blockbuster Selling Techniques

At some point everybody is selling something to somebody. Whether we are selling ourselves on a job interview or on a date, we are persuading (another) to recognize the worth or desirability of something or someone. As a mortgage broker your ability to sell is critical to the success of your career. As an owner of a

mortgage company, it's important that you learn how to identify the characteristics that make up a good loan agent.

The Enthusiastic Type

Have you ever noticed how some people can sell anything to
anybody? These individuals are energetic and enthusiastic about
what they are doing at all times. They tend to have a charismatic
personality easily capable of initiating a conversation. Many tend
to be so animated during their presentation that the client feels
inclined to give in to the excitement. A high-flying-act personality may be a good choice when selling a product but it's not nec-
essarily the best choice when seeking out a good loan agent.
These individuals are great openers, but they tend to lack in their
follow-up and closing techniques. This type of loan agent is the
reason for most complaint calls from clients. Remember, your
client is buying a *service*. This requires more than just a great
opening line; it requires diligence and follow-through.

For the enthusiastic type: Develop some patience. Focus on
taking the time to listen to your borrowers' needs. Don't dominate the conversation. You're ahead of the pack. You have
accomplished the first step by opening up the door and taking
the loan application. Now make sure you "do as you say." Follow
up, follow up, follow up, and you will be able to close the deal.

The Quiet and Methodical Type

The quiet and methodical salespeople are excellent listeners.
That's what separates them from their counterparts. They pay
close attention to detail and can better explain their product or
services. This person is excellent at follow-up. The challenge with
this type of individual is their fear of rejection. They don't like
confrontation and as a result they lack in their opening skills.
These folks may not realize it but they lack self-motivation. Their
inhibitions make it difficult for them to pick up the phone or
walk into an office and ask for referrals. This type of individual
can develop into a great loan originator if they learn how to work
on their deficiencies.

For the quiet and methodical type: By recognizing your weakness in initiating the sale, you can empower yourself by building up your personal belief system. Purchase some motivational books or audiotapes. Recondition your mind . . . to think positive.

A Positive Attitude = Positive Results

The Relationship Builder Type

A loan agent who worked for me had a distinct manner of building a friendship with her customers, and in many cases in just one conversation. Through her conversation she was able to show a genuine interest and compassion, easily forming "trust." With this trust she was able to extract certain information that would enable her to find solutions that would be right on target. People like to do business with people they like. A relationship builder is an excellent loan originator. Having an established relationship with your borrowers helps keep the loan intact through the loan process. With those loans that encounter bumps (and most loans do), they are much easier to overcome when a relationship has been established. This type of loan agent will do fewer sales calls because each sale requires more time.

For the relationship builder type: The only shortcoming for this type of individual is time management. You can waste too much time in going for the close. While trying to develop a rapport with your client, you might find yourself entangled in a long-winded discussion with no end. Learn how to develop your relationship without getting too emotionally involved and keep your calls or presentations to a time limit.

More Sales = More Loans Closed = More Money

The Shark Type

These individuals live by one rule and one rule only, and it's simple. Sell to people who want their product and ignore those who don't. This type of salesperson wastes no time. They are willing to risk the sale by testing "the close" from the beginning of the conversation. Their philosophy is No Risk = No Reward. If the client doesn't appear to be interested, they're off to the next prospect. There is something to be said about this technique of selling. You spend the majority of your valuable time on the people who will most likely become clients. But how do you determine the likely candidates in just a few minutes of your sales call or presentation? This requires a series of questions that result in positive answers. This type of salesperson is most successful in a high-volume environment where they can afford to sift through several calls or prospects a day.

For the shark type: Most of these individuals believe they already know everything. However, they may be losing some sales opportunities because they don't develop empathy for their clients. Some people may find this type of selling technique to be too aggressive and a turnoff. You might want to tone down the high-pressure close and take a little more time with your clients to ensure less fallout during the loan process.

Which of these types of individuals makes the best salesperson? It's actually a hybrid. It takes a little bit of each personality to make a great salesperson. Great salespeople are charming, persuasive, and know their stuff. They are trustworthy and know how to instill confidence in their clients. Combine this with the ability to listen and spot the right opportunity to ask for the loan and you've got yourself a winner!

Winning Qualities of a Mortgage Originator

> *Trustworthiness.* It is imperative that a mortgage originator conduct his or her business in a trustworthy and ethical manner.

> *Honesty and integrity.* Again, imperative for a mortgage originator. A necessity to fulfill licensing requirements.

> *Confidence.* A great mortgage originator is capable of being confident and self-assured without coming across as arrogant.

Good communicating skills. An effective communicator understands the power of language. You must have proper grammar skills and speak professionally so that you will be taken more seriously.

Determination. You will encounter many obstacles in today's competitive market. You'll need to be determined to overcome them.

Conviction. As we have stated many times before, you must believe in yourself and your product or service in order to sell it to your customer. You must demonstrate that you can service your borrowers better than your competitors can.

Persuasive. Great salespeople are masters of the art of persuasion.

Focus. Great mortgage originators will focus on the bottom line. Whether it's helping a borrower see the benefits of the loan or featuring their edge to a potential business referral source, they must be able to keep their focus on closing the deal.

Self-driven. Salespeople are independent souls. You must be able to motivate yourself, overcome objection, and overcome the slumps. We all encounter slow periods throughout our careers; however, we must be able to pick ourselves up, regenerate, and go back out there.

Always prepared. Preparation is key. The best salesperson plans his or her day and has a plan of attack. When meeting with your client, be prepared with answers! You can only be successful if you are prepared.

Good listener. By listening to your borrower's needs you are better equipped to provide a positive solution that should develop into a loan.

Positive attitude. It's difficult to sell with a negative attitude. Many of us start out energetic with a positive attitude, but it's easy to lose those characteristics along the way. Maintaining a healthy outlook and positive attitude is imperative to a long lasting and successful career.

Follow-through. Always follow through with what you say. I cannot stress enough how important it is to have good follow-through skills as a mortgage broker; without them, you cannot be successful.

Goal oriented. All mortgage originators are paid on production. Therefore, it's essential that you are capable of setting realistic goals and are willing to work hard to meet them!

Surround yourself with other successful people. These people are inspirational; they are a terrific influence. Learn from them. What are they doing to create their success?

To meet other successful mortgage brokers without contacting your competitors, you can join your state mortgage brokers association. Their meetings and trade shows are excellent opportunities for you to network with other professionals in your industry.

Don't sell the rate, sell the value. It's a known fact that most mortgage brokers have access to the same mortgage lenders, so you're going to have the same loan programs and rates as your competitor. What you must do is prove that your service is better than your competitor's. How do you do that? Think about it. What does your borrower want more than anything else? The loan! Guarantee that your loan process is easier and you can get the loan closed faster. And by selling the borrower on the service aspects of your product, many times you can get the loan even if your competitor's rate is a little lower. Sell the quality of your service and make sure you deliver. Delivering on service is a guarantee for more business.

Empower yourself with knowledge. I was a natural born athlete, I was not a businessman. I had to work twice as hard as everyone else all the time. I did so by reading all the books I could get my hands on, listening to audiotapes, and attending many,

many seminars. You must invest in yourself by taking the time to learn all you can.

Great Quotes from Suggested Reading Material

"Focus on those activities you do brilliantly, and from which you produce extraordinary results." From *The Power of Focus* written by Jack Canfield, Mark Victor Hansen, and Les Hewitt, March 1, 2000.

"The great football coach Vince Lombardi once said, 'Winning isn't everything, but wanting to win is.' By the same token, results are not the only thing, but are everything in business. They are the only true measure of personal ability and corporate effectiveness." From *Turbo Strategy* written by Brian Tracy, June 2003.

"You can get everything in life you want if you'll just help enough people get what they want." From *Secrets of Closing the Sale* written by Zig Ziglar, May 2003.

"The advice 'go where they ain't' is not limited to location. A Pasadena, California, attorney goes where they ain't by marketing himself as a motorcycle accident specialist, leaving other personal injury attorneys to fight for the much larger and far more competitive market of automobile accident victims...Go where others aren't." From *Selling the Invisible* written by Harry Beckwith, March 1, 1997.

"In my case, I have found that it is most effective to give value first. And give it without expectation, and give it often, and give it without expectation and give it to your best prospects. And did I mention give it without expectation?" From *Little Red Book of Selling* written by Jeffrey Gittomer, September 25, 2004.

The Art of Closing the Deal

Keep in mind that your client is no dummy. Clients can sense when you are genuinely concerned about meeting their needs or you're just concerned about earning your commission. Remember to have empathy for your borrower. Refinancing or purchasing a home is a big-ticket item, one of the largest financial transactions most people encounter in their lives. You're not simply a sales agent, you're a mortgage consultant. People are always looking for guidance. It's always necessary to guide your borrower through this major decision.

Give Your Borrower Options
You might start by giving your borrowers a couple of different loan options. This way they don't feel like they are being pressured into something they're not completely sure they want.

Always Stress the Benefits
Will the borrower be saving money by refinancing? Point out the savings. If borrowers are cashing out some equity, you should know what the purpose is. Remind them how the cash they are taking out is going to help them. If borrowers are buying a new home, how much equity are they building by buying versus renting? Borrowers always want to know what's in it for them. Always sell the benefits.

Make Sure You Are Talking to the Decision Maker
There are many times you will be talking to a spouse and you have worked up a loan, you are ready to go to docs, and you have never spoken to the significant other. Now you realize you never really had a loan because the spouse isn't willing to make the final decision. Always ask if the person you are speaking to is able to make the decision on the loan or has discussed the loan with his or her significant other.

Determine What Implications There Are If Your Borrower Does Not Move Forward
Make sure you are aware of the market—are interest rates increasing? You are an advisor, so stress to your borrower what will happen if he does not act now. If your loan approval with the lender is going to expire, make sure you inform your borrower promptly.

Set a Deadline
There are many people that can only move forward with a deadline. Even if it means risking a loan, you must be able to present your borrower with a deadline for acceptance of your loan

option. This will determine whether the borrower is really interested or not.

Go for the Close

As soon as you've determined that you have properly presented your loan proposal and have demonstrated how you can meet your borrower's needs, you must "go for the close." Don't be afraid to ask for a loan commitment. Then pause, and let your borrower give you an answer *before* you respond

High-Powered Marketing Strategies

What Is Marketing?

Marketing is how you define your product, promote your product, distribute your product, and maintain a relationship with your customers.

A marketing campaign is essential for the livelihood of a mortgage broker. After all, it's how you're going to get your prospects or leads. It's important to take the time to develop a marketing campaign that will set you apart from the competition.

Marketing is identifying your customers' wants and needs and then satisfying those customers better than your competitors can.

Success doesn't come overnight. You must take your time and see what works best for you and your business model. However, you must do some form of marketing all the time: whether it's passing out business cards, going to open houses, marketing realtors, or sending out a mailing campaign. Your marketing campaign must be consistent and continuous.

The biggest mistake I've seen with mortgage brokers is that they do not have a solid marketing plan or budget in place. I suggest dedicating a percentage of your monthly profits to advertising *each* month. Typically 10 to 20 percent is recommended, but I believe it should be the amount you are comfortable with.

Before you begin any business you should have a business plan, a proposed budget plan, and a goal plan. Then use these tools to analyze your results and adjust along the way as necessary. Track your results. Are the number of leads you're getting turning into the number of loan applications necessary to reach the amount of closed loans that you need to meet your goal plans? This is the big question you want to keep asking as you develop your business and manage your marketing budget.

Start by developing a budget for your marketing campaign. In the beginning, even if you start with a couple of hundred dollars, have some business cards and flyers printed up and go out and promote yourself and your services. Make sure you include your photograph on any marketing material so that people will know who you are.

Developing Your Personal Sphere of Influence

The most inexpensive way to begin a marketing campaign is by seeking out business from the people you already know. It has been said that the average person knows 250 to 300 people. Sort out your contacts in your database, and then start by calling them all to let them know of your new profession. Even if they do not need a loan today, you can ask for referrals and when they are considering a loan they are likely to contact you first.

Talk to everyone you encounter on a regular basis: the folks at the coffee shop, the people at your gym, church, or any other organization you belong to. You can advertise your services without being too pushy. You'd be surprised at how much business you can pick up just by letting everyone you meet know about your services.

Establish networks outside of the typical: join a bowling league, a book club, or play on a softball team. The more social you become the more people you meet and the more business you can pick up. Give everyone you meet your business card and always ask if they have any friends who might be interested in your services.

Join your local chamber of commerce and take part in any community events. Don't forget to wear your name tag. Print up a name tag that includes your name and the fact that you are a mortgage consultant. Become a walking billboard!

Establish a Professional Referral Source

Realtors

Marketing to realtors is an obvious first choice for most mortgage brokers. As a result, this can be a tough market to break into as most realtors already have an existing referral relationship in place. To get the attention of realtors, you will need to posture yourself as an expert and bring some real value to the relationship. Be prepared to go the extra mile from the beginning. You must be consistent, service oriented, and accessible. There are several marketing practices that you can try:

Begin by seeking out a realtor that is open to referrals (as most are). You begin by referring a lead; then he or she can reciprocate by referring customers to you.

Real estate offices have weekly sales meetings for their realtors. Offer your services by conducting a brief presentation at their next sales meeting. Keep your talk to 20 to 30 minutes. In your presentation, discuss topics such as any changes in the mortgage market, a new loan program, or anything that will be of value to the realtors.

If you are unable to get scheduled with a presentation, attend the weekly sales meetings and make yourself available for any questions. Take this opportunity to introduce yourself and sell your value and services.

Offer to sit in a real estate office on weekends. You can provide prequalification services and answer any questions for realtors with prospective home buyers.

Stop by open houses and be prepared to provide prequalification services.

Join the local board of realtors and attend any seminars or conferences. This is an excellent way to establish relationships in a more relaxed setting.

Choose several real estate offices that you can visit consistently every week for a couple of months. Then show up on the same day and at the same time.

If you don't get a referral after a couple of months from one of the realtors, try visiting them on a Friday afternoon and bring a pizza for them with some of your business cards.

Marketing to realtors requires innovative strategies that may require you to think outside the box. I read that one loan originator gives out a Payday candy bar, with a note reading: "Every day can be payday when you use (your name) for your clients' financing needs."

After you get a referral, it is critical that you give superior service. Remember, you are looking for a long-lasting referral source. Delivering exceptional service is the only way to ensure repeat business and establish a solid relationship. Make sure that you have properly consulted with the borrower to provide the most appropriate loan program, make sure the loan process goes smoothly, and stay in touch *constantly* with the realtor and the borrowers. I recommend that you provide the realtor with a status report that you can deliver by e-mail. This will keep the realtor apprised of the loan progress and will eliminate the need for excessive calls. To gain the confidence of a realtor, the loan must close on time so that the buyer(s) can move in on schedule. The key to creating an ongoing relationship is to couple consistency with professionalism. A happy realtor will refer you to other realtors.

Financial Planners and Accountants

Other referral sources are financial planners and accountants. You will find that as a mortgage consultant you are providing more than just a mortgage loan. By discussing with your borrower(s) their short- and long-term financial goals, you are helping them establish a financial plan. Take this opportunity to refer them to a financial planner or accountant, if necessary. This will allow you to swap leads with these professionals.

Tax Attorneys and Tax Consultants

Don't forget tax attorneys and tax consultants. These professionals work with individuals, many of whom need to refinance their home in order to pay off tax liens. These professionals are an excellent referral source.

Banks and Credit Unions

Most banks and credit unions can't offer the wide selection of loan programs that you have access to. Take this opportunity to introduce yourself to your banker and/or credit union loan officers and let them know about your services and loan programs. You'd be surprised at the positive outcome from this referral source.

Home Builders

To establish relationships with builders, you can start by developing relationships with the salespeople at the new home tracts. Stop by new model homes on the weekends. Then visit with them consistently, letting them know what hot new loan programs you have available. Loan programs with 100 percent financing are always of interest to these folks.

The Power of Free Information

It's amazing how many people respond when you are giving away information. Develop a flyer or report with some enlightening advice, consultation information, or newsy material. You can change it every few months to highlight different topics. For instance, you may start with a report on "How to Improve Your Credit." Other topics you can highlight are "The Top Ten Mistakes Homeowners Make When Shopping for a Loan" or "How to Buy with No Money Down" ... you get the message. Then place an ad in a newspaper or realtor magazine offering your Free Report and name the topic you are highlighting.

The only way this type of marketing strategy can work is by implementing a call capture system. If you begin to get more calls than you can handle, change your ad to include a toll-free number with a prerecorded message requiring the callers to leave their name, address, and phone number in order to receive their copy of your Free Report. This is a great way to start your database. Even if callers are not yet ready to buy a home, take their information and add them to your database. Then follow up regularly with these folks so when they are ready to buy, you'll be the first person they contact.

For a list of call capture system providers, please refer to Chapter 9, "The Mortgage Broker Resource Directory" under "Telecommunications/Call Capture and Voice Broadcasting."

Call capture systems allow the prospect an option to leave a message. However, the beauty of these systems is the ability to capture the caller's phone number whether he or she leaves a message or not. The system can alert you of the phone call by text messaging the phone number to your office or cell phone. This way, you can return the call immediately, providing an automated callback feature that comes in very handy.

Offer free gift certificates for a free appraisal, no closing costs, or free credit report for new customers. Then include these coupons in your ad in the paper or realtor magazine.

Provide an Educational Seminar

Develop a home buying seminar to educate prospective home buyers. Then place an ad in your local newspaper or send out mailers to neighborhood apartment complexes. A good way to attract new prospects to your seminar is by offering valuable information at no cost. Try offering a "free credit report" to each customer that attends your seminar. Don't forget to have each customer sign an authorization form allowing you to pull their credit report.

Every smart salesperson knows that to develop new business you must give *value*. At your home buying seminar, discuss topics such as:

- Steps a new homeowner must take before purchasing a home

- Prequalification versus preapproval

- How to qualify for the lowest interest rates and closing costs

- How to improve your credit score

- Financial loan comparisons made easy

Invite representatives of your strategic partners such as realtors, title companies, escrow companies, financial planners, and so on, allowing them to give a 20-minute presentation of their services. Schedule your seminars during midweek, in the evenings, and limit the presentation time to an hour to encourage a larger turnout.

Be creative with your seminars and marketing material. I read about one sample marketing piece that was a mail piece that included a free popcorn package (similar in color to a Blockbuster video flyer) with a statement that read: "Movie rental smart, Apartment renting not so smart." This is creative marketing at its best...very clever.

Seminars do not have to be restricted to prospective home buyers. Recently with a flood of nonowner real estate investments and a surge in home values, I have seen seminars offering advice on topics such as creating wealth with real estate investments, reverse mortgage strategies, and building wealth techniques with home equity.

Giving free seminars is a great way to attract new customers, develop your public speaking skills, keep your name in front of people, and help your community all at the same time.

Take a Course Yourself

Mortgage Bankers Association (MBA) last year developed a free-of-charge three-hour training program for loan originators and mortgage brokers. The program called "Creating New Customers" trains mortgage originators how to conduct home buyer education seminars and includes 100 ways to increase production. Contact: http://www.campusmba.org.

For a list of marketing tools, please refer to Chapter 9, "The Mortgage Broker Resource Directory," and a financial comparison tool included on The Mortgage Coach Web site (www.mortgagecoach.com).

Marketing FSBOs

A FSBO is a For Sale by Owner that has decided not to use the services of a realtor to sell their home. They're an excellent group to market because they're going to have many prospective home buyers coming through their home. These prospective home buyers may or may not be prequalified for a mortgage. Offer the FSBO your services by providing a "Home Buyer's Kit" for them to hand out to each and every prospect that comes through their home. In the kit, include flyers on loan comparisons, benefits of buying over renting, and information on your next home buying seminar.

FSBO leads are available for purchase on Landvoice (www. landvoice.com).

Marketing Your Existing Database for Referrals

Develop a "Customer-for-Life (CFL)" Program

It's amazing to me how many mortgage brokers do not realize the power of "the existing customer." Did you know that you spend six times more on developing a new customer than if you were to just market your existing client base? Top mortgage brokers originate from 80 to 100 percent of their business from past clients. These are exceptional brokers who understand the power of delivering superb service and maintaining a long-term loyalty with their customers.

Start your CFL program by developing a customer database with relevant information broken down into several categories. Gather information such as contact information, interest rate, loan amount, debt load, and even birthdays. Make sure you always collect an e-mail address when available. E-mail is a cost-effective way to market your database.

With the valuable information you have retained in your database, you are capable of marketing to your existing clients for a variety of reasons—for example, when interest rates drop significantly. A great service available for mortgage brokers is The Mortgage Market Guide (www.mortgagemarketguide.com). This service allows you to track market activity, which allows you to keep your clients informed about any interest rate changes.

Do not forget to update your database quarterly. Getting in touch with your clients to update their contact information allows you an opportunity to ask for any new business and/or referrals. Whatever the reason is, you want to contact your database and contact them often. People are just too busy to remember you otherwise.

For a list of customer management software providers, please refer to Chapter 9, "The Mortgage Broker Resource Directory."

In addition to the regular birthday and Christmas cards, send out a mother's day or father's day card with a personal message. This way your borrower is more likely to appreciate your extra effort.

Of course nothing works better than offering something free in exchange for referrals. After the loan closes, immediately send out a personalized thank you note with a free gift offer in exchange for a referral. What can you offer? The gift can be anything from sporting event tickets, spa treatments, or gift certificates. You can really get creative here. If your borrower just got into a new home, try sending a change-of-address stamp or a small phone book that includes your contact information imprinted on the cover and has contact information for local services like neighborhood cleaners, dentists, pizza delivery, etc. Another great and inexpensive gift is a magazine subscription. With this they are reminded of you every month when they receive their magazine. These are thoughtful and very useful gifts that your borrower will notice and appreciate. Make sure you *always* include a personalized thank you note, letting your borrower know that your business relies on referrals and any referral is personally appreciated.

Keep track of who sends you the most referrals and then offer that borrower a special treat. You'd be surprised with the results. The person sending you the most referrals might be part of a large organization with the ability to give you even more business.

Don't forget about your business referrals. Whether it's financial planners, accountants, or tax consultants, make sure you send them a thank you card and a gift every time they send you a referral. A small token of appreciation goes a long way.

A customer-for-life campaign doesn't have to be expensive or complicated. Just be consistent and take a different approach from your competitors.

The key is to give value and stay in touch.

Develop a Postcard

These days, customers are more likely to read a well-designed postcard as opposed to a letter. Postcards are very effective when marketing your existing database. Send holiday-inspired post-cards with a photograph of you and a holiday-related message asking for referrals. Holiday examples would be Valentine's Day, St. Patrick's Day, and the Fourth of July.

Develop a Newsletter

Sending out an informative newsletter is a golden opportunity to stay in touch with your past clients and your business part-ners. Sending value-added information doesn't have to be in an expensive marketing piece. There are several options available these days. You can simply use colored stock paper, or you can use any number of software programs available to create your own newsletter format.

Feature some informative articles for your reader, such as neighborhood news, a series of tips for homeowners, loan prod-uct information, etc. A good idea is to include personal infor-mation about you and your company. Maybe your company is sponsoring a Little League team, or someone in your office is getting married or having a baby. Make sure you include photos. You want to send a "personalized" message that will continue to create a bond with your customers. Your goal is to stay in constant contact with your customers so when they encounter a friend or family member who is considering buying a home or refinancing their home, they instantly think of you and will refer that customer to you.

For a list of postcard and newsletter database system providers, please refer to Chapter 9, "The Mortgage Broker Resource Directory."

Send E-Mails

One of the easiest and most cost-effective ways to maintain contact with your past clients is by e-mail. Again, include infor-mation like mortgage market watch, program highlights, and even local events. Sending out a newsletter via e-mail is a cost-effective marketing strategy. It's not so much a matter of what you send, but that you're consistent in sending something.

Voice Broadcasting

Voice broadcasting is a relatively new technology available to mortgage brokers. It allows you to leave a prerecorded message on an answering machine or voice mail. The nice feature of this service is that when your borrower plays back the message, they won't be able to tell the difference between a real message and a voice broadcast.

This service can be of great benefit when you want to keep in contact with your database, especially when you grow it into the hundreds.

For a list of voice broadcast providers, please refer to Chapter 9, "The Mortgage Broker Resource Directory."

One of the best marketing tools available for mortgage brokers is Loan Toolbox. This Web-based service provides the loan originator with invaluable tools to increase business with marketing material for lead generation campaigns, selling and presentation material, and proven techniques from some of the nation's top loan originators. In addition, there is a learning center that provides concise explanations on loan programs, techniques on how to overcome objections, and tips on how to separate yourself from the pack. The community board provides insight from mortgage originators nationwide and is a great forum for sharing ideas and marketing strategies.

A monthly teleseminar allows participants to "talk to the experts," and weekly voice broadcasts are filled with up-to-the-minute news, motivating tips, and strategies. I am particularly impressed with annual events conducted by Loan Toolbox. The second-year event includes keynote speaker Tony Robbins and is sure to be another sold-out event. For more information on Loan Toolbox, visit them at www.loantoolbox.com.

The Power of the Web

In today's world I believe the most significant marketing tool any mortgage broker can have is a Web site. Incorporating a Web site into your business model is an excellent way to reflect a professional branded business image, and it can provide a competitive advantage over your competitors.

Having an Internet presence is an excellent marketing tool that opens the door for a whole new world of doing business. You're no longer bound to your immediate area; you can market your entire state. The first thing I suggest is to get an 800 number. When you list your address on your Web site, list it as your "corporate" address; you want to project a big company image.

There are mortgage brokers out there who conduct 100 percent of their business from technology-driven leads. Keep in mind that if you plan to use your Web site as a lead-generation tool, you will need to pay careful attention to the text material on your site and the way it is organized in order to enhance your Web site's position in search engine results.

Web Site Tips

1. Make sure you provide a very detailed description of your company. Include sections such as About Your Company, Company Mission, etc. List any accomplishments.

2. Search engines prefer Web sites that are updated frequently, so make sure you go in daily, or as frequently as possible to update interest rates, etc.

3. Mention in a prominent place the geographic area you cover. If you are only interested in marketing your local area, then you would mention your county, for example, "Orange County" regularly throughout your Web pages. Keep in mind that you'll only be able to service the state in which you are licensed. If you are interested in getting licensed in additional states, check out Chapter 10 in this book for educational and licensing requirements for all states from Alabama to Wyoming.

4. Include *detailed* descriptions of loan programs you offer.

5. A descriptive title that helps confirm the relevance of each of your site's Web pages will help the text users in their search results.

6. One of the strongest features of a mortgage broker's Web site would be the capability of quoting rates.

In addition, you must be prepared to have your loan originators respond immediately to these inquiries in order to compete with other mortgage brokers and online mortgage lenders. Data-vision (www.d-vision.com) is a company that offers technology solutions for small or medium-sized mortgage brokerages, allowing them to provide online decisions on a loan similar to that of large mortgage lenders.

Your Web site should include a secure online application that is customer friendly and is capable of importing directly onto your loan origination software (LOS) program. When choosing a Web site, make sure you can customize capabilities such as:

- Automatic e-mail response to the consumer after each loan application is completed.

- Receive notification of when a borrower is actually applying for a loan online. This way you or one of your loan officers can contact the consumer immediately.

- Receive notification of loan applications completed directly to your e-mail.

- Obtain credit authorization.

- Comply with the Patriot Act

To drive traffic to your Web site, post banners on other related Web sites with an attention-grabbing headline to catch people's eyes.

Include your Web address on all of your marketing materials and advertisements so you can drive as much business to your Web site as possible. When a borrower applies directly online, this saves you time and money.

You'll want to encourage each and every customer to apply online. Let them know that your company is highly automated and tell them how much quicker the application process is by applying online. If necessary you can advertise an incentive for the consumer who applies online. For example, try offering $100 off the closing costs for all applications completed online.

The new generation of borrowers includes many consumers who begin their search for a home online. These same consumers come to expect the companies they work for to have a Web site and the ability to apply for a mortgage online. Remember, a loan application requires that consumers divulge their private financial information. Therefore, some people may feel more at ease releasing that information on a secure Web site rather than during a face-to-face interview. It is, therefore, essential for a mortgage broker to have a transactional Web site, that is, the ability to quote rates, take applications, and display loan status. In addition to providing conventional financing, a Web site allows the mortgage broker to feature unique specialties such as first-time homebuyer assistance, credit repair services, reverse mortgages, for-sale-by-owners, or small balance commercial lending. Mortgage brokers can also use their Web site to cross-market their services by exchanging links with realtors, financial planners, and other professionals.

Of course you can't expect to get a new Web site to start getting leads right away. In fact, one of the biggest concerns among mortgage brokers is how to formulate a strategy to generate traffic to their Web site. Myers Internet, Inc. one of the largest Web developers for loan originators, provides several training programs that enable mortgage brokers to increase their production. Myers also enables members of its community to help each other through Bizboard forums and collects and distributes best practices and success stories of its clients. This is an excellent forum for the new loan originator to learn from their peers and gather assistance in developing their own strategy.

Broker Perspective

"Sheer volume drove me to ask myself that age-old question, 'How do I replicate myself?' I've found the answer through Myers. My Web site gives me an extension of myself that's busy working 24/7, that doesn't lie to my clients, provides clear and concise information, and allows an easy beginning to each transaction. Right now, between 30 to 35 percent of my applications are online—and by overall, applications are up 25 percent for this year. Also taking advantage of Myers' marketing classes really lit a fire underneath me, and the Bizboard opened up my eyes to things that helped me to raise my production 2.5 times above where I was before. If I had to put a price tag on the value I receive there, it would be in the ballpark of $2,000 a month. There is more quality and value there than any other mortgage forum. I've seen some competitor sites that look sharp, but if brokers only knew the value and activity received with the Myers sites and in the Myers community, they would never have an interest in any other company," said Lee Kendrick, broker-owner of Family Mortgage of Winchester, KY and long-term Myers client.

A Web site does not have to be expensive. Myers Internet, Inc. provides very affordable templates and customized mortgage broker Web sites. Myers enables loan originators to provide their consumers with access to rate sheets or risk adjusted payments, closing costs, secure online applications, rate alerts, loan status calculators, and much more.

"In the 11+ years that I have run Myers, I've been amazed to see how mortgage companies that embraced the Internet have grown. Many of our clients have gone from being small local companies to national players. Other clients have made a lot more money and enjoyed a better lifestyle. The internet is still in its early stages as a medium. In 10 years from now—a mortgage broker that does not have a Web site will be a rare breed," said Warren Myers, CEO of Myers Internet, Inc.

The Myers platform integrates with eMagic, an MGIC subsidiary, providing easy, online access to automated underwriting (AU) decisions, mortgage insurance, contract and bundled services, rate locks, document storage, imaging, and delivery. In addition, the Myers platform complements many of MGIC's other services such as contract underwriting, home buyer education, and lead generation. For more information on Myers Web solutions, you may call (800) 693-7770 or visit them at www.myers.com.

For a list of Web site designers, please refer to Chapter 9, "The Mortgage Broker Resource Directory."

Developing a Lead Generation Campaign

The Direct Mail Campaign

One of the most effective forms of marketing for a mortgage brokerage is a direct mail campaign. That is, the mortgage broker develops a marketing piece (in the form of a letter or postcard), obtains a lead source, and picks a mail house to send out the marketing piece. Today vendors provide full service products that include a selection of direct mail pieces, targeted data, and mail service.

Choosing your marketing data is critical to a successful direct mail campaign. You must be able to deliver your message to the right people. First, you must select your targeted area (city, region, county, or state), and then identify your audience, for example, renters, current sub-prime borrowers, veterans, senior citizens, etc. To generate leads you can select specific targeted data, such as homeowners with a specific credit score range, minimum loan amounts on existing liens, revolving debt levels, and type of property (such as single-family residence or condo). Your marketing data will come in the form of a list that includes name, address, and, in most cases, a telephone number allowing for an opportunity to try tandem telemarketing techniques. An inexpensive way to obtain data is to secure public record information from title or escrow companies.

When sending out mail pieces, as a rule of thumb you can expect a 1 percent return on the amount of mailers sent out. For example, on 15,000 mailers you can expect 150 calls.

A direct mail campaign can be costly. Therefore, the most important aspect is to achieve the highest conversion rate from calls received to loans closed. To maximize your lead conversion rate, there are a few steps that you must take.

- Be prepared by ensuring that you have enough loan officers to handle a surge of calls.

- Make sure that you have loan officers covering all time slots including early morning, evening, and Saturday shifts. Don't forget to indicate your business hours of operation on your mail piece.

- Keep accurate records of all incoming calls, monitoring the number of calls, indicating which loan officer was assigned the call, to determine your conversion rate. There are software programs available that capture all incoming phone numbers with a caller ID function.

If you decide on a direct mail campaign to market potential refinance customers, try using an example of a recent transaction on one of your customers. Let's call them Mr. and Mrs. Jones. Demonstrate how you were able to save Mr. and Mrs. Jones hundreds of dollars simply by refinancing their existing mortgage. Then you can include a statement like "We were able to save Mr. and Mrs. Jones $600 off their mortgage by refinancing their existing mortgage. If saving money *and* getting cash out of your home interests you, give us a call."

 When deciding on a direct mail campaign, you must be dedicated to sending your advertising piece consistently. This type of marketing only works when the prospective client becomes accustomed to seeing your name on a regular basis.

A critical component of your mail strategy, of course, has to be the return on your investment (ROI), that is, your net profits divided by the total cost of your mail campaign. For example, on a 15,000 mail-piece campaign with a 1 percent response rate (150 calls), you could expect 60 percent of the calls to be qualified leads = 90. Out of the 90 qualified leads, you can expect 8 percent conversion rate = 7 closed loans. The net profits will depend on your total revenue per loan, your business operating expenses (including loan officer commissions), and cost for the leads. You want at least a 40 percent ROI.

For a list of direct mail list providers, please refer to Chapter 9, "The Mortgage Broker Resource Directory."

Internet Leads

Buying Internet leads can be a great source of new business for mortgage brokers. The key, however, is to purchase "fresh," untapped leads. There are hundreds of Internet sites offering mortgage leads for sale. Careful selection is advised in order to avoid unscrupulous lead originators. There are plenty of them out there. These companies sell leads that are too old, leads that have already been tapped into, or they just oversell the leads they generate.

When interviewing with a lead originating company, make sure that you ask detailed questions, for example:

- Are your leads exclusive?

- Are your leads less than 48 hours old?

- Do you have existing clients that I can speak to?

- Do you have a guarantee policy?

The best way to find a reputable lead originator is to ask other mortgage brokers for referrals. The lead-generating company should be able to provide at least three referrals.

When purchasing your leads, you can refine your selection criteria to include information such as income, loan types, property types, loan-to-value ratios, loan amount, and geographic data.

Prices vary widely and cost anywhere from $14 to $50 a lead. However, an exclusive lead less than two days old can carry an even higher cost. Buying leads can get expensive, so you will need to closely monitor your lead closing ratios. Closing 8 to 14 percent of the leads you purchase is considered to be a good return for your money.

For a list of lead providers, please refer to Chapter 9, "The Mortgage Broker Resource Directory."

Telemarketing Leads

Outsourcing

There are lead-generating companies with huge call centers that provide telemarketing services for mortgage brokers. They can either sell the actual telemarketing lead or hot-swap the lead directly to your company in real time. When purchasing telemarketing leads, you select certain parameters, for example:

- Credit rating (prime or sub-prime)
- Maximum loan to value (LTV) ratio

- Maximum loan amount

- Current home value

- Minimum current interest rate

- Type of loan desired

- Geographic location

- Property type

With the live transfer service (hot-swapping), the lead-generating company's call center will contact your prospects on your behalf, confirm their interest in a loan, then deliver the prospect to you in real time. Telemarketing leads can run from $35 to $85 per lead.

When selecting a telemarketing lead-generating company, it is imperative to ask for references and a guarantee policy.

In-House

Another option is to hire a telemarketer or several telemarketers to make outbound calls based on a prearranged script. These employees typically work for an hourly wage plus a small commission. A tiered-paying commission structure could include a small incentive to be paid for each application taken and another small incentive for each loan closed. This type of commission structure typically guarantees better results.

Your telemarketers can call off a free title company list for refinance transactions or they can call apartment dwellers for purchase money leads, or maybe to set up appointments for a home buying seminar.

For an in-house telemarketing campaign, you may consider an auto dialer. This technology allows for automatic phone dialing, mortgage message broadcasting, and "smart" message dialing. Keep in mind that you will need to support Federal Trade Commission (FTC) rules and regulations for "Do Not Call Lists." Should you use an auto dialer, make sure that the people you call are given an option to be removed from your calling list.

Advertising Your Services

There are many ways you can advertise yourself and your services. You can advertise in your local newspaper (local real estate newspapers are the best) and real estate magazines. However, other advertisement outlets include billboards, phone books, bus benches, grocery store shopping carts, and any other place where you can get your name out there. Remember to always include your photograph. You want everyone to recognize who you are and what you do. An exceptional way to cut costs and get more business is to build advertising alliances with your professional referral base.

When creating your ad, you want to start by creating a tagline that grabs your readers' attention. Your tagline should describe your business and services and could be used as a way to identify with your business as a form of building a brand. For example: The Mortgage Shoppe: Trustworthy, Reliable Service.

Remember that your services require a great deal of trust so your message should be personal as if you were simply talking to a friend. Keep the sentences short and concise. To ensure that the readers actually respond to your ad, make sure to create a sense of urgency by including a deadline date. For example, you may offer the first 100 callers a free appraisal or $500 off of their closing costs with an expiration date on the offer.

Become an Expert

As a mortgage broker you want to establish your credibility. Therefore, in order to stay on top of current mortgage trends, you should subscribe and read everything you can on the mortgage industry. Make sure you have a clear knowledge of all loan programs so you can easily give practical advice to your customers and become a trusted advisor.

For a list of trade print and online magazines, please refer to Chapter 9, "The Mortgage Broker Resource Directory."

As you become more knowledgeable in your field, try writing a short article for your local newspaper. Write about the current market condition of your local area or maybe you want to highlight a new loan product. Then start calling all the local reporters with your story ideas. Newspapers are always hungry for news and are always seeking out new items or innovative products. This is a great way to begin developing name recognition and establishing yourself as an expert in your field.

Don't forget about radio and TV. Contact your local radio talk shows, local television stations, and cable networks. If you can provide value to their viewers, these media outlets are always interested in hearing from you.

10 Powerful Marketing Tips for a Successful Mortgage Brokerage

1. "Exceed your customer's expectations" and you will maintain a relationship that will result in repeat business and referrals for more business.

2. Marketing efforts must be consistent to be successful. Your existing database should hear from you at least four times a year.

3. You will have a true "customer for life" approach when you think: "What am I going to do for this person two or three years from now?"

4. Incorporate your marketing into your everyday activities. Whether it is writing a personal thank you note after a closing or stopping in to see your realtor, complete at least one marketing strategy a day.

5. Rotate your marketing strategies. For example, the first contact could be with a personal note, the second contact could be with a postcard, the third contact could be with voice broadcast, and the last contact could be a newsletter.

6. Develop your name recognition with business cards, your Web site, flyers, pens, and anything else you can think of.

7. Use a buddy marketing strategy. Joint advertising with a realtor or builder is a great way to team up and expand your business.

8. You should not be selling rates and fees; you should be selling yourself and your expertise.

9. Have fun with your marketing campaign. Share ideas with your loan agents, business partners, etc. Don't be afraid to try different marketing campaigns. Just make sure to measure your results to know what works and what doesn't.

10. Realize that referrals are the lifeblood of your business. Don't just think about closing the loan at hand. Stop thinking of this business as a *transaction* business and think of it as a *relationship* business!

CHAPTER 5

MANAGING YOUR BUSINESS

Management Principles

Developing a Niche Market

Sample Business Models

Management Principles

Motivation + Teamwork = Making a Difference

Dwight Eisenhower once said, "Motivation is the art of getting people to do what you want them to do because they want to do it." It is the fuel that allows common people to attain uncommon results. Teamwork is the ability to work together toward a common goal.

It makes no difference whether you are a sole proprietor working from home or a large mortgage brokerage. You can't provide exceptional service without having the proper systems in place. A system is just a set way of doing things, so that every demand that is made of you can be channeled in a certain direction and dealt with in a planned way.

When the loans start rolling in and the workload increases, work begins to pile up. Between rate quotes, qualifying the borrowers, reviewing credit and appraisal reports, handling escrow, and investigating titles, the details can become overwhelming if not handled properly. The days begin to fly by, and mortgage brokers find they don't know where all their time was spent. Their days are focused on returning phone calls and working out problems on current loans. They don't go out and seek new business until their current load is depleted. Over and over again, they find themselves doing just one deal at a time. The only way to break this cycle is to learn and implement the disciplines of time blocking.

Time Blocking

A time block system begins by identifying and breaking down your daily activities into categories. A mortgage broker's income-producing activities can be broken down into three categories:

1. Learning time

2. Growth time

3. Processing time

Learning time is the time you spend learning new loan products, lender and other operational procedures, software systems, and the time you spend on strategic planning, necessary for your growth and your company's growth. This is a very important category. Only you can make yourself an expert in this field. You must know your stuff in order to become a trusted advisor.

Obviously when you first start out in your career, you will want to be learning at least half of every day. Our ever-changing marketplace requires even seasoned mortgage brokers to spend several hours a week in this category. The seasoned mortgage broker can consider this category as continuing education.

Growth time is the time you spend on prospecting new clients. This category includes taking applications, prequalifying your borrowers, sending out rate quotes, and recruiting and meeting with your strategic partners.

As mentioned in Chapter 4, the key to a successful mortgage brokerage is to do some form of prospecting *daily* to bring in new business. Often what happens to mortgage brokers when they get too busy is they become too complacent, believing that the business will just keep coming in on its own. Believe me, it doesn't. No matter how busy you get or how many loans you are carrying in your pipeline, you need to dedicate a *minimum* of one hour every day to prospecting new business.

Processing time is the time you spend on making sure the loans in your pipeline get closed. Returning phone calls, following up with your processor and underwriter to make sure all conditions have been met and keeping your borrowers and referral sources notified about the status of the loan. Although critical, this category produces the least income and could be assigned to an assistant if you have proper follow-up procedures in place.

Spend the majority of *your* time doing the things that make you more profitable.

You will quickly learn that the most valuable commodity you have in life is your time. Only you can determine how much time to spend in each category. Develop a schedule and don't forget to include your personal activities. I believe it's extremely important to not lose sight of your personal life in an attempt to grow your business. It's imperative to incorporate personal priorities and include them in your schedule. I personally cannot conduct my business activities without putting in a good workout in the mornings. For me my daily workouts have helped me overcome even the most difficult of circumstances. However, your personal priority can be coaching your child's Little League team or spending time on a hobby. Develop a schedule and get it down on paper.

Now that you have your daily schedule, you need to stick to it. If you've decided to devote an hour a day to your prospecting time, then check yourself out for that time. Don't read your e-mails or answer your phones for that hour. Allow yourself a half hour in between your time blocks to address any emergencies. This way you will be able to meet your time block goals and still have time to handle the unexpected.

As you begin to apply your time blocking disciplines, you will realize how much more you're able to accomplish on a daily basis. Taking control of your daily structure is a guarantee for more production and a successful career as a mortgage broker.

Develop a Plan

Before you begin hiring anyone, whether assistants, processors, or loan agents, you'll need to start with a plan. What do you want your business to look like? Where will you get your business? How big do you want to grow your business? Do you want to develop your business around a team? Do you want to hire loan originators? Will you need telemarketers? Select three to five goals that you want to reach in three to five years. Then write down your strategic business plan and develop a business flow chart...a road map that you want to follow.

Without a road map you won't know where you're going and therefore you'll never get where you want to go.

Be specific when developing your plan. Don't just simply make your goal to become the largest-producing mortgage broker. By developing specific goals in numbers you can measure whether or not you're on track in reaching those goals.

Don't just draw up a business plan and file it away. Keep that plan out where you can see it and refer to it often. With a business plan in place, as your company evolves you'll be better prepared to respond to any changes in conditions or resources.

Implementing Your Systems

It is important to remember that getting the loan in the door is just half the battle. Getting the loan closed will depend on whether you have a competent processing team that can get the loan funded on time and at the promised rate and fees.

The loan process can be arduous at times, requiring that every single detail be carefully reviewed and examined. Without a good team and effective systems in place, you could find yourself facing delays or, even worse, a deal that falls apart at the closing. The key to overcoming these negative situations is to develop and implement a proper system that ensures any potential problems are taken care of before they turn into unwelcome surprises.

Even a sole proprietor working from home should have a system. It can be as simple as a checklist that he or she completes on each application. The checklist contains all the necessary information required to hand over the file to the processor. The mortgage broker may not look at this file again until the loan is closed, but it is a system nevertheless.

Each system is unique to the business model, and each mortgage brokerage must determine how many systems are necessary to properly run his or her business. Systems should include:

- *Origination system.* This includes your database management system for marketing your existing database, your technology system to provide your borrowers with a rate quote, or maybe even a preapproval system. It should also include your system for prospecting business from your strategic partners.

- *Processing system.* This is the system designed for proper communication between your loan originators and processors. This system can be automated and may be accessible via your software.

- *Closing system.* This system should include your record management system. This system will properly add the customer to your database for future marketing. This is also the system for sending out thank you notes and/or a survey to your customer and referring partners.

Don't ever let your customers go in to sign loan documents without your loan originator and loan processor first reviewing the estimated HUD. Make sure the interest rate and fees are the same as quoted. This system avoids any negative situations at the closing.

Time management and organization are critical to the success of a mortgage broker business. Your goal will be to implement basic workflow systems that will enable your company to run like a well-oiled machine.

Creating a Job Description

After you determine what systems you need to put into place, you must decide if you have the right people to carry out these systems. Careful choice of personnel is essential.

To select the right employees, you must begin by creating a job description for each position you intend to fill. You can't expect to just hire people as you become busy, put them at a desk and expect them to know what to do. You must do a task analysis and clearly define what job functions are required of each position. A job description should be in writing, and there should be a job description for each desk.

Top 10 Traits to Look for When Hiring Your Staff

1. Highly money motivated

2. Eager to learn

3. Appreciates a challenge

4. Great listening skills

5. A team player

6. Able to cope with criticism

7. Extremely organized

8. Confident

9. Persistent

10. Competitive

With a job description comes accountability. You can easily evaluate someone's performance when everyone involved is aware of his or her job functions.

Of course this requires constant evaluation, which can be accomplished with effective communication and regular meetings.

Conducting Regular Meetings

I believe the best way to manage a successful mortgage brokerage is to conduct regular weekly meetings. Providing an opportunity for open communication means you are developing a foundation for a trust-based relationship. You are creating positive relationships between yourself and your staff. With the increased use of technologies, people are having fewer and fewer personal interactions. Do away with e-mail and memos and conduct weekly face-to-face meetings.

Setting aside a specific time for regular communication in your office allows everyone involved plenty of time to be prepared with their ideas, input, and any grievances they might want to air.

Regular meetings are an opportunity for you to keep a close eye on your business. You can assess workloads and determine whether any work needs to be reassigned or delegated to someone else, or maybe the workload requires hiring another person. It's important for you to treat your employees with the respect they are due. Listen to their needs and respond to them. By showing genuine concern, you're allowing them to feel comfortable approaching you in the future.

During these meetings, take the opportunity to get close to your staff:

- Encourage your people to participate with their ideas.

- Keep your employees engaged in your business. Let them know what the company's values and visions are. The more your employees feel that they are part of your vision, the better chance you have of retaining your employees.

- Take a genuine interest in your employees' personal interests and life goals. By doing so, you learn what motivates your employees and you establish a bond.

- Constantly ask for feedback. Ask your employees direct questions, for example... "What can I do to make your job easier?"

- Be consistent with your monthly meetings. No matter how busy you get, take at least 10 minutes to meet weekly so everyone can air out the previous week's issues.

This is the time to build camaraderie among your staff and develop a true team spirit. Good communication will assure your ongoing success.

Good communication and trust are closely related. Therefore, in order to have good communication in your business, you must make sure that you do what you say you are going to do. Create high levels of credibility and trust.

Managing Your Team

Everyone is aware that the cost of high turnover is enormous, not only in terms of out-of-pocket expenses related to recruitment and training but also in lost productivity. The key to holding on to employees is to have them be satisfied, or, better yet, loyal to you. Loyal employees become a real asset to your business because they act in your best interests and they are less likely to leave.

Train, Train, Train

Building loyalty requires building a solid support system for your employees, and this begins with an in-house training program. Loan officers and loan processors alike will benefit from a training program that incorporates their individual needs as they relate to your company systems and procedures.

Your loan originators in particular need training in order to ensure they have sufficient knowledge to properly explain and sell your company's loan products. It's also a good idea to encourage your sales team to attend outside sales training and mortgage origination seminars. For an excellent training tool, check out my book *The Mortgage Originator Success Kit*, currently available in bookstores or on my Web site at www.mortgage-smarts.com.

Providing a solid support system adds value to your loan staff because you are providing them with the tools necessary to achieve success. It's simple...

Their Success = Your Success

Motivating Your Sales Team

Develop a Sales Recognition Program

Everyone wants to feel acknowledged and recognized in the workplace, and loan originators are no exception. There's no better way to motivate and encourage your sales team than to recognize the top performers with a symbol of achievement. For example, you can design a plaque that includes the loan originator's name and has a statement such as Top Producer for the Month of...and include your company name and logo if you have one. Gifts for Professionals has a good selection of employee recognition gifts (www.giftsforprofessionals.com).

To enhance your program, include a special reward for the originator who receives top recognition for 12 consecutive months. You should make this a highly desirable item such as an all-inclusive weekend getaway, or maybe a gift certificate. Take a look at www.800giftcertificate.com. They have a program for employers called "Everyone Gets What They Want" that allows recipients to choose any number of rewards that are sure to fit just about anyone's taste.

Generate Excitement with Public Celebration

Hold a monthly awards ceremony in which the entire staff gathers to celebrate the previous month's achievements. At the ceremony provide lunch or just snacks and drinks and then distribute the awards. Send out a survey to your customers after the closing that asks the customers to score their experience with their loan originator and loan processor. Then include an award for the person(s) with the highest scores and maybe a certificate for a free lunch at a local restaurant. Share the information provided in these surveys so that your staff can really get motivated to provide the best customer service.

Conduct Monthly Goal-Setting Meetings

Once a month meet with your sales staff to praise the results for the previous month's numbers. Then ask each salesperson to set his or her own individual goals for the current month. Competition drives salespeople to set higher goals in an open forum. Individual higher goals are a strong motivation for salespeople.

Stay in Constant Touch

You or your sales manager should stay in constant contact with your sales team. Have frequent open forums to discuss triumphs. Encourage your salespeople who are encountering challenges to meet with you or your sales manager in private one-on-one meetings to discuss their personal challenges and develop ways to directly help create a solution.

Environment Matters

Take a look at your workplace. Is it an upbeat, exciting place to work or is it dull and depressing? Are you and your managers walking around enthused or are you bringing in baggage from your personal lives? If you've hit a slump, turn yourself around with positive affirmations. Try motivational tapes and books.

Truly successful employers make sure they value their salespeople. Always thank your salespeople for a job well done.

Just recently a sales manager who formerly worked for me and who now owns his own mortgage company asked me, "How did you get your staff to be so loyal to you?" I responded simply, "I was so loyal to them."

Developing a Niche Market

Specializing in one or two areas and strategically selecting a market segment can create an excellent mortgage broker. If you talk to top mortgage producers today, you'll find they have selected one or two mortgage products to specialize in and have selected a particular group to market. In other words, you want to develop a niche.

So, what products can you specialize in? There are government loans, such as FHA or VA, first-time home buyer programs, conventional, jumbo, Alt-A, and sub-prime loan programs.

Trying to specialize in all of these loan programs is like being a jack-of-all-trades and a master of none. Narrow your product selection and become an expert in a specialized market. You'll quickly be known, for example, as the person who does FHA loans. You'll end up making more money and getting more referrals.

Here we will review various loan programs.

FHA

Federal Housing Administration (FHA) is a government-insured loan program designed for low- to moderate-income borrowers, with average loan amounts at $117,776. FHA is specifically attractive for first-time home buyers and credit-impaired borrowers because it provides better pricing (on 30-year fixed-rate term) than a sub-prime loan program. FHA's leniency on credit is another reason for its popularity. A minimum 500 score is required but when there is no credit, FHA allows for nontraditional credit (such as utility bill records) to be used. Even more attractive is the allowance of nonoccupying co-borrowers to assist in qualifying purposes. Other notable benefits for FHA are

- No prepayment penalties.

- FHA loans are fully assumable.

- Funds necessary for closing can come from cash on hand or sweat equity.

What are the negative factors of FHA? First and foremost, you must be a HUD-approved lender, and this can be a costly and cumbersome process. In addition, loans are restricted to a 97 percent loan to value (LTV) ratio. That means that your home buyers must have 3 percent of their own money to qualify for an FHA loan. Then there are the loan amount restrictions, and these vary with each county! The last two negative factors are the mortgage insurance (required regardless of the LTV) and the fact that FHA requires the use of their own approved appraisers (resulting in conservative appraisals). Despite these negative factors, there are many mortgage brokers that have made FHA their very profitable and worthwhile niche.

To become an FHA expert, you must thoroughly learn the 4155 FHA guidelines.

Automated underwriting is available through Loan Prospector (LP) or Designated Underwriting (DU), but many loans will still need traditional underwriting due to lack of credit, low credit, or lower credit scores. My book *The Mortgage Originator Success Kit* includes detailed lending guidelines for FHA, VA, Conforming, and Non-Conforming loan programs. For more information on FHA guidelines, take a look at the resource guide "FHA Practical Guide" available online at www.allregs.com. A subscription service for FHA guidelines is available at Mortgage References, Inc., (763) 878–2247. For training courses, you may visit the Mortgage Bankers Association (MBA) Campus for online courses such as "FHA Fundamentals."

VA

Veterans Administration (VA) is a government-guaranteed loan program. VA is currently going through modifications that will make this loan program even more popular.

Previously the maximum guaranty amount was $60,000 for certain loans in excess of $144,000. However, as of December 10, 2004, President Bush signed the Veteran's Benefit Acts of 2004 changing the maximum guaranty amount to an amount equal to 25 percent of the conforming loan limit. For 2006 VA's guaranty of 25 percent guarantees a lender $104,250 on a loan amount up to $417,000. Thus a military person could qualify for a VA loan of up to $417,000 with no down payment required.

In California, Governor Schwarzenegger signed bill AB1439, increasing the loan limit for a CalVet loan to 125 percent of the current conforming loan amount or $521,250, effective January 1, 2006.

The benefits of VA loan programs include:

- Typically require no down payment and no monthly mortgage insurance (even up to 100 percent LTVs).

- VA loans are often assumable (to another veteran).

- Easier qualifying ratios than conventional loans.

VA loans deterred lenders in the past with restrictions on allowance of third-party closing costs. Currently modifications are in place to allow for third-party closing costs, resulting in more lenders revisiting VA loan programs.

VA loans require a mortgage broker to have thorough knowledge of VA guidelines and a familiarity with military terminology and military pay grades. VA loans require a veteran's certificate of eligibility and a VA-assigned appraiser.

VA provides short informational videos online at: http://www.homeloans.va.gov/ondemand_stream_video.htm.

First-Time Home Buyers

Some mortgage brokers elect to specialize in first-time home buyers, requiring knowledge of Down Payment Assistance (DPA) loan programs and state- or county-specific funding through bonds and grants.

DPA loan programs through nonprofit agencies pool funds to help people purchase a home. Statistics show that 90 percent of DPA recipients require an FHA loan. When seeking out DPA providers, make sure they are part of the Homeownership Alliance of Nonprofit Downpayment providers (HAND) who have formed the best practices and "code of ethics" for their service. Among those participants are the following:

AmeriDream, Inc., www.ameridream.org, (866) 263–7437

The Nehemiah Program, www.nehemiahprogram.org, (877) 634–3642

Futures Homes Assistance Program, www.fhap.org, (800) 672–4055

Neighborhood Gold, www.neighborhoodgold.com, (888) 627–3023

The Federal Bond Subsidy Act authorized state and local governments to issue tax-exempt revenue bonds to assist first-time home buyers with low to middle income. These programs generally pay all or a portion of the closing costs and prepaids, and other bond programs assist or provide the down payment. Typically a soft second is placed on the property. A soft second is a subsidized second mortgage. Basically the interest rate on the "soft second mortgage" is paid through the use of public or private funds, and in some cases the mortgage can be forgiven entirely if the borrower exhibits responsible home ownership over a fixed period of time (5 years in some communities and 10 or 15 in others). The only point of contention applies to the recapture fee encountered should the home be sold before the incentive period expires. For more information you will need to check with your state and local government to learn what bonds are available for your area. Other first-time home buyer programs are

- Fannie Mae Community Homebuyer Program
- Freddie Mac HomeSteps Program
- Freddie Mac Home Possible

Other Government Programs

Other government loan programs you can specialize in include:

Section 502—The Guaranteed Rural Housing loan program assists borrowers with the down payment (borrowers must have decent credit and income) in rural areas. Cities and towns with a population of less than 10,000 and most "nonmetro" communities with populations between 10,000 and 25,000 are considered to be rural. The program provides 100 percent financing with no mortgage insurance and no loan limits. Must be a 30-year fixed-rate term and can only be used for the purchase of a residential owner-occupied property and does not provide financing for farms. For details, visit www.rurdev.usda.gov/rhs.

Section 184—Indian Housing Loan Guarantee Program offers homeownership for eligible tribes and Native Americans located in 26 states across the country. The program can be used for purchases, refinancing to a lower interest rate, remodeling, or to build a new home. For details, visit www.hud.gov.

Conventional Loans

A conventional loan is *any* loan that is *not* insured by the government. Under conventional loans there are two subcategories: conforming and nonconforming loans. Conforming loans are loans that follow the guidelines and are eligible for purchase by Fannie Mae and Freddie Mac, the two largest procurers in the country.

Fannie Mae (FNMA) and Freddie Mac (FHLMC) establish strict guidelines that include maximum loan amount, borrower credit and income requirements, and down payment and property requirements.

The conforming loan amount changes annually at the beginning of the year. In 2006 the conforming loan limit is $417,000. If a loan does not meet FNMA or FHLMC guidelines, it is considered to be nonconforming (jumbo loan or sub-prime).

In the past the biggest negative factor of conventional prime loans was the mortgage insurance (MI). Most prime loans require mortgage insurance when the LTV is more than 80 percent. However, MI is changing and to remain competitive, MI companies have come up with new options such as discounted and lender-paid (LPMI). This allows for one mortgage loan rather than an 80/20 or 80/10 combo loan. A larger first mortgage loan means more profits for the loan originator. (Typically lenders do not allow for any fees to be charged on the second mortgage of a combo loan.)

To learn more about conforming Fannie Mae guidelines, visit http://www.fanniemae.com.

Jumbo Loans

With today's home prices, it's no wonder jumbo loans are so prevalent. Jumbo loans are any loans exceeding the conforming loan amount (for 2006 that is $417,000). These loan programs typically come in a variety of adjustable rate mortgages and most recently include interest-only loan programs. Other well-known products include the London Interbank Offered Rate

(LIBOR)-based adjustable, prime rate–based first mortgage, and the Cost of Funds Index (COFI) product that is especially good for $1 million-plus loans.

Jumbo loans typically require good credit with interest rates at a quarter to a half percent higher than conforming rates.

This is a very profitable niche to specialize in because of the obvious: a higher loan amount = a higher profit. Jumbo borrowers are even more concerned with the originator's expertise and role as a trusted advisor. Therefore, you will need to be extremely knowledgeable about the various jumbo loan programs that lenders have to offer. Each lender carries its own guidelines; therefore, you would need to do some research to find which lenders handle jumbo (to $1.5 million) and super jumbo ($2 to $3 million-plus) loan products.

Alt-A Loans

These loan programs were designed for the borrower with adequate income, credit, and reserves but who may lack a substantial paper trail to provide as work or collateral history. The Alt-A market is the fastest-growing sector with an increase in 2004 of 137 percent from 2003. A recent study conducted by Wholesale Access reports that Alt A loans consisted of 40 percent of all loans originated in the first quarter of 2005. The anticipated interest rate increase and an ever-increasing entrepreneurial environment should only spur the growth as prime lenders begin to seek out other niches. The predominant use of "verbal verification" or "no documentation" loan programs and investor property loan programs will no doubt continue to dominate this market sector.

Sub-Prime Loans

Sub-prime loans are nonconforming loan programs that did not fit into Fannie Mae or Freddie Mac guidelines because of either credit or property restrictions. These loan programs normally require more work for the originator but typically bring in a higher compensation.

Sub-prime loans carry a higher risk for the lender with higher qualifying ratios than conforming loans and thus carry a higher interest rate. These loans almost always include a prepayment penalty.

Sub-prime loans are another very profitable niche market. Again each lender carries its own set of guidelines and most lenders don't do everything. Every sub-prime lender has its own niche. For example, some are good at loans with 500 to 550 credit scores for stated income borrowers. Another's niche might be 80/20 combo loans, etc. So find several sub-prime lenders and then learn their guidelines inside and out to become a sub-prime loan specialist.

Reverse Mortgages

The older population 65+ numbered 36.3 million in 2004. An estimated 80 percent own their own homes and of those, an approximate 72 percent own their homes free and clear. With an average income of $20,000 or less and a longer life expectancy for seniors, the popularity of reverse mortgages in recent years has increased significantly. A reverse mortgage is an obvious choice for many seniors as it allows a homeowner (62+) to convert his or her home equity into tax-free income without having to sell his or her home, give up title, or take on a mortgage payment. No repayments are due until the borrower moves out of the home.

To learn more about this loan product, visit www.reversemortgage.org.

HELOCs and Second Mortgages

A second mortgage is any lien placed on real estate property after a first lien is already in place. A second mortgage can be a loan that is placed concurrently with a first mortgage, for example, when purchasing a home and two loans are obtained: 80/20 or 80/10. This type of transaction is typically encountered to avoid mortgage insurance.

Another option for a second mortgage is a stand-alone second. This is a second mortgage that carries a term. A HELOC (home equity line of credit) does not carry a term; it is a revolving open line of credit.

It's important to have these loan products available for your customers as an addition to your specialized market. Even though a second mortgage or HELOC brings a smaller commission, you are providing your customer with a service so that they don't end up as someone else's customer in the future.

Selecting a Market Segment

Property Niche

Finding your niche doesn't have to be daunting. Your niche should complement your business, and it may be as easy as looking right in your own backyard. Try specializing in providing financing for a certain property type. For example, if you live in Miami or Las Vegas, you may want to specialize in high-rise condos. What type of property is most prevalent in your primary market: manufactured homes, rural homes, or new home developments? Maybe there's a need for a specialist in construction loans. Take a look at your environment and identify which segment currently has a *need* for your services.

Industry niche

Another option is to consider specializing in a specific industry. What is your background? For example, if your background is in the health industry, start by targeting doctors and nurses. Your health background should help open doors within this specialized market. The same applies if your background is in finance, entertainment, education, etc.

Consumer Niche

You can consider specializing in specific consumer niches such as farm workers, immigrants, senior citizens, or first-time home buyers. Determine who the people are that you *already know* who can help get you to where you want to go.

The point is you want to determine which loan program and market segment you're most comfortable with. Selecting a niche includes doing some research. Explore your market segment for the least amount of competition in your area. Then check out your competitors. What are they doing to be successful and how can you do it better? Developing your niche market requires commitment and originality.

We're all aware of the fact that the most successful people are the people who enjoy what they're doing. After that, just focus on your target and you're sure to be on the road to success.

Sample Business Models

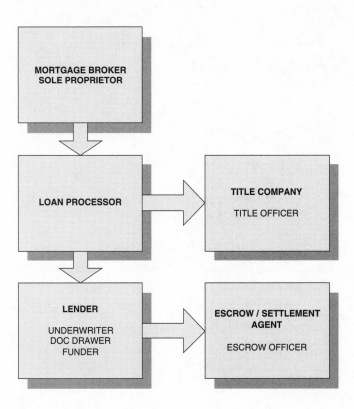

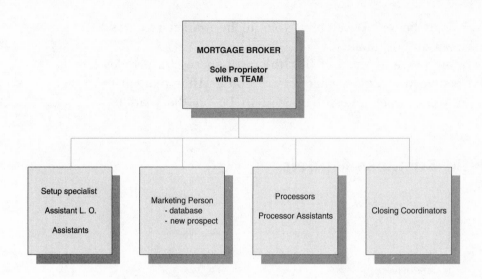

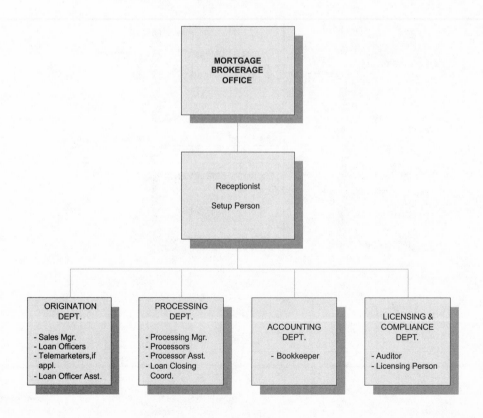

CHAPTER 6

LENDER AND THIRD-PARTY PROVIDERS

The Relationship Between the Mortgage Broker and the Lender

Identifying the Third-Party Providers

Title and Escrow Terms and Their Definitions

The Relationship Between the Mortgage Broker and the Lender

Communication + Expectation = Excellence

Communication is the art of using words effectively to impart information. Great things happen when expression is held at the highest level. Expectations are prospects of success. As Michael Jordan says, "You have to expect things of yourself before you can do them."

As a mortgage broker, perhaps the most important affiliation you will establish is the relationship with your wholesale mortgage lenders. It is your job as a mortgage broker to shop your borrower's loan for the best product and price. However, it is the relationship between the mortgage broker and mortgage lender that will ensure a smooth and timely loan process.

Let's begin with the basics.

Before you can broker any loans, you must get approved by a wholesale mortgage lender. Most brokers establish relationships with several wholesale lenders, because one lender cannot provide all of your lending needs. After you have determined your niche market, your next step would be to seek out the wholesale lenders that provide the best product, price, and service.

So what will you need to get approved by a wholesale lender? The approval requirements vary from lender to lender, but in most cases you will need the following:

- An original completed broker application and agreement

- A copy of your current mortgage broker's license

- If the mortgage brokerage is an entity, a copy of proper organizational documents

- A copy of principal's resume

- A W9 form

- A copy of current company P&L statements

Wholesale mortgage lenders are paying more attention to broker relationships than they used to. These lenders evaluate a mortgage brokerage's performance by keeping track of certain variables such as the quality of loans submitted and the ratio of loans submitted to loans closed and loan turnover. Lenders do not want to have early payoffs or early payment defaults on loans just acquired by your company. Lenders pay you a yield spread premium (YSP) based on the projected life of the loan (typically 4 years). If the borrower pays off this loan or defaults early on the loan, the lender loses money.

The loan process takes a lot of effort and resources from all parties involved. Whether it's wholesale lenders or title and escrow, everyone in the industry is paid on loans closed, not on loans submitted. Therefore, a considerable effort from the mortgage broker is expected when representing a loan package.

So how can mortgage brokers maintain a good relationship with their lenders? I believe this begins by understanding the broker-lender relationship. This is a relationship where neither party can survive without the other. The relationship can only work as a team, each party working toward a common goal: to get the loan funded. The wholesale lender will have certain expectations for the mortgage broker, and the mortgage broker will have certain expectations for the wholesale lender.

What Can a Mortgage Broker Do to Maintain a Good Broker-Lender Relationship?

Be Conscientious of Your Work

This begins with your loan submissions. Take the time to be as accurate and complete as possible. Any wholesale account executive will tell you that one of the key reasons for delay when requesting a loan approval is an incomplete loan application (1003). Be sure to include an accurate 1008—and double-check your ratios!

The quality of your work will begin with the loan originator. Make sure that proper training and proper setup systems are in place to ensure that loans are submitted *only* when they are complete and accurate.

Be Prepared

A successful loan originator is familiar with the lender guidelines. That means that all the proper questions were asked up front. By questioning the borrower, you can determine which program best suits his or her needs. By questioning the lender, you can ensure that the loan fits into their parameters. Therefore, the loan originator will be aware of what conditions will be required from the lender in order to fund the loan.

Your borrower has a private-party first lien holder. In response, the loan originator has already requested from the borrower 12 months of canceled checks and complete contact information for the first-party lien holder. This will allow the processor to request a Verification of Rent (VOR) and allow escrow to request a notarized reconveyance. By being prepared, the loan originator has successfully avoided any undue delays at closing.

Become Technology Savvy

Take advantage of the technology tools your lender has to offer. Most wholesale lenders have excellent Web sites allowing potential borrowers to submit a loan for approval and lock the rate directly on their Web site. The loan is exported from the mortgage broker's loan origination software program (LOS) and transported directly onto the lender's Web site. How easy can it get?

Wholesale lenders are clearly aware of the importance of speed, and there is no better way to obtain a fast loan approval than to submit your loan online and have an instantaneous response.

If that's not enough, lender Web sites allow brokers to check the status of their loans by providing a loan pipeline. Brokers can then track the status of their loans, check on loan conditions, and in some cases they can even order loan docs, all from the lender Web site.

Keep Control of the Loan Process

As a mortgage broker you don't just want to slam a lot of paperwork into a lender's pipeline. You want to submit a viable loan package and you want to ensure that the loan actually closes. This means that you don't just take a loan application, assign it to your loan processor, and go play golf. Make sure that you are in constant contact and control of the loan process.

The loan originator or mortgage broker should be aware of any conditions requested by the lender. If the loan processor typically requests conditions from the borrower, the loan originator or mortgage broker should review them in detail *before* the loan processor contacts the borrower.

You are refinancing a condominium, and a lien from the condo association appears on the title report. Before your processor calls and asks the borrower about the lien, you contact the association and determine that the lien has already been satisfied but the reconveyance has not been properly recorded. The reconveyance is requested and forwarded to escrow for recording—all without contacting, and possibly upsetting, your borrower.

By providing this type of personalized service, the loan originator or mortgage broker is maintaining control of the loan transaction and the relationship with the borrower.

Keep Your Lender from Becoming Your Competitor

Maintaining a healthy and long-lasting relationship with your borrower is extremely important. As we mentioned earlier, your goal is to establish a customer for life. Yet your biggest competitor may well be the lender to whom you are sending your loan. Many wholesale lenders also have a retail operation and a servicing division. That means that once the lender becomes the loan servicer, the borrower is now *their* customer and periodically the lender will solicit the borrower for further business.

The only way to avoid losing your customer in the future to the new servicing lender is to stay in constant contact with your borrower. If your borrower receives an enticing offer from the lender, he or she should be able to come to you first to determine whether it's a good idea for them to accept the offer or whether you can provide them with a better solution.

If you have provided your borrower with excellent service and you have become a trusted advisor by providing valuable information, you should be able to maintain the loyalty of your borrower.

Choosing a Lender

When seeking out a lender relationship, it's all about speed, efficiency, and ease. Most important, even more important than pricing, should be the ease in getting the loans closed. Once again, a mortgage broker is paid on closed loans. As a mortgage broker, you may be losing a quarter of a point on revenue but if you're able to get the loan closed sooner, you are now free to work on another loan. The more loans you can close, the more money you will make.

Technology Is a Big Factor

The use of technology has given mortgage brokers and mortgage lenders the ability to enhance the loan process and lower costs, passing the savings on to the consumer. In today's business world, time is of the essence and this is never more the case than in the mortgage industry. Interest rates, loan approvals, and loan documents are all time sensitive. Therefore, having access to a highly user-friendly lender Web site is imperative.

Take a look at the lender's Web site. Is it highly usable? You want the lender Web site to have the ability to:

- Price the loan online

- Lock in the rate online

- Check the status of a loan online

- Allow the broker to order loan documents online

- Deliver loan documents via e-mail

Look for even more technological advances in the future for wholesale lenders as the industry strives for a paperless society. Read more in Chapter 7 about what's in the future for the mortgage broker.

Wholesale lenders are continuously seeking ways to retain broker loyalty. They realize that in today's fiercely competitive market, brokers must be better educated in loan products and in marketing. In the competition among lenders to retain broker business, wholesale lenders are providing "educational and marketing tools" for their mortgage brokers. Currently Countrywide's Web site allows a mortgage broker to customize rate sheets and provides educational conference-call seminars. Argent Mortgage's Web site enables mortgage brokers to develop their database, prepare custom postcards and flyers, and contains many more marketing tools. WMC Mortgage and New Century provide "boot camp" broker and loan originator training to enhance the broker's business of closing more loans.

The Importance of the Account Executive

One important factor in choosing a lender should be the quality of the account executive. All wholesale lenders have account executives that work as a liaison between the mortgage broker and the lender. Account executives either solicit you for business or if you are contacting the lender directly, an account executive is assigned to you.

The account executive should have a good amount of experience and background in the mortgage industry. He or she should have a thorough knowledge of product features and guidelines, and a working knowledge of the mortgage business in general. The reason is that the account executive will be representing your best interests with the lender. An account executive with a solid background will most likely have the best internal support staff, consisting of account managers, underwriters, and funders, all working together to ensure a smooth loan process. The account executive and his or her team can make or break a broker-lender relationship.

What Should You Look for in an Account Executive?

- Returns your calls promptly

- Frequently contacts you or your loan originators

- Can readily be reached by telephone or e-mail

- Provides fast responsive answers

- Provides reliable prequalifications

- Has impeccable follow-through

- Can provide training for your loan officers concerning loan products and features

- Has a sterling reputation

An account executive is never more important than in the nonprime business. In this business, borrowers don't normally fit into a perfect mold. Many times certain loans may need more attention. This is when your account executive's expertise and experience becomes critical to ensuring a smooth loan process.

Remember that your wholesale lenders are your lifelines. Nurture your relationships and you will find that these wholesale lenders will respond by adding value to your business day in and day out.

Some mortgage brokers prefer to choose just one or two wholesale lenders to send the bulk of their business. By doing so they are better equipped to build a more solid and long-lasting relationship and reach a preferred broker status. Your preferred wholesale lender should have the most innovative products with competitive pricing and provide the best service for a smooth loan process, a user-friendly Web site, ongoing training and support for you and your staff, and marketing tools that can help you build your business.

PRIME AND ALT-A WHOLESALE LENDERS

Wholesale Lender	Web site
Countrywide Wholesale	www.cwbc.com
Wells Fargo Home Mortgage	http://ilnet.wellsfargo.com/ilonline/whole
Washington Mutual	www.wamubroker.com/wholesale
Chase	www.chaseb2b.com
Citimortgage	www.brokercitimortgage.com
Indymac Bank	www.indymacb2b.com/whole
Impac Lending Group	www.impaclending.com
Greenpoint Mortgage	www.greenpointwholesale.com
Loan City	www.loancity.com
American Brokers Conduit	www.abcconduit.com

SUBPRIME WHOLESALE LENDERS

Wholesale Lender	Web site
New Century Financial	www.ncen.com
Argent Mortgage	www.argentmortgage.com
Decision One Mortgage	www.D1online.com
Option One Mortgage	www.optiononemortgage.com
WMC Mortgage Corp.	www.wmcdirect.com
Fremont Investment & Loan	www.1800fremont.com/Wholesale
BNC Mortgage	www.bncmortgage.com
First NLC Financial	www.firstnlc.com

SECOND MORTGAGE WHOLESALE LENDERS

Wholesale Lender	Web site
Secured Funding	www.securedwholesale.com
Aegis Home Equity	www.aegishomeequity.com

For a complete list of wholesale lenders, I recommend the following Web sites:

http://www.scotsmanguide.com: an excellent resource for residential and commercial lenders and their matrixes.

http://www.weirdloans.com: allows you to search their lender database and enter a particular loan scenario.

http://www.mortgagegrapevine.com: allows you to post your particular loan scenario and have lenders respond.

In addition, most wholesale lenders advertise their services in all trade magazines. For a full list of trade magazines, please refer to Chapter 9, "The Mortgage Broker Resource Directory."

The Net Branch Mortgage Company

In some cases a mortgage broker may not be ready or willing to pursue self-employment or lender approvals because of lack of mortgage experience or financial requirements. In this case, using the services of a net branch company is certainly an option. Net branch companies offer a full range of support services including human resources services (such as benefits and payroll), processing, and compliance. Basically the net branch company is a large lender or mortgage brokerage that has lender and third-party approvals. The mortgage broker acts as a *branch* of the company by originating and closing loans under the net branch company name. Most net branch companies are approved in several states, allowing the mortgage broker to expand business to these states as well (check compliance requirements for certain state restrictions). Compensation packages vary between 80 and 100 percent of commissions earned to one flat fee per loan. There are many, many net branch companies. You should always ask for references and interview with some of their existing clients.

Identifying the Third-Party Providers

Let's not forget about the other team players involved in the mortgage process. Building and maintaining relationships with third-party providers is equally as important to a mortgage broker who wants to provide fast and reliable service. The top mortgage brokers realize that the other members of their team must offer the same excellent service to ensure a smooth loan process and a happy customer. Therefore, a careful selection process is warranted. Let's take a look at our team players.

The Credit Reporting Company

One of the first third-party vendor relationships that a mortgage broker will need is with a credit reporting company. Before you can originate any mortgage loans, you must be capable of running the customer's credit report.

The key factor in selecting a credit reporting company is the product itself. You want a credit report that is easy to read and reasonably priced. In many cases mortgage brokers will run a tri-merged credit report. This means that the information gathered on the credit report will be merged from all three credit bureaus: Experian, Equifax, and Transunion. The cost for a tri-merged credit report can run between $14 and $18. This cost may seem minimal but keep in mind that a typical mortgage broker's office will run several hundred credit reports a month. The cost of running credit reports can easily get out of control, so a mortgage broker will need to keep a close eye on the ratio of credit reports that are requested to loans that are closed.

What Type of Services Are You Looking for in a Credit Reporting Company?

You are looking for helpful and prompt customer service from all account representatives. There will be cases when you will encounter a credit report–related problem; for example, a credit score is missing on the credit report. In this case, you want a company that can be reached easily and can provide fast solutions. You want a credit reporting company that

Provides an easy-to-read credit report.

Has a simple system to order the product and can easily link the credit report onto your LOS (loan origination software) system. Most credit reporting companies will have the capability of importing the credit report information from their Web site onto your LOS system.

The ability to update many types of consumer credit information with the credit bureaus within a few days. In some circumstances, borrowers may have inaccurate information on their credit report, which will require a correction or update. In many cases, borrowers are not aware of these inaccuracies especially in the case of first-time home buyers or nonprime borrowers. The credit reporting company should have the ability to forward supplemental information obtained from your borrower, present it to the credit bureaus, and obtain a new score within a few days. In the industry this is known as a "re-score." This is a very important tool for a mortgage broker. Take, for example, a borrower who has an outstanding collection appearing on his credit report that has already been paid. A re-score can possibly increase his score and may change his loan status from a decline to an approval, depending on the loan program selected. So what type of information can be re-scored? Update account balances, or accounts paid in full, update any collection status, correct inaccurate derogatory information, or update an account that should be included in a bankruptcy.

In addition, several credit reporting companies are now offering wider services such as producing credit reports in Spanish for Hispanic or immigrant borrowers and score simulators that allow a consumer to reach his or her targeted credit score. A score simulator is a new tool available to the mortgage broker. It's an excellent marketing tool for first-time home buyers. If you have a borrower that does not have a good enough credit score to qualify for a certain loan program, you can use a score simulator to show your borrower what actions he or she can take in order to reach the desired credit score.

One of the best credit report providers is Advantage Credit. They have very useful, innovative products at a very competitive price. Their tools include: Spanish credit reports, ScoreMor, CreditXpert, Bilingual postcards for lead generation, and more. For more information visit their Web site at www.advantagecredit.com.

For a full list of credit report providers, please refer to Chapter 9, "The Mortgage Broker Resource Directory."

The Appraiser

The appraiser is a licensed or certified professional who establishes a carefully documented opinion of value on a home in compliance with U.S. Standards of Professional Appraisal Practices (USPAP). The value of a home is commonly derived by using recent sales of comparable properties. A full residential appraisal report (Form 1004) includes interior and exterior photos of the subject property. Form 2055 is used for an exterior-only inspection.

The appraiser plays a key role in the mortgage process. His or her function is to determine the value of the property in order to establish whether there is a viable loan solution for your customer. For that reason you want to make sure that the appraiser selected maintains the proper credentials, adheres to the standards of professional practices and ethics, and can provide you with fast reliable appraisals.

Typically a mortgage broker will order an appraisal for the customer. Keep in mind that if *you* are ordering the appraisal, *you* are responsible for payment of the appraisal unless you clearly specify that the customer is responsible for payment at the door (referred to as a COD request).

The appraiser will prepare the appraisal in the mortgage broker's or lender's name. Even if the customer pays for the appraisal, the appraisal is, in fact, legally owned by the broker or lender, unless the broker or lender "releases its interest" in the document. Keep in mind consumers must be given a copy of the appraisal report, upon written request, under the Equal Credit Opportunity Act. The cost for an appraisal varies among regions; however, they generally run between $300 and $500.

What Should You Look for in an Appraiser?

1. Make sure the appraiser has proper credentials and check for current licensing. In addition, most appraisers carry errors and omissions (E&O) insurance. Some lenders have requirements for the amount of E&O insurance an appraiser must carry. E&O insurance is typically $500,000 to $1,000,000. A handy Web site, www.appraiserguide.com,

is a nationwide appraiser directory that verifies appraiser credentials. The listing includes the amount of E&O insurance coverage the appraiser holds.

For a list of other appraisal referral services, please refer to Chapter 9, "The Mortgage Broker Resource Directory."

2. Make sure the appraiser can provide fast reliable service. It is best when the appraiser is up to date on technology and has a Web site allowing for online appraisal requests. This way you are more likely to receive e-mail status updates and electronic delivery of the actual appraisal.

The appraiser should be able to provide:

Short turnaround times (from ordering appraisal, to inspection, to delivery of final product)

Online status reports

Electronic ordering and delivery of product

Highest-quality appraisal reports

Competitive pricing

Remember to always collect an invoice with the appraisal even if the appraisal was paid by the customer at the door. The lender will require a copy of the invoice to reflect either an amount due or a zero balance.

The Title Company

The title company provides a title commitment, which is always required by the lender. The title commitment provides the lender full coverage of the mortgage and includes a title search. The title search includes researching a chain of title and examining any public records. If any liens are placed on the property, they will appear on the title commitment. A title commitment consists of the following:

Provides information on who is being insured. Generally the lender and any future investors are the insureds. On a purchase transaction, an owner's policy is issued and thus the purchasers of the property are also the insured.

Provides the amount of the insurance. This is the loan amount for the mortgagee and the sales price for the owner.

Provides vesting information. This is the manner in which a person takes title of the property.

Provides information on what is being insured. In this section you will find the legal description of the property.

Provides information on what is required to insure the property. In this section the title company will note property tax information. If any property taxes are outstanding, the borrower will need to pay them current in order to close the loan. If the loan transaction is a cash-out refinance, the taxes due can be paid at closing through the loan proceeds. Also included in this section are any liens or judgments placed on the subject property. Liens can include the existing mortgage lien holder. A request for payoff information (referred to as a "demand for payoff") is requested from the current lien holder by escrow or settlement agent. The demand provides an exact amount due the current lien holder in order to satisfactorily release the lien on said property. An abstracter is the person who prepares a summary (or abstract) of public records relating to the title to the a specific property.

Provides information on what is not insured. Most notably labeled as "exceptions and/or exclusions," these could typically include servitudes or easements; restrictions or covenants; and any oil, gas, or mineral titles.

Title Insurance

Title insurance is very important to both the lender and the homeowner because it protects against any problems that might affect title ownership. For example, it protects against forgery, fraud, missing links in the chain of title, unknown heirs to the property due to successions, improper identification of owners, surveyor errors, etc.

The Title Officer

When a mortgage broker opens title, a title order is made with the title company. A title officer is assigned, and an order number is issued. The title officer is your contact person for billing, status, and clearance of any liens or judgments.

What Should You Look for in a Title Company?

Commitment to provide prompt, accurate, and efficient service.

If you conduct business in several states, you want a title company that can provide nationwide coverage.

A modernized title company that allows for online title requests and ensures title orders to be tracked and retrieved online.

What Services Does a Title Company Perform?

Issues title insurance policies for lenders and owners

Examines title abstracts and surveys

Drafts deeds, mortgages, subordination agreements, and any other related legal documents

Records deeds and any other loan documents

For a list of title providers, please refer to Chapter 9, "The Mortgage Broker Resource Directory."

The Settlement Company/Escrow/Closing Attorney

Title and escrow work hand in hand and, in many cases, title and escrow will exist within the same company. The settlement company you choose is an integral part of your team. That's because the settlement agent has the important duty of handling the monies in a mortgage transaction. It's important that the settlement company has all the proper errors and omissions insurance and fidelity bonds. When selecting a settlement company, you might want to check that they are already approved with the lenders you will be working with.

Keep in mind that settlements vary from state to state. Some states require an attorney to conduct the closing of a mortgage transaction and other states, such as California, use an escrow company to conduct closings. Title and escrow work together to process the transaction of a residential purchase, refinance, or equity loan.

A round table closing refers to the "wet settlement" act requiring that actual cash be at the closing table. At a round table closing, mostly conducted on the East Coast, the involved parties meet around a settlement table and after the paperwork is signed, the new homeowners are handed over the keys.

In escrow states, such as California, they do not require the involved parties to meet. In this case the borrower will sign the loan documents and bring in any money necessary a couple of days before the loan is closed. The loan documents are returned to the lender for review, and then the lender wires the money to escrow. After the money is received by escrow, escrow orders the deed to be recorded at the county courthouse. Monies are only distributed *after* the recording of the deed. This is typically a 2- to 3-day process.

What Functions Does a Settlement Agent Perform?

Receives and holds all monies, instructions, and documents pertaining to the purchase transaction.

Requests a payoff demand from the existing mortgage lien holder.

Orders loss payee clause from the homeowner's insurance.

If a purchase transaction, orders home inspection, survey, and pest reports.

Coordinates signing of the loan documents.

Calculates the funds needed and prepares an estimated HUD-1 (see below). Supplies most of the information; however, the closing agent compiles the information and prorates expenses.

Disburses the funds to all parties.

Taking Title to Property

Early in the escrow process your borrower(s) will be asked how they would like to *take title* to their property. Your escrow officer may also refer to this as your *vesting*. The vesting will be indicated on the *deed,* which the seller will sign in order to convey title to the property to the new owner. The deed is the original loan document that will be recorded at the local land records in the jurisdiction where the property is located. The type of deed may affect the owner's interest; there is a *General Warranty Deed*, which conveys the property with the seller's guarantee that the title is good. A *Special Warranty Deed* is basically a statement from the seller of the property, that as far as he or she knows, the title is good. A *Quit-Claim Deed* releases a seller of any liability of ownership.

There are four common forms of ownership:

Joint tenants with the right of survivorship. A joint tenancy exists whenever two or more persons own an entire, undivided interest in a particular piece of property. The right of survivorship means that upon the death of one of the joint tenants, the surviving joint tenant continues to retain an undivided ownership interest in the property.

Tenants in common. The major difference between a tenancy in common and joint tenants with right of survivorship is that a tenancy in common is concurrent ownership with no right of survivorship. Each individual owner is assigned a percentage of ownership in the property. For example, A and B own a parcel of property as tenants in common. A has an undivided forty percent (40%) ownership interest and B has an undivided sixty percent (60%) ownership interest, although each owner is entitled to possession of the whole property. Each owner's undivided interest is freely transferable by inheritance and is subject to the claims of the creditors of the particular owner. Unless otherwise stated, however, each tenant in common is presumed to take an equal share in the property.

Tenants by entirety. Ownership as tenants by the entirety is a form of ownership reserved for married couples. Neither the husband nor the wife can sever his or her ownership interest in the property without the consent of the other. This means that one spouse cannot sell or mortgage any part of the property without the consent of the other spouse. The only ways to terminate the co-ownership interest of tenants by the entirety are by the death of either spouse, divorce (in which case the parties become owners as tenants in common), or mutual agreement. One significant reason why married couples take ownership in this manner is because the ownership interest of one tenant by the entirety cannot be reached by the other spouse's individual creditors.

Sole and separate. When a person takes title as sole and separate, that means there is no other titleholder. In order for a married person to hold title as his or her sole and separate property, a disclaimer deed from the spouse must be recorded after the acquisition deed (except for property acquired by gift, devise, or descent). Example: A, husband of B, as his sole and separate property.

The Closing Statement

The closing agent will prepare a Uniform Settlement Statement (known as a HUD-1). The HUD-1 is the closing statement that is issued to both the buyer and seller on a purchase transaction and to the borrower in a refinance and equity loan transaction. The HUD-1 is a three-page form, and includes the following:

Page 1 is a summary that shows where the money for closing came from and how it was spent.

Page 2 contains the details of the charges to the buyer and the seller.

Page 3 is a statement signed by the buyer and seller concerning the accuracy of the information.

The closing agent prepares an estimated HUD-1, which is available for the buyer and seller to review at least 24 hours prior to the closing. The mortgage broker is responsible for requesting and reviewing the estimated HUD-1 *prior* to the borrowers receiving a copy to check for accuracy. For example, the mortgage broker will review all closing costs to ensure the costs are correct and that there is sufficient cash available to close.

Title and Escrow Terms and Their Definitions

A

Abatement
A reduction or decrease; usually applying to the decrease of assessed valuation of property taxes after an assessment and/or levy.

Abstract
A summary prepared by a licensed abstracter of all documents recorded in the public records of the subdivision where the subject property is located. In some states an abstract is reviewed by an attorney or other experienced title examiner to determine the status of title.

Accommodation Recording
When the title company records instruments with the county recorder merely as a convenience to a customer and without assumption of responsibility for correctness or validity.

Acknowledgment
A formal declaration made by a notary public or judicial officer, certifying that the maker(s) of such instruments appeared before the notary or judicial officer and acknowledged that they signed the instrument (document). An acknowledgment is necessary to entitle an instrument to be recorded and to entitle the instrument to be used as evidence without further proof. The certificate of acknowledgment is appended or incorporated within deeds, mortgages, leases, and other related estate instruments.

Administrator
A person appointed by the probate court to carry out the administration of a decedent's estate when the decedent has left no will.

Adverse Possession
The unauthorized occupation of land belonging to another, by a person who does not have consent of the owner. In most states, by operation of law, title to real property becomes vested in such occupier after a certain (statutory) period of time of peaceful occupancy.

Affidavit

A written statement or declaration made under oath before a notary or judicial officer.

All-Inclusive Rate

The rate, which includes charges for title insurance and escrow fees.

Allodial Tenure

The absolute ownership of real estate that is subject to inheritance by the owner's heirs or to disposition by the owner as he or she sees fit. Typical of ownerships in the United States.

ALTA

American Land Title Association; an organization composed of title insurance firms, which sets standards for the industry including title insurance policy forms used on a national basis.

Amendment

Changes to alter, add, or correct part of an agreement without changing the principal idea or essence.

Approved Attorney

An attorney whose opinion is acceptable to a title company as the basis for issuance of a title insurance policy by the insurer.

Appurtenance

A minor right or privilege that is incident to, but outside of, the principal property such as a right-of-way to a highway across the land of another. Another example is water rights.

Assessed Valuation

The estimated value of property for tax purposes, usually fixed by the tax assessor.

Assessment

The amount of taxes or special improvement charges. Special improvement charges are usually for the costs of streets, sidewalks, sewers, etc.

Assignee

The person who receives ownership of a mortgage by transfer from another. *Assignment* is the instrument by which one person transfers ownership to another. *Assignor* is the person who transfers ownership of a mortgage to another.

Assumption

The act of conveying real property; taking title to a property with the buyer assuming liability for paying an existing note secured by a deed of trust against the property.

Attorney's Opinion

The written statement of an attorney regarding the condition of real estate title. Commonly required in new condominiums and home developments.

B

Back Title Letter

In some cases where titles have been previously examined by a reliable examiner up to a certain date, the title company can give subsequent examiners a letter, which sets forth the condition of the title at the time of the previous examination. The back title letter or certificate authorizes subsequent examination with the terminal date of the previous examination.

Binder

Also referred to as a "prelim" or preliminary certificate. It is a preliminary report as to the condition of a title and a commitment to issue a title insurance policy in a certain manner when certain conditions are met.

Blanket Mortgage

A mortgage that covers more than one lot or parcel of real property and often an entire subdivision. Typically, as individual lots are sold, a partial reconveyance from the blanket mortgage is obtained.

Building Code

Laws specifying the type, kind, area, and manner of construction of buildings, and prohibiting construction or repair of buildings in violation of such specifications.

C

Certificate of Title

In states where attorneys examine abstracts, the certificate of title is a written opinion executed by the examining attorney, certifying that title is vested as stated in the abstract.

Chain of Title

A chain of title will start with a conveyance (transference) out of an original source of title, and each succeeding deed constitutes a link in the chain of title. The chain of title is the amalgam of all such links.

Close of Escrow

The date the documents are recorded and title passes from seller to buyer. On this date, the buyer becomes the legal owner and title insurance becomes effective.

Closing

The final procedure in the real estate sales process, where the sale and/or mortgage are completed by the execution of documents for recording. In some states, such as California, this procedure is known as the closing of escrow.

Closing Service Letter

Also referred to as the Closing Protection Letter (CPL). A letter of authorization from a title company, for an individual or agency conducting a settlement on behalf of the title company and lender which includes the execution of all documents and disbursements of funds.

Cloud on Title

An irregularity; a possible claim or lien, which, if valid, would adversely affect or impair the title.

Commitment

A binding contract with a title company to issue a specific title policy showing only those exceptions contained in the commitment. The commitment contains all information included in the preliminary title report plus a list of the title company's requirements to insure the transaction. Also included are the standard exceptions from coverage that will appear in the policy.

Condemnation

The taking of private property for public or quasi-public use with compensation to the owner under the right of eminent domain.

Conservator

A person appointed by the court to care for the person and/or property of an incompetent adult or an adult unable to care for his or her person or property because of health.

Constructive Notice
Notice imparted by the public records of the county when documents entitled to recording are recorded.

Conveyance
An instrument in writing (such as a deed) that is used to transfer (convey) title to property from one person to another.

Covenants, Conditions, and Restrictions
Commonly referred to as CC&Rs; a written recorded declaration which sets forth certain covenants, conditions, restrictions, rules, or regulations established by a subdivider or other landowner to create uniformity of buildings (such as condominiums) and use within tracts of land or groups of lots.

Curtesy
A right which a husband has in his wife's property at her death (does not apply to all states).

D

Deed
A written document by which an interest in real property is transferred from one person to another. The person who transfers the interest is called the *grantor*. The one who acquires the interest is called the *grantee*. Examples of deeds are grant deeds, administrator's deeds, executor's deeds, quit claim deeds, etc. The appropriate deed to use depends on the language of the deed, the legal capacity of the grantor, and other circumstances.

Deed of Trust (DOT)
A written instrument by which the title to land is conveyed as security for the repayment of a loan. It is a form of mortgage. The borrower (debtor) is called the *trustor*. The party to whom the legal title is conveyed (and who has the power to foreclose if the loan is not paid) is the *trustee*. The lender is the *beneficiary*. When the loan is paid off, the trustee issues a reconveyance, releasing the hold on the mortgage.

Deed Restrictions
Limitations in the deed to a property that dictate certain uses that may or may not be made of the property.

Default
Failure to pay an obligation when due. For example, default on a mortgage.

Defect
A blemish, imperfection, or deficiency. A defective title is one that is irregular and faulty.

Defective Title
A defective title could be (1) title to a negotiable instrument obtained by fraud or (2) title to real property, which lacks some of the elements necessary to transfer good title.

Deficiency Judgment
When property at a mortgage foreclosure sale does not bring enough money to pay the mortgage debt (plus costs of foreclosure), the court will enter a deficiency judgment against the mortgage debtor for the difference between the sales price and the mortgage debt plus costs.

Demand Note
A note having no date for repayment but due on demand of the lender.

Deposit
The money given by the buyer with an offer to purchase to show good faith; also known as *earnest money*.

Description
The exact location of a piece of real property stated in terms of lot, block, tract, or metes and bounds. This is also referred to as *legal description of property*.

Devise
A gift of real estate made by a will. *Devisee* is the person who is given real estate under a will.

Dominant Estate
The property of which a right-of-way easement exists across another's adjoining piece of land is said to be the dominant estate. The land across which the easement runs is said to be the *servient estate*.

Dower

A right which a wife has in her husband's property effective at the time of his death.

E

Easement

The legal right the owner has to a piece of land to use another person's land for a limited purpose. Although an easement lasts in perpetuity, it doesn't give the owner of the easement the right to improve or modify the subservient land.

Eminent Domain

The right of a government to take privately owned property for public purposes under condemnation proceedings upon payment of its reasonable value.

Encroachment

The extension of a structure such as a wall, fence, or other fixture, which overlaps an adjoining property.

Encumbrance

A lien upon the title to real estate held by someone other than the real estate owner.

Escheat

The reversion of property to the state when an owner dies leaving no legal heirs, devisees, or claimants.

Estoppel

A legal restraint which stops a person from reneging on previous commitments.

F

Fee Simple

The highest degree of ownership a person can have in real estate. An interest in real estate which gives the owner absolute ownership and full power of disposition.

Filing

For the title industry, this term means the delivery of real estate instruments to a recorder for recording.

Foreclosure

A legal proceeding for the collection of real estate mortgages which involves a judicial sale of the property to pay the mortgage debt.

Forfeiture of Title

A penalty for the violation of conditions or restrictions imposed by the seller upon the buyer in a deed or other proper document. For example, a deed may be granted upon the condition that if liquor is sold on the land, the title to the land will be forfeited (that is, lost) by the buyer (or some later owner) and will revert to the seller.

Forged

Fraudulently executed, counterfeited.

Freehold

A life estate or a fee simple estate.

G

General Warranty

A type of deed where the grantor (seller) guarantees that he or she holds clear title to real estate and has a right to sell it. The guarantee is not limited to the time the grantor owned the property; rather it extends back to the property's origin. This type of warranty contains all of the common-law items of warranty.

Grant

A transfer of real estate between individuals by deed. The *grantee* is the one to whom a grant is made. The *grantor* is the one who makes the grant.

H

Hiatus

In the title industry, this term refers to a separation, gap, or unaccounted-for area. Usually a strip of land between two tracts.

Homestead

Property designated by a head of a family as his or her home, which is protected by law from forced sale to pay his or her debts. Florida, for example, is a homestead state.

I

Index

An alphabetical listing in the public records of the names of parties to recorded real estate instruments together with the book and page number of record.

Instrument

Any written document by which something is done regarding rights or interests in real estate.

Interests

Estates, rights, or legal claims in and to real estate.

J

Judgment

A determination by a court of law awarding payment of money to one of the parties to a lawsuit.

Jurisdiction

A geographical area in which a court has power and authority to act.

L

Land Contract

A contract between a buyer and seller for the purchase and sale of land; the purchase price is typically paid in installments over a considerable period.

Lease

An agreement granting the use or occupancy of land during a specified period in exchange for rent. A *lessee* is a tenant holding a lease. A *lessor* is the person who gives a lease to a lessee.

Lien

The liability of real estate security for payment of a debt. Such liability may be created by a contract such as a mortgage, or by operation of law such as a mechanics lien.

Life Estate

An estate of ownership in real estate which exists only during the term of a certain person's life.

M

Mechanics Lien
A lien on real estate created by operation of law, which secures payment of debts due to persons who perform labor or services on the construction of buildings and improvements on real estate property.

Metes and Bounds
A land description in which boundaries are described by courses, directions, distances, and monuments.

Mortgage
A temporary conditional pledge of property to a creditor as security for payment of a debt which may be canceled by payment in full. A *mortgagee* is the person to whom a mortgage is made. A *mortgagor* is the person who executes the mortgage.

N

Note
Also referred to as *promissory note*. A written promise to pay a specified sum of money (to include the interest) at a stated time (or demand) to a named person.

O

Owner's Policy
A policy of title insurance insuring the owner of real estate against loss because of defects in title.

P

Parol
Orally, or by word of mouth. For example, when verbal permission is given, it is considered to be a parol license. *Parol gift* is a gift made orally in contrast to a gift made in writing.

Partition
In the title industry, this term refers to a lawsuit between joint owners of real estate in which the court either divides the property between the owners or orders the property sold and divides the proceeds between the owners.

Perimeter

The boundary lines (or length of boundary lines) enclosing a tract of land.

Plat Book

One in a set of books in the public records in which maps, plats, and copies of surveys are recorded.

Premium

The amount payable for an insurance policy.

Probate

A legal procedure in which the validity of a document such as a will is proven.

Public Records

The transcriptions in a recorder's office of instruments which have been recorded and include the indexes pertaining to them.

Public Trustee

A public official to whom title of real estate may be conveyed by trust deed to be held by him as security for repayment of a loan.

Q

Quietus

Final disposition, settlement, or elimination of a claim or debt.

Quit Claim Deed

A type of deed where a grantor transfers all of his interests to someone else. The grantor offers no guarantees about the title to the grantee (recipient). This is a simple method used to give up interests in a property; for example, in a divorce, a husband or wife would use a quit claim deed to transfer all of his or her rights over to the other.

Quite Title Suit

A lawsuit brought by an owner of real estate for the purpose of canceling unenforceable claims and interests which cloud his or her title.

R

Recording

The act of receiving and transcribing a book or film of public record instruments affecting the title to real estate, by a recorder.

Release of Lien

The instrument by which a lien is released from the real estate which it encumbers.

Reversion

The return of an estate or interest to a grantor after the grant has expired.

Riparian Rights

The many rights of a person in, to, and over the banks, shore and water of a stream or body of water that the land borders.

S

Satisfaction

The payment of a debt or the fulfillment of an obligation.

Servitude

A right or interest in a piece of real estate, which benefits another unrelated property.

Subdivision

An area of land laid out and divided into lots, blocks, and building sites, and in which public facilities are laid out (such as streets, parks, and easements for public utilities).

Subjacent

A term applied to land or property lying contiguous to, but at a lower level than, another piece of property.

Subordination Agreement

A recorded document used to establish lien position when more than one lien exists on a property. When a borrower wants to refinance his existing first lien and does not want to pay off his existing second lien, then a subordination agreement would be required from the existing second lien holder before the refinance can take effect.

Surety

A person who agrees to be responsible for a debt of another.

Survey

The map or plat drawn by a surveyor, which represents the property surveyed and shows the results of a survey.

T

Tax Lien
The lien that is imposed on real estate property to secure the payment of real estate taxes.

Tenement
A building containing residential rental units.

Title
The rights of ownership recognized and protected by law.

Title Examination
The review of instruments on a chain of title to determine their effect and condition in order to reach a conclusion as to the status of the title.

Title Insurance
Insurance against loss resulting from defects in or liens upon title.

Title Search
The careful exploration and review of the public records in an effort to find all recorded instruments that affect the title to a particular piece of land.

W

Warrant
To legally assure that the title conveyed is good and possession will be undisturbed.

Warranty Deed
A warranty deed conveys title to a grantee with a guarantee of good clear title to the property free from any interests held by other people.

Writ of Execution
A direct command from the court to the sheriff to carry out the action required in the writ. For example, requirement to seize a property and sell it to pay a money judgment.

Z

Zoning Ordinance
Laws passed by local governments regulating the size, type, structure, nature, and use of buildings.

CHAPTER 7

WHAT DOES THE FUTURE HOLD?

What's in the Future for the Mortgage Broker?

The Emerging Immigrant and Minority Market

Broker to Banker

What's in the Future for the Mortgage Broker?

Insight + Vision = Destiny

Insight is the act of perceiving in an intuitive manner. Kahlil Gibran: "Progress lies not in enhancing what is, but in advancing toward what will be." Vision is intelligent foresight; it is the unusual capability of perception. To succeed in business you must be willing to travel down new roads with nothing but your own vision. Richard Hovey: "I do not know beneath what sky nor on what seas shall be thy fate; I only know it shall be high; I only know it shall be great." This is your destiny!

It has been said that "looking back, everyone is a genius." It seems everyone has an opinion about what should have been done, or what could have been done better. However, making future decisions is not always so easy; it takes strong will and conviction. In order to rally the troops, a true leader must be confident and he or she must have a clear vision. But as we all know, no one truly knows what the future will bring.

Experts and analysts can make predictions about the future movement of interest rates and the real estate market. Even so, no one predicted that interest rates would drop to such historical lows. Because experts make predictions based on past history, the housing boom that lasted 13 consecutive years left experts scratching their heads. So what can you do to prepare for the future? Keep yourself well informed. Today it seems every newspaper or television news program has at least one story relating to the mortgage industry. At the very least you want to read the industry press, so that when it does come time for decision-making you can make sound, intelligent choices.

It's inevitable that most mortgage brokers jump on the bandwagon and follow current trends. Take, for example, the ever popular interest-only and option adjustable rate mortgages. However, retired Fed Chairman Alan Greenspan warned these risky products may bring potential problems. ARMs are under fire as well. The Option ARM gives borrowers flexibility to decide how much they want to pay each month on their mortgage. With home prices skyrocketing, these loan programs have given many borrowers an opportunity to buy a home they would normally not have qualified for. Fears are that when given a choice, too many consumers are deciding to take the minimum payment option and are thus only covering a *portion* of the interest. Should housing prices drop, the borrower would owe more than the house is worth and should the rates rise, the loan would be too expensive to pay off.

A loss of appeal in the secondary market for these risky loans (interest-only with stated income and high loan-to-values) will surely bring tighter underwriting constraints and possibly higher costs. You can expect these loan programs to lower their loan-to-value restrictions and require a higher Fair Isaac & Company (FICO) credit score. A mortgage broker would look at current events and then diversify his loan product portfolio and marketing segment.

With the loss of one "hot" loan product there always comes a new one. One thing is for certain: mortgage lending is cyclical and another upturn is sure to come. Mortgage brokers are for the most part made up of small and nimble businesses, and that's a big advantage over mortgage lenders with huge overheads. Mortgage brokers can quickly adjust to market conditions by simply shifting their marketing to a different loan product. On the other hand, when the market switches, mortgage lenders are forced to acquire one another and find other ways to cut overhead in order to compete. The U.S. mortgage market is the largest debt market in the world, even larger than the U.S. Treasury market. There is plenty of business for us all, as long as we stay just a few steps ahead of the game.

What's on the Horizon for Mortgage Brokers?

Going Paperless

Without a doubt, the mortgage process is cumbersome and paper-saturated from the loan origination stage to the closing stage. It all begins with the initial application stage. The loan originator must collect all the necessary conditions from the borrower, then fax or e-mail them to the processor, who in turn has to send them by overnight mail, fax, or e-mail to the underwriter. A loan originator can find most of his or her time spent just on follow-up to make sure that all the information was received by the respected parties to ensure a smooth loan process. This antiquated manner of conducting business causes high costs, poor service, and, as we all know, long turnaround times.

With the continued use of technology in the mortgage industry, look for software systems to allow better integration between the mortgage broker and wholesale lender to allow for a better document-collection and sharing process and tracking abilities.

So how can you start the process of going paperless? A good way to start is with an imaging system. When conditions from the borrower, loan approvals, title reports, appraisal reports, etc., are received, they can all be scanned and placed into an electronic folder. Eventually a loan originator will not only have the capability of delivering loan files electronically in folders but there will also be universal access over the Internet (on a secure site) for access to a loan file by all mortgage participants. In addition, capturing an entire loan file into an electronic folder will allow for easy electronic storing of loan files.

Electronic Loan Documents and Signatures (eMortgage)

There are many collaborative efforts in place striving to achieve greater efficiency through electronic transactions. Already the majority of loans today involve the electronic delivery of loan documents from the wholesale lender to the closing agent.

Even though the electronic delivery method has been implemented, paper loan documents and physical shipping are still the norm. There are numerous legal issues to consider in going paperless. Due to the high sensitivity of mortgage loan documents, our industry is not quite ready for a paperless industry. However, I believe it is just around the corner.

In the future look for eMortgage documents that will be generated, transferred, signed, sealed, registered, and stored electronically. eMortgages will ultimately eliminate the need for printing, scanning, shipping, couriers, data re-entry, manual data certification, and other costly steps of the mortgage loan process.

The legal framework for electronic signatures was established in 1999 with the Uniform Electronic Transactions Act (UETA). This act allows for the use of electronic signatures by notaries. In 2000 the Electronic Signatures in Global and National (Esign) Commerce Act was passed. Since then the Mortgage Industry Standards Maintenance Organization, Inc. (MISMO) has developed the technical specifications needed to create digital documents known as the SMART Document specification. eMortgage technology will include eDisclosure, eNote, eClosing, eDelivery, eRecording, eServicing, and eCompliance. For more information, visit www.mismo.org.

As our industry continues to replace paper documents, the electronic signature technology that you choose will become an increasingly important investment. Currently there are two common types of signature technology that are already in use. On the Internet, consumers use a "click-to-sign" or "I accept" method. For face-to-face transactions such as in retail stores, parties sign using a small LCD signature pad to capture an electronic handwritten signature. UETA and Esign call for authentication and nonrepudiation of an electronic signature.

Loan Processing Overseas

We all have encountered the use of offshore outsourcing. Whether you are calling your credit card company or some other type of support service, you will likely be connected to someone overseas. The surge of offshore outsourcing is for obvious reasons—lower cost of personnel. An abundant supply of educated labor and low operational costs have made India the prime outsourcing destination for many large companies, including mortgage lead-generation companies.

A few large mortgage lenders have begun to use offshore loan processing. With offshore loan processing, files can be worked on 24 hours a day, and technology has made it easy to submit loan packages overseas. Will this catch on? Only time will tell. For more information, visit www.eops.com, a 24/7 paperless mortgage-processing service.

Bundling of Settlement Costs

All the technological advances coming our way will likely result in a significant reduction of loan processing time and inevitably lower loan costs. An earlier Real Estate Settlement Procedure Act (RESPA) proposal for the bundling of loan costs was attempted with terminal opposition. However RESPA reforms are back on the table and in 2005, the Department of Housing and Urban Development (HUD) proposed reforms to streamline mortgage closings. The proposal would require a quote to the consumer at the start of the loan shopping process that would guarantee the price for the bundle of settlement services needed to close the loan. The bundling of loan costs seems to be a good idea. It would be less confusing for the borrower when reviewing the Good Faith Estimate, and it should be easier for lenders who then have to account for only one fee rather than tracking and reconciling multiple fees. For example, the appraisal fee, credit fee, inspection fee, tax service, private mortgage insurance (PMI), and all title and escrow fees would come from one vendor. The bundling of costs requires all these companies to become bundling partners in an effort to offer competitive services in an increasingly aggressive marketplace. The trend toward the bundling of closing costs is gaining momentum as the market continues to streamline the mortgage process. In the future one-stop shopping of settlement services will be offered through home builders, realty firms, and settlement service providers.

Commercial Real Estate

Ever since the bursting of the tech-stock bubble, yield-oriented investors have flocked to real estate in record numbers. Couple this with today's surplus of capital flow and you have the most competitive commercial real estate market environment in recent history. Today while the housing market is slowing down, the commercial sector of real estate continues to grow.

Commercial real estate loans are made on apartment complexes (5+units), mixed-use properties, office buildings, industrial properties, retail centers, hotels and/or motels, self-storage facilities, RV and mobile parks, and health care facilities such as assisted living and senior housing.

According to the Mortgage Bankers Association, commercial and multifamily loan originations hit a record $136 billion in 2004, up 16 percent from $117 billion in 2003, and reached a whopping $345 billion in 2005. On MBA's Commercial/Multifamily Newslink, Doug Duncan, MBA chief economist and senior vice president of research and business development noted, "Capital continues to flow into the commercial and multifamily real estate markets on both the debt and equity sides, and so far, no significant obstacles to that flow have appeared, whether in the form of higher interest rates, declining loan performance or declining property performance." MBA's chief economist predicts a strong outlook for 2006, with both total volume and average deal size continuing to climb.

*Small-Balance Commercial Loans: Are They the Next
"Alternative Product" Boom?*
Evidence has mounted to suggest that one of the next "big" products residential brokers will consider is the small-balance commercial loan. Why? It's a story of consumer need-meets-emerging industry innovation; new, borrower-focused programs have been introduced within a traditionally fragmented and unpredictable commercial marketplace. Experts agree that brokers who study the potential of small-balance commercial

loans (loans under $5 million) and take advantage of innovative programs in the category will bring themselves new business and become more profitable.

The Small-Balance Commercial Market

In stark contrast with the large commercial market, originations in the small commercial segment are driven by the demands of small business owners and property investors. Yet traditional lenders ignored this segment, presumably because these smaller deals are conventionally cumbersome and require the same amount of effort as their larger counterparts, for less profit. Brokers have generally been cautious as well with roadblocks to entry such as a complicated process, long transaction timelines, complex approvals, and tedious approvals.

But the consumer need is proven. Deal volume in the small-balance loan market (loans under $5 million) topped $118 billion in 2005, a sizeable 11-percent increase over the previous year, according to mortgage research firm Boxwood Means, Inc. Loans up to $1.5 million comprise nearly one-third of that number, translating to vast untapped potential and opportunity for mortgage brokers. In fact, industry research now suggests that the small-balance commercial loan is a top product to replace residential mortgage brokers' diminished refinance business; however, the majority of professionals are not taking advantage of commercial opportunities.

New Product Enters the Scene, and Wakes Up the Market

In 2003, a new category of small balance commercial loans emerged with the launch of Silver Hill Financial, LLC, a subsidiary of Bayview Financial, L.P. Silver Hill introduced a program that challenged the traditional commercial underwriting model to make small-balance loans more accessible for borrowers and easier for residential brokers to offer. A cornerstone of the program is the company's keen interest in increasing the comfort level of residential brokers working with commercial transactions. By applying the residential-style debt-to-income (DTI) underwriting approach to commercial loans up to $1.5 million, Silver Hill's CLEAR (Commercial Lending Easy as Residential) approach would serve as a home for the commercial loan requests that cross the desks of nearly every residential mortgage professional. And it worked.

In the first three years of business, the wholesale lender amassed a network of thousands of brokers across the country who learned how to earn more money by offering small-balance commercial loans—often to borrowers already in their residential client base. Silver Hill provides in-depth broker training and education on the commercial market and how to sell its program, in addition to free marketing tools to help brokers promote their commercial offering. Silver Hill's program has served as the forerunner in an evolving, opportunity-rich segment of the commercial real estate lending market.

Broker Perspective

Robert Tanner, a mortgage broker from Lakeland, Florida, says that Silver Hill's program allowed him to increase his compensation and profits with half the effort. "Prior to working with Silver Hill, I had always focused on residential exclusively." He admits that fear of the unknown was probably the toughest part of the transition, "but Silver Hill took me through the process step by step, and I saw how easy it was, I began to ask myself why I waited so long." Tanner goes on to say that Silver Hill handles much more of the process than what he was accustomed to, overseeing the entire deal from start to finish. Tanner's positive experience with the lender's small-balance program has prompted him to look at his business with new eyes. "I've been giving a lot of thought to making the transition to 100-percent commercial," he concludes.

Indeed the future for small-balance commercial deals is bright. According to industry observers, growth is sizeable given the relative absence of capital market pressure associated with the larger institutional mortgage market. And with the market-share leader garnering just 4 percent in 2005 (the top four banks accounted for just 11 percent of total commercial loan originations), there is still widespread fragmentation and inefficiency—which translates to plenty of opportunity for lenders and brokers alike.

Silver Hill foresees growth with more access to capital via mortgage-backed securities and a convergence of factors including increased broker awareness and interest. With a record flow of funds into commercial real estate, you can expect a growth in commercial broker activity in the future.

"Silver Hill's program provides a great alternative to bank financing for small commercial investors and is ideal for self-employed borrowers; as a result, we've really opened up the market with our unique approach to small-balance," says Joanna Schwartz, managing director of Silver Hill Financial. "We expect that trend to continue as more borrowers discover the DTI approach to commercial lending through the thousands of brokers who are offering programs like ours."

For more information on Silver Hill's product you may call (888) 988-8843 or visit their Web site at www.silverhillfinancial.com.

For courses and workshops on commercial lending, visit www.mbaaa.org or www.namb.org and for a full list of commercial lenders visit www.scotsmanguide.com.

The Emerging Immigrant and Minority Market

When I began my career as a loan officer over two decades ago, I dressed in a three-piece suit and my colleagues were predominantly white and male. Times have certainly changed; today, dress requirements have become much more lenient. A lax dress environment allows employees to comfortably work long hours and to have a sense of identity. These days, employees, management, and their employers come from diverse backgrounds creating a better lending environment for the people they serve.

As the mortgage industry continues to evolve, a strong emphasis has been placed on serving an emerging market often referred to as the "underserved" population. So who are the so-called underserved consumer groups? They are made up of minorities such as Hispanics, African-Americans, Native Americans, Asians, immigrants, people with low income, and people from the rural parts of the country.

You might wonder why there is so much interest in minorities. Well, the reason is quite simply the numbers. In 2005 home sales defied expectations and grew to 8.3 million. An all-time high of 69 percent homeownership was reached with well over 1 million owners added in 2005, much due in part to minorities who contributed nearly half of the gain in homeownerships. Data released by the US Census Bureau shows the first quarter of 2005 with minority homeownership reaching a record rate of 51.6 percent meaning 15.7 million minority families now own their own home. A new quarterly record was made by Hispanic homeownership reaching 49.7 percent meaning now 5.8 million Hispanic families own their own home.

Of course home sales growth was also due in part to the U.S. mortgage finance system. Lower financing costs and the wide array of mortgage products helped give millions of people an opportunity at homeownership, which previously they might not have had.

> Continued population growth has leading experts predicting 8.3 to 8.8 million home sales in 2013.

> Even with the expected slowdown industrywide, that is, post-refinance boom, the National Association of Realtors remains optimistic with a steady pace of home sales expected. Purchase origination volumes will continue to grow, largely due to the underserved consumer groups that make up the emerging market.

Looking to the future, it's hard to avoid the staggering numbers released by the 2005 State of the Nation's Housing Report. There has been a record number of immigrants entering the United States over the past two decades, with now one in five heads of households either foreign-born or the native-born child of an immigrant. Immigrants will account for one-third of net household growth over the next ten years.

Especially noted in the report is the economic progress incurred by minorities. The report states that 6.2 million minority households joined the ranks of middle-income earners—a number nearly equal to that of whites. In fact it is our nation's strong income and wealth gains that have fueled the housing demand.

The foreign-born population of the United States is currently 33.1 million, which is 11.5 percent of the U.S. population with an additional 1.3 million immigrants expected each year. The U.S. Census Bureau projects that immigration will cause the current population of the United States to increase from 300 million to more than 400 million in fewer than 50 years. With the overall population living longer and the flood of immigrants, the next 10 years may see the highest level of homeownership growth since the baby boomers swept into the housing market in the 1970s.

Of importance is the increased numbers of second-generation Americans, Those ages 11 to 20 grew by an outstanding 63 percent, with Hispanics making up about half of second-generation heads of households age 40 and under.

It's clear to see that the immigrant and minority market will play an important role in the future housing market. In 2005, the number of minority first-time homeowners has risen 32 percent. With second-generation Americans reaching homeownership age, that number is likely to increase. According to the U.S. Census Bureau, minority families will account for over 60 percent of all first-time home buyers over the next decade.

The real estate and mortgage industry and their providers are already planning to take advantage of the business opportunities in this market niche.

> The National Association of Realtors (NAR) is working with the White House and the Congressional Black Caucus Foundation in its efforts to increase minority homeownership by 5.5 million over the next 10 years.

> The National Association of Mortgage Brokers (NAMB) has introduced its "Emerging Markets Initiative," which is designed to reach minority home buyers and those with low-to-moderate income. The key component to this initiative includes an educational course called "Are You Prepared to Head Down the Road to Homeownership?"

> Freddie Mac has an initiative aimed at both African-Americans and Hispanics called "Homeownership: Let the Truth Move You" to educate minorities about many misconceptions regarding homeownership.

One of the biggest challenges immigrants and minorities face when seeking a home loan is the lack of a traditional credit history. To fill the need, First American has introduced a new credit suite called Anthem. Anthem—the acronym for assisting nontraditional home buyers in emerging markets—allows lenders to take a nontraditional credit history borrower and establish that customer as a qualified borrower, based upon other criteria such as rental payment history, rent-to-own contracts, or payday loan contracts.

How Do You Reach the Minority and Immigrant Market?

Studies show that ethnic and minority groups do not typically respond to traditional marketing. Foreign clients are more likely to seek home financing through word-of-mouth. They like to work with trusted sources such as family or friends. Other types of trusted sources are their church congregations and other local community or cultural organizations. For example, Bridgeport HOME (homeownership made easy) is a faith-based initiative effort made up of African-American and Hispanic churches that will provide access to low down payment mortgages and home-ownership counseling.

It has been shown that ethnic or immigrant customers prefer to work with real estate brokers or originators of their own nationality when working on a mortgage transaction. Recognizing the interests of an ethnic or minority group, and at the very minimum understanding their language, reflects a respect and sensitivity for their culture. Many large lenders have begun strong recruitment programs to increase their number of bilingual staff. Wells Fargo Home Mortgage is capitalizing in the Hispanic Market by hiring 100 loan consultants in Los Angeles, California (their fastest-growing market), with Hispanics making up approximately half of that growth.

In order to make a genuine effort to reach an ethnic or immi-grant community, try to provide some of your marketing and mortgage material in their native language. Freddie Mac has a trademarked bilingual financial literacy curriculum called

CreditSmart that helps prepare Spanish-speaking communities for the financial responsibilities of homeownership. United Guaranty (www.ugcorp.com) has developed its version of "The Road to Homeownership," an Internet-based home buyer education course in Chinese Mandarin. Translation Source (www.translation-source.com) can provide certain loan documents such as the note, deed of trust/mortgage, HUD-1, and Truth-in-Lending in various languages. Online quotes are also provided.

How should you begin your communication efforts with an ethnic or minority community? The least expensive method is to post flyers in local community and cultural centers, even ethnic markets, anywhere your target audience congregates. Another inexpensive method is to hire ethnic loan originators who are already embedded in their communities who can easily target these groups. Advertising in ethnic newspapers and on radio and cable channels is another excellent communication source. These sources are generally less expensive than comparable English-language sources.

A lack of knowledge of U.S. financing systems is one of the major barriers an immigrant encounters when contemplating homeownership. Therefore, providing educational seminars would be an effective strategy in capturing this type of customer. Offer free home buying seminars through faith-based organizations. Additionally, you could contact any company that employs a large number of minorities (e.g., hotels, restaurant chains, manufacturing companies, etc.). Homeownership offers a great opportunity for employers to stabilize their workforce.

Once you have decided to cater to the minority and immigrant market, you will need to have access to the proper loan programs to serve them. Having access to a variety of 100 percent financing and zero down loan products is essential. Most recently some lenders have begun to provide 103 percent financing to help consumers cover the closing costs. In addition, there are the nonprofit organizations that offer gift funds for down payments, the largest being AmeriDream, Inc. (www.ameridream.org). Futures Home Assistance Program (www.fhap.org) now has a department specifically addressing the needs of the Hispanic community in all 50 states.

Purchasing a home is extremely important to the minority and immigrant client. In fact, minorities and immigrants rank buying a home as their number one priority. Therefore, a loan originator plays a very important role in these communities. You become more than just a loan originator; in many cases, you will be playing an extended consultant role. By expanding homeownership to minority and immigrants, you will be performing an invaluable service for your community and your nation. So even though an ethnic or minority customer expects more from you and may even require much more upfront work, minority and immigrant customers are *very* loyal and thus will require less customer retention efforts. Providing an ethnic or minority customer with a positive experience will not only gain you a loyal customer but can also provide you with an unending supply of referrals!

WHERE THE FOREIGN-BORN POPULATION LIVES	
State	Population
California	8,864,255
New York	3,868,133
Texas	2,899,642
Florida	2,670,828
Illinois	1,529,058
New Jersey	1,476,327
Massachusetts	772,983
Arizona	656,183
Washington	614,457
Georgia	577,273
Virginia	570,279
Michigan	523,589
Maryland	518,315
Pennsylvania	508,291
North Carolina	430,000
Connecticut	369,967
Colorado	369,903
Ohio	339,279
Nevada	316,953

Source: U.S. Census Bureau Census 2000.

TOP 10 COUNTRIES OF ORIGIN FOR THE FOREIGN-BORN	
Country of Origin	**Population**
Mexico	9,177,487
China	1,518,652
Philippines	1,369,070
India	1,022,552
Vietnam	988,174
Cuba	872,716
Korea	864,125
Canada	820,771
El Salvador	817,336
Germany	706,704

Source: U.S. Census Bureau Census 2000.

Interesting Statistics from U.S. Census Bureau Census 2000

- The foreign-born population in the United States increased by more than half between 1990 and 2000, from 19.8 million to 31.1 million.

- In 2000 over half of the foreign-born population was from Latin America for a total of 16 million, representing a total 52 percent of the total foreign-born.

- The South experienced the most rapid growth of foreign-born population, increasing by 88 percent in the South between the years 1990 and 2000.

- More than one-third of the foreign-born live in the West. In 2000 38 percent of the foreign-born lived in the West, 28 percent in the South, 23 percent in the Northeast, and only 11 percent in the Midwest.

- The foreign-born increased by 200 percent or more in North Carolina, Georgia, and Nevada. In 16 states the foreign-born grew by 100 percent to 199 percent; in 12 states this group grew by 57 percent (the national average) to 100 percent and by less than 57 percent in the remaining 19 states and the District of Columbia. The only growth rate below 10 percent was in Maine (1.1 percent).

- The foreign-born represented 26 percent of the total population in California in 2000, the highest proportion in any other state: 20 percent in New York, 18 percent in New Jersey and Hawaii, 17 percent in Florida, 16 percent in Nevada, 14 percent in Texas, 13 percent in the District of Columbia and Arizona, and 12 percent in Illinois and Massachusetts.

| FOREIGN-BORN POPULATION BY WORLD REGION ||
Area	Population
Latin America	16,086,974
Asia	8,226,254
Europe	4,915,557
Africa	881,330
North America	829,442
Oceania	168,046

Source: U.S. Census Bureau Census 2000.

Broker to Banker

Inevitably there comes a point in time when a mortgage broker considers becoming a mortgage banker. Making the transition from a broker to a banker has never been easier. These days, correspondent lenders encourage even the smallest mortgage brokerage to become a mortgage bank by providing access to a warehouse line of credit. Even though there are lots of benefits to becoming a mortgage banker, it doesn't come without risk. It's important to carefully evaluate your reasons for wanting to become a banker. You must understand the risks associated with this method of doing business before taking the plunge.

What Exactly Is a Mortgage Banker?

The term generally refers to an originator of loans that has the capability to close the loan in its own name with the use of a warehouse line of credit. A true mortgage banker originates, closes, services, and sells the loan to the secondary market. However, even a mortgage broker with a warehouse line of credit from a correspondent lender can assume the term of mortgage banker.

The Benefits

There are many reasons why brokers want to become bankers Primarily,

> *They want to be more profitable.* Correspondents and whole-sale lenders typically pay more for closed loans and charge less in fees. Many of the fees charged and passed on in a traditional transaction can flow to you as additional income. A mortgage banker can also sell loans "in bulk" to the secondary market at possibly higher premiums.

> *They want more control of the loan process.* A mortgage banker makes underwriting decisions without the need to refer to third parties. In addition, the mortgage banker schedules and controls the settlement and funding date.

> *They want more credibility.* Mortgage bankers, unlike mort-gage brokers, are not required to disclose yield-spread pre-miums on certain disclosures like the Good Faith Estimate and Broker Fee Agreement. Closing transactions in this manner provides for a "cleaner" transaction. Eliminating the need to explain yield-spread premiums helps maintain integrity in the eyes of the consumer.

Qualifications

There are three primary requirements to consider when becom-ing a mortgage banker.

1. *Net worth.* The net worth of a company is determined by an audit from a licensed CPA firm. My suggestion is to seek out a CPA firm that is experienced working with mortgage lenders and familiar with preparing audited financials for the purpose of acquiring a warehouse line of credit.

   It is much easier to qualify for a warehouse line of credit with a correspondent lender, such as Countrywide or New Century. In this case a mortgage broker is capable of fund-ing loans in their own name, but the file is actually approved and underwritten by the correspondent lender prior to the actual funding of the loan. Since there is less risk involved, it is easier to qualify.

If you are seeking a warehouse line of credit through a traditional warehouse bank, be prepared for net worth leveraging. Leverage is expressed as a ratio whereby you multiply the net worth of a company by a fixed number. Typically a warehouse bank will leverage your net worth by 15 to 20 times. For example, if your net worth is $100,000 and the ratio is 15 to 1 or 15:1, then you would qualify for a line of credit of $1.5 million. If your net worth were $200,000, then you would qualify for a line of credit of $3 million, and so forth. An appropriate net worth requirement for a warehouse bank is $250,000.

2. *Credit history*. Undoubtedly a warehouse bank is going to consider the credit history, character, and credibility of an individual before a warehouse line of credit is offered. For this reason, you individually will be held responsible for these lines, and a personal guaranty will most likely be required.

3. *Experience*. One of the significant challenges when transitioning from a mortgage broker to a mortgage banker is the need for an experienced operations team that includes underwriting, quality control, and closing. Keep in mind that you are now *personally* responsible for every loan that is funded on your warehouse line of credit, and, therefore, there is little room for error. You will need to be prepared to handle postclosing functionality that includes the transfer of servicing, trailing documents, Home Mortgage Disclosure Act of 1974 (HMDA) reporting, quality control, and trust accounting. It's important to have a strong business plan in place that includes a well-thought-out strategy for the cycles that mortgage bankers encounter.

Be prepared with a good-quality control plan and a risk management plan in place.

The Warehouse Line of Credit

A warehouse line of credit is a real estate–secured short-term line of credit. The warehouse line of credit provides the mortgage banker with the necessary funds to close the loans. All of the loans are presold in the secondary market and the warehouse line funding will cover approximately a 15- to 30-day period between the closing and the sale of the loans to the end institutional investor.

The mortgage banker earns interest at the note rate during the warehouse period (from the original funding date to the date the funds are received from the mortgage purchaser), and it generally offsets the interest and fees charged by the warehouse lender.

The first step to making the transition from a mortgage broker to a mortgage banker is to secure a warehouse line of credit, be it through a correspondent lender or a warehouse bank. This first step requires a lot of research, as not all warehouse line providers are created equal, and your profits and service will vary depending on the choice you make.

What you should look for when selecting a warehouse line:

> Look for a warehouse bank that allows for higher warehouse line leverage-to-net worth ratios. As we mentioned before, a warehouse bank will lend at a multiple of your net worth. Look for a warehouse bank that lends 15 to 20 times net worth.

> Look for a warehouse bank that primarily purchases the types of loans you are closing, for example, FHA, nonprime, seconds, etc.

> Avoid a warehouse bank that requires you to sell exclusively to a certain investor.

> Avoid "haircuts." A *haircut* is when a warehouse banker wants a percentage of the mortgage banker's own finances to fund loans as added security.

The Risks

In my opinion the biggest risk in becoming a mortgage banker is the repurchase risk. Mortgage brokers will start funding their own loans and think that more volume equals more money, not realizing the risk of repurchase until they are faced with their first incident. That's right. If for some reason you sell a loan or loans to an end investor and that investor finds any quality deficiencies, you may be asked to repurchase that loan or, in some cases, several loans.

Other risks include:

> *Secondary market/interest risk.* If you decide to hold loans on your warehouse line "at market" during the "warehouse period," interest rates may fluctuate and the price that you get may move significantly, up or *down*.

> *Prepayment risk.* As a correspondent you will most likely be responsible for prepayment risk, which can vary anytime between four to six months from the settlement date. This means that you will share in the risk with the end investor should the borrower refinance during this period.

> *Fraud risks.* As we mentioned before, fraud is prevalent in our industry. If you do not have the proper quality control plans in place and fund a fraudulent loan in your name, a proper execution plan will be necessary. This includes the chain-of-title risk.

> *Investor and product risk.* You may be working with one particular lender for a niche product and even though you are provided with a purchase commitment, that lender may stop buying those loans at any time. In the meantime if you are holding loans on your own warehouse line, you will need to find another purchaser immediately.

Finally there is the overhead risk. As previously mentioned, becoming a mortgage banker will require additional fixed costs for operations staff. This additional salary expense will have to be taken into consideration when evaluating the profits versus the risks and costs involved with this transition.

Another challenge with this type of business model is the delay in revenue. As a mortgage *broker* you are paid at settlement from the settlement company. As a mortgage *banker* you are paid after the loan is purchased with your warehouse line of credit and after the postclosing process that can generally take one to two weeks.

Then of course there are state licensing rules to consider. You must decide what states you want to fund loans in. Just as there are mortgage broker licensing fees, there are mortgage banker licensing fees that can cost between $750 and $1,000 for each state. Many mortgage brokers and bankers retain the help of outside law firms to assist with state licensing compliance.

As you can see, there is a lot to consider when deciding on becoming a mortgage bank, and it may require the enlistment of an outside consulting service. You want to clearly understand the risks and decide whether you are capable of managing those risks versus the benefits and profits that can be made.

CHAPTER 8

LAWS AND ETHICS

Preventing Fraud

What Is Predatory Lending?

Why Is Compliance Important to Mortgage Professionals?

Lending Laws

Preventing Fraud

Integrity + Character = Credibility

Integrity is the steadfast adherence to a strict moral or ethical code. To reach great heights, a person must have great depth. Character is moral or ethical strength with truthfulness being the main element. A mortgage broker must have integrity and character to earn credibility and trust.

Fraud is a dirty word in the mortgage industry. The mere mention of this word will raise the hackles of even the most seasoned mortgage professional. Fraud can be viewed as cancer. The only way to fight it is to have routine checkups for early detection. Protective measures that include quality control procedures will enable early detection of unlawful activities.

Unfortunately, fraudulent activities are prevalent across the nation. No one has any idea how big a problem it really is. What we do know is that mortgage fraud causes severe damage in our communities and costs our industry billions of dollars annually.

I cringe every time a story appears in the news about yet another mortgage broker committing some type of fraudulent activity. These unscrupulous individuals force all the honest, hardworking mortgage brokers to work twice as hard to reassure an already untrusting public.

What Are Some Fraudulent Practices?

Unfortunately, there are many kinds of fraudulent activities. With the new technologies, there are probably more that haven't even been invented yet. Below I have listed some of the fraudulent practices conducted within the mortgage brokerage industry.

Falsifying Information

Many people think of fraud as complex schemes involving identity theft and straw deals. Actually fraud can be as basic as lying about the borrower's occupancy of property. Many times a loan originator is aware that a borrower does not intend to occupy the property that he or she is purchasing and will look away in order to get a lower rate. This is not only dishonest but is also considered fraud. Needless to say, you should not encourage or allow a borrower to lie about any representations made on the loan application. This includes participating in the falsification of income or employment for the purpose of obtaining a loan or lower interest rate that the borrower would not qualify for.

Inflated Appraisals

Appraisers have complained for years about the pressure they receive from loan originators, brokers, and lenders to bring in a certain property value, especially in the case of a purchase money loan. Telling a mortgagee that a house is worth more than it is in order to close a larger loan and make a bigger commission is just plain wrong. Who are the perpetrators of this type of mortgage fraud? It can be the realtor, the loan originator, the appraiser, or the collusion of all three. However, appraisal fraud does not end there. Appraisal fraud can include the alteration of an honest professional appraisal report.

Appraisal fraud can hurt the lender because if the borrower defaults on the loan, the collateral used to secure the loan does not really have enough value to cover their loss. Appraisal fraud hurts the borrower because if something catastrophic happens such as death, severe illness, or divorce, and the borrowers are no longer able to make the mortgage payments, they will not be able to sell the home for the amount they mortgaged.

Most lenders have their own quality control procedures in place. One is that they can pull their own backup appraisal report to ensure the property value is in line with the appraisal report.

Identity Theft

There are countless charges made across this country against individuals who either forge legal documents or steal a person's identity for the purpose of illegally acquiring a mortgage loan. This type of mortgage fraud usually involves a pyramid of perpetrators involving real estate agents, investors, appraisers, and title closers.

One such case involved a husband, wife, and daughter, operating Global Mortgage Investors, who orchestrated a string of schemes involving title companies and real estate investment companies. A total of $3.8 million was stolen. All three were sentenced to six years in prison and were ordered to pay $7 million in restitution.

Another case involved a perpetrator who was the buyer and seller of a single transaction and the principal beneficiary of the proceeds from those transactions. The man involved in this case is serving a 3- to 6-year jail sentence.

However, mortgage fraud can also include individuals maintaining ownership under false pretenses. For example, an elderly man (a realtor) out of Connecticut was sentenced to five years in prison for illegally receiving monies from a mortgage on two properties he no longer owned.

Property Flipping

Property flipping happens when an unscrupulous investor buys a home under market value (usually a run-down property in a low-income urban area), then immediately sells it (after little or no rehabilitation) for a severely inflated price. The classic scheme of property flipping has the seller and appraiser agreeing to inflate the value of the property. These transactions may involve the real estate agent, appraiser, and mortgage broker, who all conceal the initial transaction and submit a loan with a bogus appraisal. In many cases the buyer of the property is in on the deal. The buyer gets a mortgage and then quickly defaults on the loan.

Property flipping affects an entire neighborhood because other sellers and buyers in the same housing market may reference a flipped property value without realizing that it is not a true market sale. So eventually prices in the entire market move upward—but only temporarily. In a case where the buyer is in the fraud scheme, they immediately default on the loan, so the high amount of foreclosures rebound in the form of depressed property values and promote urban decay in affected neighborhoods.

The Department of Housing and Urban Development (HUD) signed a rule against flipping in 2003, making properties sold at a significant price hike within a short time of purchase ineligible for Federal Housing Administration (FHA) mortgage insurance.

So how do you know when a property is being flipped? Here are some signs to look for:

The property being sold was purchased by the seller within the past few weeks or months.

The settlement statement shows funds going to an individual or company not listed as a lien holder or on the title commitment.

The owner of the title commitment is not the same person on the appraisal report, or the seller on the sales contract, or you find that a phrase "owner of record" takes the place of a name on any of these documents.

The comparable properties on the appraisal report have had their own titles transferred within the last year (indicating these properties might have been flipped also).

Misappropriation of Mortgage Funds

In a case where a mortgage broker collects money up front from a borrower for a credit report and appraisal fee, a trust account is required. There are state-specific laws that regulate the proper handling of trust accounts.

Unfortunately the mishandling of monies from a trust account often involves a mortgage broker at a vulnerable moment, facing a bad financial situation and making a bad choice by deciding to dip into the trust account. Any officer or employee who wrongfully takes any money or funds held in trust without authority risks severe fines and imprisonment, not to mention being fired immediately.

Such was the case with Mike Davis of Ameribanc Mortgage from Columbus, Ohio. A small mortgage broker, Davis faced the decision to either shut his doors or take some funds from the escrow account to pay for his business and personal expenses. In 2005, he pleaded guilty to theft, engaging in a pattern of corrupt activity and using others to deceive clients. He now faces nine years in prison and will owe $7 million in fines.

It's very simple. Mishandling monies from a trust account even for just a minute, is committing fraud. Don't do it...ever!

How Do You Prevent Fraud?

Fighting fraud is a national campaign that we all must embark on and fight together. Start by resolving to run a zero tolerance policy for fraud in your office. When you first begin to hire employees, don't forget to conduct a background investigation on all of your prospective employees. It's not a bad idea to let the prospective employees know of your zero tolerance policy while conducting your employment interview. Perpetrators usually seek an office with least resistance, meaning no policies are in place. This policy is not guaranteed to prevent fraud in your office, but it can help to discourage any "bad apples" that may come your way.

It's not enough to just have a zero tolerance policy for fraud in your office and believe that you are done. Necessary quality control procedures and orientation plans need to be put into place. Teach your processors how to detect fraud and, if need be, provide an incentive for reporting any fraudulent activities.

Here are just a few quality control tools available in the fight against fraud:

AppIntelligence

A quality control tool for fraud prevention delivers an integrity score to each loan file.

www.appintelligence.com
Tel: (363) 300-2500

Mortgage Asset Research Institute

Has a database of information relating to mortgage fraud. For a fee, you can access the Mortgage Industry Data Exchange (MIDEX) to cross-reference applicant, broker, or appraiser information to check for instances of fraud.

www.mari-inc.com

Platinum Data Solutions

Collateral Expert identifies potentially flipped properties and identifies the relationship between buyers and sellers. Can be used as a stand-alone report or integrated into your loan origination system (LOS).

www.platinumdatasolutions.com
Tel: (877) 711-1200

QC-Mac

Postclosing loan file reviews is a quality control tool that helps assure the quality of the loan transaction. Department of Housing and Urban Development–Department of Federal Housing Administration (HUD-FHA), Veterans Administration (VA), Fannie Mae (FNMA), and Freddie Mac (FHLMC) require that all mortgage brokers with whom they do business have quality control reviews conducted on at least 10 percent of their closed loans.

www.qcmac.com
Tel: (888) 483-2834

Rapid Reporting

Income verification with IRS form 4506 and borrower identity verification with DirectCheck tool.

www.rapidreporting.com
Tel: (888) 749-4411

For a list of other QC service providers, please refer to Chapter 9, "The Mortgage Broker Resource Directory."

What Is Predatory Lending?

Even though there is no generally accepted definition of *predatory lending*, the term essentially refers to unfair and abusive loan terms imposed on borrowers through deceptive sales tactics and sometimes fraud. As you may imagine, predatory lenders target the poor, elderly, and minorities, and they take advantage of borrowers' lack of understanding of complicated mortgage transactions with outright deception. Predatory lending tactics are unfair, unethical, and sometimes illegal.

Predatory lending schemes include credit insurance packing, forced refinances, property flipping, equity stripping, balloon payments, negative amortization, and mandatory arbitration. Mandatory arbitration in some loan contracts does not allow borrowers to seek legal remedies in court if they find that their home is threatened with a loan containing illegal or abusive terms.

The issue of predatory lending comes up often when discussing the sub-prime market because predatory loans contain higher interest rates and fees than those set by fair lending institutions. It's true that since the mid-1990s, the sub-prime mortgage market has grown substantially, providing access to credit for borrowers with less-than-perfect credit histories and to other borrowers who are not served by prime lenders. But somewhere along the way, there have been increased variations in loan pricing and increased reports of predatory lending. According to The Center for Responsible Lending, "not all sub-prime loans are predatory, but nearly all predatory loans are sub-prime."

Often predatory loans carry high upfront fees and may be based on the homeowners' equity in their homes, not their ability to make the scheduled payments. When homeowners have problems repaying the debt, they are often encouraged to refinance the loan. This is referred to as *loan flipping*. Frequently this leads to another high-fee loan that provides little or no economic benefit to the borrower.

Another hot topic for predatory lending is the issue of prepayment penalties. Prepayment penalties are allowed, as long as there are alternative products offering an option, which does not carry a prepayment penalty.

There are federal laws such as the Home Ownership and Equity Protection Act (HOEPA), the Truth in Lending Act (TILA), and the Real Estate Settlement Procedures Act (RESPA) that govern predatory lending. These laws will be discussed in detail later in this chapter. Additionally, however, many states continue to pass and implement their own set of unique statutes for extra protection. Georgia has recently passed one of the toughest predatory lending laws in the country. Penalties include criminal charges, fines, and in some cases the loan can become void during the first years (3 to 5) of maturity for violations.

Why Is Compliance Important to Mortgage Professionals?

As mortgage professionals make transactions in their home state and across state lines, compliance increasingly becomes a big concern to their business. Each state has different licensing rules, fees, mortgage regulations, continuing education requirements, and more. To stay compliant, mortgage brokers must remain aware of the ever-changing legislative behaviors of every state in which they do business. This can be a daunting task, even when doing business in just one state, not to mention multiple states.

Tracking State Compliance with AllRegs

One solution to tracking state legislative changes and regulations is AllRegs' State Compliance product. AllRegs is the preeminent electronic publisher of guides, regulations, analyses and forms for the residential mortgage lending industry. All of the official information from agencies such as Fannie Mae, Freddie Mac, FHA, and VA, as well as Federal and State Compliance information is compiled in an electronic database, updated daily and maintained on a feature-rich, online application. Subscribers benefit from a logically organized online collection of searchable information, priced at a fraction of the cost of alternative sources.

The State Compliance package includes state-by-state plain-language analyses and interpretive summaries for origination through servicing of first and second mortgages and home equity lines of credit for both lender and broker issues. There are links directly to supporting statutes and regulations, references to federal preemptions, state specific disclosures and other forms, and e-mail notification of updates. Enhanced by years of experience and user feedback, the search feature allows users to quickly find the information they are seeking. In addition, users can insert personal annotations that remain private or put in public notes that everyone in the firm can see. There is also a comprehensive library of mortgage-related forms and state-specific disclosures.

What's on the Horizon?

To provide additional opportunities to learn about compliance, AllRegs launched an education division known as AllRegs Academy in September 2006. AllRegs Academy combines these timely resources with various training opportunities and delivery modes to provide students with a unique educational experience—quality curriculum and learning activities enhanced with the most current regulations and industry updates. The goal of AllRegs Academy is to offer industry professionals convenient, relevant, and affordable mortgage training. Upcoming courses include the School of Mortgage Compliance classroom program.

The Mortgage Professional's Perspective

With AllRegs State Compliance package, mortgage professionals can find everything they need to know to do business within the state — the requirements for licenses, education and fees, as well as any restrictions regarding advertising, specific transactions, fees, interest rates, and more.

For example, a class action lawsuit was filed in New Jersey on behalf of individual consumers who were illegally charged a

$60 statement fee when requesting a written payoff calculation, required for closing.

New Jersey Statute 46:10B-25: Creditors, Prohibited Practices Relative to Home Loans states that "No creditor shall charge a fee for informing or transmitting to any person that balance due to pay off a home loan or to provide a release upon prepayment. Payoff balances shall be provided within seven days after the request." The plaintiff's attorney estimates that as many as 10,000 borrowers may be affected.

AllRegs' State Compliance Guidelines include specific information concerning this prohibited practice. To learn more about AllRegs and the State Compliance Package, visit www.allregs. com or call (800) 848-4904.

Additional references include:

Center for Responsible Lending
www.responsiblelending.org

Department of Housing and Urban Development
www.hud.gov

**Association of Community Organizations
for Reform Now (ACORN)**
www.acorn.org

National Fair Housing Alliance (NFHA)
www.nationalfairhousing.org

Lending Laws

A mortgage broker must abide by the laws, rules, and regulations required under the mortgage broker licensure code. In addition to the federal laws discussed here, there may be state laws to abide by. To avoid violation, a complete knowledge and understanding of all laws is necessary. The material contained here is to be used for informational purposes only. There may be other provisions that are applicable, which may require additional counsel.

Alternative Mortgage Transaction Parity Act

The Alternative Mortgage Transaction Parity Act, better known as the Parity Act, is regulated by the Office of Thrift Supervision

(OTS). The Parity Act was adopted in 1982 to grant certain state-chartered housing creditors parity with federally chartered lenders when making alternative mortgages. An alternative mortgage is a loan with payment features such as variable rates or balloon payments that vary from conventional fixed-rate, fixed-term mortgage loans.

A new rule enacted in 2003 removes the prepayment and late fee rules from the list of OTS regulations as applicable to state housing creditors. What this means is that state housing creditors such as mortgage bankers will once again be subject to state laws and regulations concerning prepayment penalties and late fees, rather than OTS rules. Federally chartered thrifts supervised by OTS will continue to follow OTS rules.

> For full details, contact the OTS at www.ots.treas.gov.

Community Reinvestment Act

The Community Reinvestment Act was enacted by Congress in 1977 to encourage depository institutions to help meet the credit needs of the communities in which they operate. This act requires financial institutions to abide by the Fair Housing Act and to give back to their communities by providing programs specifically targeted to low-to-moderate-income neighborhoods.

> For full details, contact the Community Reinvestment Act Web site at www.ffiec.gov/cra/.

Equal Credit Opportunity Act (ECOA)

The Equal Credit Opportunity Act and the Federal Reserve Board's implementation of Regulation B prohibit discrimination in any aspect of a credit transaction on the basis of:

- Race

- Color

- Religion

- National origin

- Gender

- Marital status

- Age

- Receipt of income from a public assistance program

- Good faith exercise of any right under the Consumer Credit Protection Act

The ECOA and Regulation B require creditors and/or lenders to:

Notify applicants of action taken on the applications within 30 days of application.

Provide the applicant with a copy of the appraisal if the applicant requests the appraisal in writing within a reasonable period of time from the date of application.

Retain records on credit applications.

Collect information in applications about the applicant's race and other personal characteristics for monitoring purposes.

The Housing Financial Discrimination Act of 1977 requires that all lenders provide a Fair Lending Notice to mortgage applicants. See also the section on the Fair Housing Act below.

Penalty for violation of this act includes actual damages, punitive damages to $10,000 for individual actions, and the lesser of $500,000 or 1 percent of the creditor and/or lender's net worth for class actions, and the recovery of costs and legal fees.

> For full details, contact the Board of Governors of the Federal Reserve System or www.fdic.gov/regulations/compliance/manual/part3/p3-h1.pdf.

Fair Credit Reporting Act

The Federal Trade Commission (FTC) enforces the Fair Credit Reporting Act. The purpose for the Fair Credit Reporting Act is to ensure that the reporting agencies are reporting accurate information and that no one can view a person's credit report without authorization.

As a mortgage broker or loan originator, before you request a credit report on any consumer you must first obtain authorization. The consumer should sign a credit authorization at the time of the loan application and/or when the credit report request is made.

The mortgage broker cannot share this information with other agencies or use it for marketing purposes. If the mortgage broker wants to share the information on the credit report with affiliates, the consumer must be given the opportunity to "opt-out." It is permissible to share this information with lenders or investors that are part of the lending process.

> For full details, contact the Federal Trade Commission at www.ftc.gov/os/statutes/fcra.htm.

Fair Housing Act

The Fair Housing Act was enacted in 1968 and prohibits discrimination by lenders, realtors, as well as other entities of persons because of race or color, religion, gender, national origin, family status, or disability.

HUD enforces this act and an applicant has up to one year to file a complaint. Penalties for violating this act are

- Civil penalties of $10,000 to $50,000 can be imposed.

- Criminal penalties can be added for those who do not adhere to the action recommended by HUD or who hinder an investigation.

> For full details, contact the U.S. Department of Justice or visit www.usdoj.gov/crt/housing/housing_coverage.htm.

Flood Disaster Protection Act

The Flood Disaster Protection Act is a federal legislation that in 1973 amended the National Flood Insurance Act of 1968.

The Flood Disaster Protection Act of 1973 made the purchase of flood insurance mandatory if the subject property lies in an area deemed by the National Flood Insurance Program to be in a flood zone. Typically lenders will contract with a flood certification service that has maps published by the government. Lenders cannot lend on any property that is in a flood zone without flood insurance in place upon funding the loan.

> For full details, contact FEMA or visit www.fema.gov/fhm/dl_acts.shtm.

Financial Institution Reform, Recovery, and Enforcement Act (FIRREA)

Congress enacted the FIRREA legislation in 1989 for the purpose of protecting real estate–related transactions by requiring that real estate appraisals in connection with federally related transactions are performed in writing, in accordance with uniform standards, and by individuals whose competency has been demonstrated and whose professional conduct will be subject to effective supervision by a subcommittee. The subcommittee ensures that all appraisers are properly licensed or certified.

> For full details, contact The Appraisal Foundation or visit www.appraisalfoundation.org.

Gramm-Leach-Bliley Act

The GLB Financial Modernization Act of 1999 requires "financial institutions" that offer financial products to give consumers a privacy disclosure that explains the institutions' sharing of nonpublic information to third parties or affiliates. This gives the consumer the opportunity to opt out if he or she does not want this information shared.

The FTC enforces the law and has jurisdiction over nonbank mortgage lenders, mortgage brokers, debt collectors, financial and investment advisors, tax preparers, and providers of real estate settlement services.

In addition this law requires that financial institutions protect information collected about individuals.

For full details, contact the FTC at www.ftc.gov/bcp/conline/ pubs/buspubs/glbshort.htm.

The Home Mortgage Disclosure Act

HMDA was enacted by congress in 1975 and is implemented by the Federal Reserve Board's Regulation C. It is designed to prevent any and all discrimination by the lender and to determine whether financial institutions are serving the housing needs of their communities.

HMDA requires lenders to gather certain information from the loan application. The loan data is submitted to the Federal Financial Institutions Examination Council (FFIEC) who in turn provides a disclosure statement. The disclosure statement is available to the public by both the lender and the FFIEC.

The information the lender is required to gather from a loan application is

- Loan type
- Property type
- Purpose of the loan or application
- Owner-occupancy
- Loan amount
- Report whether the application is a request for preapproval
- Type of action taken
- Date of action
- Property location

The information the lender is required to gather from the applicant is

- Method of application (mail, Internet, telephone, or in person)
- Ethnicity of the borrower or applicant

- Race of the borrower or applicant

- Gender of the borrower or applicant

- Income (from the application)

- Type of loan purchaser (FNMA, FHLMC, GNMA, etc.)

- If denied, reason for denial

The government monitoring information found toward the bottom of page 3 of the application (Form 1003) is voluntary and does not have to be provided by the applicant. However, the lender is required to fill in the information based on visual observation.

In addition the lender must report:

- If the loan is subject to Regulation Z, the spread between the annual percentage rate (APR) and the applicable Treasury yield.

- Home Ownership and Equity Protection Act (HOEPA) status.

- Lien status (first or second).

For full details, contact the FFIEC at www.ffiec.gov/hmda.

Homeowners Protection Act

The Homeowners Protection Act was enacted in 1998 for the purpose of defining the guidelines for the mandatory (automatic) cancellation of private mortgage insurance (PMI) on home loans when the following requirements have been met:

The mortgage balance is scheduled to reach 78 percent of the home's original value.

The borrower is current on his or her mortgage payments.

In addition, the borrower can submit a written request of cancellation of his or her private mortgage insurance when any of the following requirements have been met:

- The mortgage balance reaches or is scheduled to reach 80 percent of the home's original value.

- The borrower has a good payment history.

- There are no other liens on the property.

- The property value of the home has not declined.

The act also requires financial institutions to provide borrowers with certain disclosures to inform the borrower at the time of closing as to how and when to cancel mortgage insurance.

> For full details, contact FDIC at www.fdic.gov/news/news/financial/1999/fil9950.hmtl.

Homeownership Equity Protection Act (HOEPA)

HOEPA was enacted in 1994 for the purpose of curbing predatory lending practices in the home-equity lending market. The Federal Reserve Board amended Regulation Z to include the following:

- Extend the scope of mortgage loans subject to HOEPA protection

- Restrict certain acts or practices

- Strengthen HOEPA's prohibition on loans based on homeowner's equity without regard to payment ability

- Enhance HOEPA disclosures received by consumers before closing

The rule also prohibits a creditor from refinancing any HOEPA loan made to a borrower into another HOEPA loan within the first 12 months. Lenders are also prohibited from exercising "due-on-demand" or call provisions on a HOEPA loan.

To avoid presumption of violation of the statutory prohibition of making an equity loan without regard to payment ability, a lender must verify and document the borrower's income.

> For full details, contact the Federal Trade Commission at www.ftc.gov/be/v010004.htm.

Real Estate Settlement Procedures Act (RESPA)

RESPA was first passed in 1974 as a consumer protection statute. RESPA covers loans secured with a mortgage placed on a one- to four-family residential property. The purposes of RESPA are the following:

> Provide consumers with pertinent disclosures that include the nature and cost of all settlement services enabling the consumer to shop for the best loan scenario.

> Eliminate kickback and referral fees that may unnecessarily increase the fees for settlement services.

> Protect borrowers by placing limitations on the use of escrow accounts and requiring specific disclosures of applicable charges and disbursement dates.

What Disclosures Are Required by RESPA?

The number 1 violation of RESPA is the timing of disclosures. RESPA requires that each borrower receive at the time of application or *no later than* three business days of receiving the loan application, the following disclosures:

> A Good Faith Estimate

> A Mortgage Servicing Disclosure Statement or Notice of Possible Transfer Disclosure

> A Settlement Cost Booklet (for purchase transactions only)

> An Affiliated Business Arrangement Disclosure (if applicable)

Let's take a closer look at RESPA guidelines.

Section 6 of RESPA provides borrowers with important consumer protections relating to the servicing of their mortgage loans. Under Section 6 a borrower has the right to contact his or her loan servicer in writing if the borrower is having a problem with the servicing of the loan or has any escrow questions. Within 20 business days of receipt of the complaint, the servicer must acknowledge the complaint in writing. Within 60 days the servicer must resolve the complaint by correcting the account or giving a statement of the reasons for its position.

A borrower has up to three years to bring a lawsuit against any servicer in violation of Section 6 and can obtain actual damages as well as additional damages if there is a pattern of noncompliance.

Section 8 of RESPA prohibits anyone from giving or accepting a fee, kickback, or anything of value in exchange for referrals of business. Additionally, fee splitting and receiving money for services not actually performed are prohibited.

Violations of Section 8 include criminal and civil penalties with fines up to $10,000 and imprisonment of up to one year. In a private lawsuit the violator could be liable to the person charged for the settlement service an amount equal to three times the amount of the charge paid for the service.

Section 9 of RESPA prohibits a seller from requiring the home buyer to use a particular title insurance company as a condition of sale. This violation of Section 9 allows the buyer to sue a seller for an amount equal to three times the charge for title insurance.

Individuals have up to one year to bring a private lawsuit to enforce violations of Sections 8 and 9. HUD, a state attorney general, or state insurance commissioner may bring an injunctive action to enforce violations of Sections 6, 8, or 9 of RESPA within three years.

Section 10 of RESPA sets limits on the amounts that a lender may require a borrower to put into an escrow account for the purposes of paying taxes, hazard insurance, and other charges related to the property.

Once servicing starts for the mortgage loan, the lender cannot require a borrower to pay more than one-twelfth of the total of all disbursements payable during the year. The only time a lender is allowed to charge over the one-twelfth limit is when there is a shortage in the impound account and there are insufficient monies to pay the yearly premium once it becomes due.

The lender may require a cushion in the event that the taxes, insurance, etc., are not an accurate amount, but the cushion is not to exceed one-sixth of the total disbursements for the year. Lenders are also required to perform an audit on all impounded accounts each year. If there is an excess of $50 or more, a refund is due to the borrower.

Under Section 10, HUD has authority to impose a civil penalty on loan servicers who do not submit initial or annual escrow account statements to borrowers.

Mortgage loans that are exempt from RESPA rules are

- An all cash sale
- A sale where the individual home seller takes back the mortgage
- Agricultural, business, or commercial use
- 25 acres or more regardless of the purpose of the loan or whether or not there is a structure of the property
- Temporary financing, such as construction loans with a term of two years or less
- Loans transferred in the secondary market (excluding table funding)
- Nonlender-approved assumptions

For full information and illustrations of requirements of RESPA, visit http://www.hud.gov/offices.

The Right to Financial Privacy Act

The Right to Financial Privacy Act of 1978 protects the confidentiality of personal financial records by creating a statutory Fourth Amendment protection for bank records. The act was Congress's response to a U.S. Supreme Court decision finding that bank customers had no legal right to privacy in their financial information that was held by financial institutions.

The law specifies when, and under what conditions, a financial institution may release customer financial records to a federal government authority, pursuant to customer authorization, a search warrant, judicial subpoena, administrative subpoena, or summons.

For full details, visit http://www.epic.org/privacy/rfpa.

Truth in Lending Act (TILA)

The Truth in Lending Act (TILA), which is implemented by Regulation Z, is a federal law whose main purpose is to assure that creditors provide uniform disclosure of consumer credit to allow the consumer to easily comparison shop loan products.

Transactions that fall under Regulation Z are defined as any open-end (such as credit cards) or closed-end transactions (such as mortgage loans).

A short list of some of the requirements of Regulation Z include the following:

All oral or written disclosures of the interest rates be provided as annual percentage rates

Disclosure of a number of terms and conditions (i.e., amount financed, annual percentage rate, finance charge, late fees, and payment schedule) to a borrower prior to being obligated under a contract

Borrower to have a three-day rescission period to cancel the loan when using his or her primary residence as collateral

Certain disclosures for advertising loan products

Regulation Z defines *annual percentage rate* or APR, as the "cost of credit" to the borrower. The APR calculates the interest rate and other fees and charges that may be associated with obtaining credit. On a mortgage loan, certain fees are not affected by the APR since they are *not* associated with obtaining credit, for example, fees paid by the borrower for recording and taxes.

If credit approval on a mortgage is given, a truth-in-lending (TIL) disclosure must be provided to a borrower within three days of the application and again at closing. In the case of open-end transactions, a disclosure must be provided to the consumer before the transaction along with the periodic billing statement.

Any lender that does not adhere to the disclosure requirement is subject to penalties that can include all costs, attorney fees, and twice the amount of the finance charge.

CHAPTER 9

THE MORTGAGE BROKER RESOURCE DIRECTORY

Resource Directory

State-by-State Association Directory

Resource Directory

Wisdom + Power = Wealth

Wisdom is the sum of learning through the ages. A wise person knows the power of knowledge. Wealth is a profusion of material possessions or resources. Benjamin Franklin said, "Wealth is not his that has it, but his that enjoys it."

Mortgage Smarts, LLC, does not recommend or endorse any of the below-mentioned vendors, nor do we assume any liability for the products or services provided by any of the below-mentioned vendors. The directory is intended for guidance and informational use only.

Appraiser Referral Services

Appraiser Guide.com
www.appraiserguide.com

A nationwide appraiser referral service that provides the appraiser's license information and errors and omissions (E&O) insurance.

AppraiserSource.com
www.appraisersource.com
A national directory of real estate appraisers.

AppraiserUSA.com
www.appraiserusa.com
A national directory of real estate appraisers.

National Association of Real Estate Appraisers
www.iami.org

Automated Property Valuation Companies

Automated property valuation companies use multiple databases that cross-reference resources in order to provide a high probability range of property value within just minutes.

AAA Insured AVM Co.
www.aaainsuredavm.com

Appraisal Management Co. (AMCO)
www.amco.net

Case Shiller Wise (CASA)
www.csw.com

C&S Marketing
www.csmarketing.com

Background Check Providers

Mortgage Asset Research Institute (MARI)
www.mari-inc.com
Provides preemployment background screening.

Other background screening companies include:

Accurateinformationsystems.com

Backgroundsonline.com

Ceridian.com

Instantcriminalchecks.com

Intelius.com

Sentrylink.com

Business Cards

The companies listed below provide business cards, business thank you cards, and other marketing tools specific to the mortgage industry.

Business Greetings Express
www.businessgreetingcards.com

CCI Cards, Inc.
www.ccicards.com

Great FX
www.greatfxbusinesscards.com

LoanFuel.com
www.loanfuel.com

Closing Gifts

AdStamp
www.adstamp.com
Self-inking address stamp for new home buyers (includes your contact info).

DebitAmerica Incentive Services, Inc.
www.debitamerica.com
Business thank you card with a prepaid dining card available at any restaurant that accepts MasterCard.

Elite Corp Gifts
www.elitecorporategifts.com
Gift cards and certificates, private labeling for gourmet gifts.

Commercial Lender

Silver Hill Financial

4425 Ponce De Leon Boulevard
Fifth Floor
Coral Gables, Florida 33146
Tel: (888) 988-8843
www.silverhillfinancial.com

Headquartered in Miami with regional offices throughout the country, Silver Hill Financial is a nationwide commercial real estate lender. Since introducing the first-of-its-kind residential-style commercial program in 2003, the national lender has championed the small-balance loan among the residential broker community by providing training and education on the market opportunity. The company's innovative residential-style program makes commercial lending as easy residential, using flexible underwriting criteria ideal for borrowers seeking loans from $100,000 to $1.5 million.

Compliance

AllRegs

2975 Loan Oak Drive
Suite 140
Eagan, Minnesota 55121
Tel: (800) 848-4904
www.allregs.com

The leading online publisher of reference material, providing plain-language analysis of state laws and compliance, forms for the mortgage lending industry, a Practice Guide to FHA, and much more.

Icomply

www.icomply.com

Credit Reporting Companies

Advantage Credit

15 West Strong Street
Suite 20A
Pensacola, Florida 32501 Tel: (800) 600-2510
www.advantagecredit.com

Easy to read credit reports, Spanish credit reports for your bilingual clients, bilingual marketing material provided, ScoreMor, and CreditXpert.

Credit Plus, Inc.
Tel: (800) 258-3488
www.creditplus.com

First American Credco
Tel: (888) 819-2608
www.credco.com

Kroll Factual Data
Tel: (800) 929-3400
www.factualdata.com

NCO Credit Services
Tel: (800) 925-6691
www.ncocreditservices.com

Customer Management Software Programs

Act
www.act.com
Customer management software system.

Front Range Solutions
www.frontrange.com
Goldmine; customer database system.

Mortgage Advisors
www.mortgageadvisors.net
Contact management system.

The Turning Point
www.turningpoint.com
Customer management system.

Direct Mail/List Providers

3G Marketing Group
www.3gmktg.com

Altair Data Resources
www.altairdata.com

Century List Services
www.centurylist.com

Data Marketing Resources Inc.
www.4DMRInc.com

Data Warehouse Corp.
www.dwcsolutions.com

Debroux Marketing Inc.
www.debrouxmktg.com

Direct Marketing Associates
www.dmaleads.com

Parasec Interact
Tel: (866) 972-7732
www.parasecinteract.com

Pioneer Info & Marketing Inc.
www.pioneerinfo.com

QuantumMail.com
www.quantummail.com

Red Clay Media
www.redclaymedia.com

SmartLeads, Inc.
www.smartleadsusa.com

TMONE Leads
www.Tmone.com

For Sale by Owner Web Sites

www.fsbo.net
www.forsalebyowner.com
www.landvoice.com

Interpretation Services

Language Line Services
www.languageline.com
Provides interpretation services 24/7 in 140 languages and specializes in translating financial documents such as credit and loan documents.

Lead Providers

Alansis
www.alansis.com

Buyleads.net
www.buyleads.net

Eleadz.com
www.eleadz.com

Ileads.com
www.ileads.com

Impact Web Enterprises, Inc.
www.impactleads.com

LeadsToLoans/First American Real Estate Solutions
www.firstamres.com
Under Products Section click leads to loans.

Lender Lead Solutions
www.lenderleadsolutions.com

LSI/Fidelity National Financial Company
www.leadlocatorplus.com

Loanbright.com
www.loanbright.com

LocalLender, LLC
www.locallender.net

mLeads.com
Tel: (888) 43-LEADS
www.mleads.com

MoneyNest.com
www.theloanconnection.com

Myers, Internet, Inc.
www.myersinternet.com

Loan Officer Employment Web Sites

www.brokeruniverse.com   **www.monster.com**
www.careerbuilder.com   **www.mortgageboard.com**

www.indeed.com   www.mortgagejobs.com
www.jobmag.com   www.mortgagejobstore.com
www.lendercareers.com   www.mortgagemag.com
www.loanofficerjobs.com   www.mortgagerecruiters.com
www.loancloserjobs.com   www.nationalmortgagenews.com

Loan Origination Software Programs

Calyx Point
www.calyxsoftware.com

Ellie Mae E-Pass
Encompass Mortgage Automation System
Ellie Mae, Inc. 4140 Dublin Blvd., Suite 300
Dublin, California 94568 Sales: (888) 955-9100
Customer Support: (800) 777-1718
www.elliemae.com
Headquartered in Dublin, California, Ellie Mae launched its innovative loan origination system Encompass in 2003. Now, the Encompass Mortgage Automation System has established itself as the new standard for loan origination. Within the first two years after its introduction, over half of the top 250 brokerages were using the technology. Encompass is used for origination, marketing, and processing of loans.

Marketing Tools

LoanToolbox
2625 Townsgate Road
Suite 300
Westlake Village,
Ca. 91361
Tel: (877) 684-8665
www.loantoolbox.com
An excellent marketing tool for both the new and existing loan originator. LoanToolbox provides tools for time and database management, direct marketing and follow-up campaigns, and includes explanations on several loan programs.

Mortgage Advisors

www.mortgageadvisors.net

Customer presentation material (loan analysis presentations).

The Mortgage Coach

www.mortgagecoach.com

Provide mortgage planning advice with detailed cost and loan analysis.

Mortgage Market Guide

www.mortgagemarketguide.com

Provides you with daily market updates and instant repricing alerts.

Mortgage News and Magazines

Broker Magazine

www.brokermagazine.com

A monthly publication and a great sales and management resource for the mortgage broker.

Mortgage Broker Magazine

www.nationalmortgagebroker.com

The official publication of the National Association of Mortgage Brokers.

Mortgage Originator Magazine

3990 Old Towne Avenue
Suite A203
San Diego, California 92110
Tel: (619) 223-9989
www.mortgageoriginator.com

Monthly publication that produces articles covering all topics pertaining to mortgage originators. A special topic is featured monthly along with an annual highlight of the nations top loan originators.

Origination News

www.originationnews.com

The largest publication servicing mortgage originators, it is a monthly publication delivering the latest news and trends in the mortgage industry.

Scotsman Guide

18912 North Creek Parkway S.

Suite 205

Bothell, Washington 98011

Tel: (800) 297-6061

www.scotsmanguide.com

An excellent resource for both residential and commercial wholesale lenders includes loan-product underwriting matrixes. A residential and commercial edition is published monthly at no cost to every mortgage loan origination office that brokers loans in the United States.

Other mortgage news and magazines include:

www.bankrate.com

www.nationalmortgagenews.com

www.mortgagedaily.com

www.mortgagemag.com

www.mortgagepress.com

Newsletter and Postcard Marketing

DC Marketing Specialists

www.dcmspec.com

Gooder Group/LoanLetter

www.goodergroup.com

In Touch Today

www.intouchtoday.net

LoanFuel.com

www.loanfuel.com

My Mortgage Newsletter

Mymortgagenewsletter.com

Newsletter Company

www.newslettercompany.com

Postcard Mania

Postcardmania.com

RealMarCom.com
www.realmarcom.com

Right Side Marketing
www.rightsidemarketing.com

Sendsations Power Marketing
www.sendsations.com

Touchpoint Communications
www.touchpoint.com

Payroll Service Providers

ADP
www.adp.com

Intuit Payroll Services
www.payroll.com

Paychex
www.paychex.com

SurePayroll
www.surepayroll.com

Quality Control Services

AppIntelligence
www.appintelligence.com
DISSCO, a quality control tool used to detect fraud and deliver an integrity score.

Callender Mortgage Services
www.callenderqc.com
Provides quality control preparation, pre- and post-closing loan file reviews, and annual on-site HUD compliance audits for loan correspondents.

C&S Marketing
www.csmarketing.com
HistoryPro identifies potential flip properties and markets.

ComplianceEase

www.complianceease.com

Provides 4506 verification through their 4506Xpress program and validates a customer's identity through their Identifier program.

Ingrian Networks

www.ingrian.com

Encrypts your database including your borrower's sensitive financial information. Can also encrypt Web sites and more.

Platinum Data Solutions

www.platinumdatasolutions.com

Collateral Expert identifies potential flip properties and identifies the relationship between buyers and sellers.

QC-MAC

www.qcmac.com

Conduct postclosing loan file reviews to comply with HUD requirements. Great source for HUD approval.

Rapid Reporting

www.rapidreporting.com

Verify borrower's income directly from IRS, with IRS Form 4506. Also verify borrower's identity with DirectCheck tool.

Sysdome, Inc.

www.sysdome.com

4506 verification, SafeCheck SSN verification, address validation, and prefunding audits.

TeleTrack, Inc.

www.teletrack.com

Specializes in sub-prime consumer credit information. Fraud detection, risk assessment, and scoring and decisioning tools.

TruApp

www.truapp.com

Fraud prevention product that screens for property flipping, inflated sales price, inflated appraisals, borrower identity fraud, non–"arms-length" transactions, and more.

VMP

www.vmpmtg.com

Provides a wide range of fraud management solutions including IDFlag, a product that authenticates a borrower's identity. Designed to combat identity theft.

Registered Agent Company

Parasec

www.parasec.com

Resourceful Web Sites

BankRate

www.bankrate.com

Department of Housing and Urban Development

www.hud.gov

Fannie Mae

www.fanniemae.com

Freddie Mac

www.freddiemac.com

Inman News

www.inmannews.com

Mortgage Bankers Association

www.mbaa.org

Asian Real Estate Association of America

www.areaa.org

National Association of Hispanic Real Estate Professionals

www.nahrep.org

National Association of Realtors

www.realtor.org

National Association of Real Estate Brokers

www.nareb.com

Surety Bond Companies

American Manufacturers Mutual Insurance Co.
178 Castleton St.
La Puente, CA 91748
Tel: (626) 369-7700

Burch Marcus Pool
229 Heymann Blvd.
Lafayette, LA 70503
Tel: (337) 235-8866

Company of Maryland
1333 Betterfield Rd., #410
Downers, IL 60515
Tel: (630) 719-6800

Fireman's Fund Insurance Co.
777 San Martin Dr.
Novato, CA 94998
Tel: (415) 899-2000

Grammercy Insurance Company
7616 LBJ Freeway, Ste. 720
Dallas, TX 75251
Tel: (972) 404-0022

JW Bond Consultants
9 Village Row
New Hope, PA 18938
Tel: (215) 862-6100

Liberty Mutual Insurance
175 Berkley
Boston, MA 02116
Tel: (617) 357-9500

Lumbermen's Mutual Casualty
2877 Brandywine Rd.
Atlanta, GA 30341

Ohio Casualty
136 M 3rd Hamilton
Hamilton, OH 45025
Tel: (513) 867-3000

Patterson Insurance Company
1325 Barksdale Blvd.
Bossier City, LA 71111
Tel: (318) 746-5060

Querbes & Nelson
(Independent Insurance Agents)
214 Milam St.
Shreveport, LA 71101
Tel: (318) 221-5241

Safeco Insurance Company
Three Bala Plaza East, Ste. 416
Bala Cynwyd, PA 19004
Tel: (215) 839-3530

Scott Insurance Company
1301 Old Graves Mill Rd.
Lynchburg, VA 24506
Tel: (804) 832-2100

Shelter General Insurance Co.
1817 West Broadway
Columbia, MO 65218
Tel: (573) 445-8481

State Farm Fire & Casualty Co.
One State Farm Plaza
Bloomington, IL 61710
Tel: (309) 664-7000

**The North River
Ins. Co.**
c/o Crum & Foster Ins.
Bond Dept.
Box 1973
Morristown, NJ 07960
Tel: (770) 513-7393

**Traveler's Property
Casualty**
Nationwide locations
www.stpaultravelers.com/bond/
    index.html

Trinity Universal Insurance
P.O. Box 655028
Dallas, TX 75265
Tel: (214) 360-8000

Universal Surety
950 Echo Lane, Ste. 250
Houston, TX 77024
Tel: (713) 860-4600

Western Surety Company
4006 Belt Line Rd., Ste. 100
Dallas, TX 75265-5908
Tel: (972) 702-8802

Technology Systems

Data-Vision, Inc.
www.d-vision.com
LoanQuoter; provides innovative products, to include online decision-making.

QuickQualifier
www.mortgagesoftware.com
Marketing tools and calculators for mortgage professionals.

Telecommunications/Call Capture and Voice Broadcasting

Arch Telecom
www.archtelecom.com
Lead generation and follow-up; call capture with Powerline.

Database Systems Corp.
www.databasesystemscorp.com
Mortgage marketing software and auto dialer.

Five 9
www.five9.com
Predictive dialer

FreedomVoice Systems
www.freedomvoice.com

Information Now, Inc.
www.callcapture.com
Call capture service.

Smart Reply
www.smartreply.com
Voice messages.

Stratasoft
www.stratasoft.com
Voice broadcasting software solutions.

Tele-messenger Systems
www.auto-dialers.com
Voice broadcast automated dialing equipment.

Title and Settlement Companies

First American Title Insurance Company
3 First American Way
Santa Ana, CA 92702
Tel: (800) 525-3633
www.firstam.com
First American has a wide array of services available for the mortgage originator, including title and closing, property valuation reports, and much more.

Chicago Title
601 Riverside Ave.
Jacksonville, FL 32092
Tel: (888) 934-3354
www.ctic.com
Provider of national title and escrow services.

Fidelity National Title Insurance Co.
601 Riverside Avenue
Jacksonville, Florida 32204
Tel: (888) 866-3684
www.fntic.com

Title, escrow, and closing service with nationwide service available. Fidelity also provides; real estate information, foreclosure publishing, credit reporting, attorney services, flood certification, real estate tax service and more.

LandAmerica Financial Group, Inc.
101 Gateway Centre Parkway
Gateway One
Richmond, Virginia 23235
Tel: (800) 446-7086
www.landam.com
Provider of title and escrow services, appraisal, inspection, flood insurance and more.

Old Republic National Title Insurance Group
400 Second Avenue South
Minneapolis, MN 55401
Tel: (800) 328-4441
www.oldrepublictitle.com
Provider of title insurance with nationwide coverage.

Stewart Title
1980 Post Oak Blvd., #800
Houston, TX 77056
Tel: (800) 783-9278
www.stewart.com
Stewart provides a wide range of services and technology for the mortgage originator including title, property data, flood zone, pre-employment screening, and more.

Transcontinental Title Company
2605 Enterprise Rd. East, #150
Clearwater, FL 33759
Tel: (888) 853-6347
www.tctitle.com
With offices nationwide, Transcontinental provides title and escrow services.

Translation Service Providers

Translation Source

www.translation-source.com

Can provide translated loan documents such as note, deed of trust/mortgage, HUD-1, and Truth-in-Lending.

Web Site Designers

Ellie Mae

www.elliemae.com/products/websites.asp

Lion MTS

www.lionchoice.com

LoanBright.com

www.loanbright.com

Myers, Internet, Inc.

2160 Lundy Avenue

Suite 128

San Jose, California 95131

Tel: (800) 693-7770

www.myersinternet.com

Headquartered in San Jose, California, Myers is the leading provider of Web-based solutions to mortgage originators, and has delivered affordable state-of-the-art, customized mortgage Web sites since 1995. Their low-cost Web sites make them the top choice among the mortgage and real estate industry. Currently hosting over 7,000 mortgage Web sites, Myers has been ranked as the Number One Web Design firm in Silicon Valley for seven consecutive years.

State-by-State Association Directory

The most prestigious and powerful organization representing mortgage brokers is the National Association of Mortgage Brokers. NAMB has a professional publication, *National Mortgage Broker*, which is full of valuable information. NAMB also provides continuing certified education and updates on state legislation. Membership is an excellent resource for current changes in the mortgage industry. Their contact information is

National Association of Mortgage Brokers (NAMB)
8201 Greensboro Dr., Ste. 300
McLean, VA 22102
Tel: (703) 610-9009; Fax: (703) 610-9005
www.namb.org

Local representation is equally as important; becoming a member of your state's broker association will keep you informed of local issues and is an excellent way to network. Below is a state-by-state mortgage broker association guide.

Alabama
Alabama Mortgage Brokers
  Association
108 Windsor Lane
Pelham, AL 35124
Tel: (866) 845-2622
www.almba.org

Alaska
Alaska Association of Mortgage
  Brokers
224N. Yenlo, Suite 3B
Wasilla, AK 99654
Tel: (907) 357-9640
www.akamb.org

Arizona
Arizona Association of Mortgage
  Brokers
P.O. Box 487
Peoria, AZ 85380-0487
Tel: (623) 972-6180
www.azamb.org

Arkansas
None known.

California
California Association of Mortgage
  Brokers
1730 I St., Ste. 240
Sacramento, CA 95814
Tel: (916) 448-8236
www.cambweb.org

Colorado
Colorado Association of Mortgage
  Brokers
9200 W Cross Dr., Ste. 404
Littleton, CO 80123
Tel: (720) 377-0410
www.camb.org

Connecticut
Connecticut Society of Mortgage
  Brokers
26 Broad St.
Milford, CT 06460
Tel: (203) 874-3090
www.csmbct.com

Delaware
Delaware State Mortgage
Association
Contact President Bill Betit
Tel: (302) 494-7405
Toll Free (800) 272-3477

District of Columbia
None known.

Florida
Florida Association of Mortgage
    Brokers
1292 Cedar Center Dr.
Tallahassee, FL 32301
Tel: (800) 289-9983
www.famb.org

Georgia
Georgia Association of Mortgage
    Brokers
4630 Clary Lakes Dr.
Roswell, GA 30075
Tel: (770) 993-5507
www.gamb.org

Hawaii
Hawaii Association of Mortgage
    Brokers
P.O. Box 1074
Honolulu, HI 96808
Tel: (808) 377-3456
www.hamb.org

Idaho
Idaho Association of Mortgage
    Brokers
600 N. Curtis, Ste. 247
Boise, ID 83706
Tel: (208) 321-9309
www.idahomortgagebrokers.org

Illinois
Illinois Association of Mortgage
    Brokers
350 W. 22nd St.
Lombard, IL 60148
Tel: (630) 916-7720
www.iamb.org

Indiana
Indiana Association of Mortgage
    Brokers
212 W. 10th St., Ste. A-309
Indianapolis, IN 462
Tel: (317) 964-1225
www.inamb.com

Iowa
Iowa Association of Mortgage
    Brokers
3636 Westown Parkway, Ste. 217
Des Moines, IA 50266
Tel: (515) 223-9701
www.iowamortgagebrokers.org

Kansas
Kansas Association of Mortgage
    Brokers
14904 W. 87th Parkway
Lenexa, KS 66215
Tel: (913) 492-5262
www.kamb.org

Kentucky
Kentucky Mortgage Brokers
    Association
Box 4584
Frankfort, KY 40604
Tel: (502) 223-4840
www.kmba.net

Louisiana
Louisiana Mortgage Lenders
    Association
8550 United Plaza Blvd.
Baton Rouge, LA 70809
Tel: (225) 922-4642
www.lmla.com

Maine
None known.

Maryland
Maryland Association of Mortgage
    Brokers
720 Light St.
Baltimore, MD 21230
Tel: (410) 752-6262
www.mamb.org

Massachusetts
Massachusetts Mortgage Association
607 North Ave., Bldg. 16
Wakefield, MA 01880
Tel: (781) 246-0601
www.massmort.org

Michigan
Michigan Mortgage Brokers Association
3300 Washtenaw Ave., Ste. 220
Ann Arbor, MI 48104
Tel: (734) 975-4426
www.mmbaonline.com

Minnesota
Minnesota Association of Mortgage
    Brokers
5200 Willson Rd., Ste. 300
Edina, MN 55424
Tel: (952) 345-3240
www.mnamb.org

Mississippi
Mississippi Association of Mortgage
    Brokers
P.O. Box 195
Clinton, MS 39060
Tel: (866) 844-6262
www.msamb.org

Missouri
Missouri Association of Mortgage
    Brokers
4700 South Lindbergh Blvd.
St. Louis, MO 63126
Tel: (314) 909-9747
www.mamb.net

Montana
None known.

Nebraska
None known.

Nevada
Nevada Association of Mortgage
    Professionals
6130 Elton Avenue #224
Las Vegas, NV 89107
Tel: (702) 216-0430
www.namp.us/

New Hampshire
Mortgage Bankers and
    Brokers Association of
    New Hampshire
91 North State St., Ste. 101
Concord, NH 03301
Tel: (603) 226-4486
www.mbba-nh.org

New Jersey

Mortgage Bankers Association of New
  Jersey
385 Morris Ave.
Springfield, NJ 07081
Tel: (973) 379-7447
www.mbanj.com

New Mexico

New Mexico Association of Mortgage
  Brokers
P.O. Box 3967
Albuquerque, NM 87190
Tel: (505) 489-7610
www.nmamb.org

New York

New York Association of Mortgage
  Brokers
25 North Broadway
Tarrytown, NY 10591
Tel: (914) 332-6233
www.nyamb.org

North Carolina

North Carolina Association of
  Mortgage Professionals
3901 Barrett Dr., Ste. 202
Raleigh, NC 27609
Tel: (919) 783-0767
www.ncmortgage.org

North Dakota

None known.

Ohio

Ohio Association of Mortgage Brokers
170 Bancorp Building
5686 Dressler Rd. NW
North Canton, OH 44720

Tel: (330) 497-7233
www.oamb.org

Oklahoma

Oklahoma Association of Mortgage
  Professionals
Tel: (918) 760-4950
www.okamb.com

Oregon

Oregon Association of Mortgage
  Professionals
P.O. Box 2042
Salem, OR 97308
Tel: (800) 650-9076
www.oamb.com

Pennsylvania

Pennsylvania Association of Mortgage
  Brokers
2405 Park Dr.
Harrisburg, PA 17110
Tel: (888) 311-7262
www.pamb.org

Rhode Island

Rhode Island Mortgage Bankers
  Association
14 Circlewood Dr.
Coventry, RI 02816
Tel: (401) 421-2338
rimba.org

South Carolina

South Carolina Mortgage Brokers
  Association
1122 Lady St., Ste. 914
Columbia, SC 29201
(803) 771-0416
www.scmba.org

South Dakota
South Dakota Association of
   Mortgage Brokers
421 West 18th Street
Sioux Falls, SD 57105
Tel: (605) 330-6033
www.sdamb.org

Tennessee
Tennessee Association of
   Mortgage Brokers
25 Century Blvd., Ste. 602
Nashville, TN 37214
(615) 695-5234
www.tnamb.org

Texas
Texas Association of Mortgage
   Brokers
502 E. 11th St., Ste. 400
Austin, TX 78701
(800) 850-8262
www.tamb.org

Utah
Utah Association of Mortgage
   Brokers
60 South 600 East, Ste. 150
Salt Lake City, UT 84102
(801) 493-2990
www.uamb.org

Vermont
None known.

Virginia
Virginia Association of Mortgage
   Brokers
P.O. Box 71197
Richmond, VA 23255
Tel: (804) 285-7557
www.vamb.org

Washington
Washington Association of
   Mortgage Brokers
P.O. Box 2016
Edmonds, WA 98020
Tel: (866) 425-7250
www.wamb.org

West Virginia
None known.

Wisconsin
Wisconsin Association of Mortgage
   Brokers
16 North Carroll St., Ste. 900
Madison, WI 53703
(608) 259-9262
www.wambrokers.com

Wyoming
None known.

CHAPTER 10

EDUCATIONAL AND LICENSING REQUIREMENTS FOR THE MORTGAGE BROKER

State-by-State Guide for All 50 States

Sample State Disclosures for Mortgage Brokers

State-by-State Guide for All 50 States

Alabama

Regulatory agency: Alabama State Banking Department

Contact info: http://www.banking.alabama.gov/bol_applications.htm or call (334) 242-3452

Requirements

Education

An application for a mortgage broker's license will need to include evidence of satisfactory completion of 12 hours of approved continuing education in first and second mortgage transactions by the officers and principals who are or will be actively engaged in the daily operation of the company. Approved courses can be those approved by:

Alabama Mortgage Brokers Association

Alabama Bankers Association

Alabama Mortgage Bankers Association

Education Committee of the National Association of Mortgage Brokers

For a list of approved courses and facilitators, visit http://www.banking.alabama.gov/Applications/bol_applications_ambla.htm and press Continuing education provider list.

Licensing fee

$500 Annual license fee

$100 Investigation fee

A licensee shall obtain a license for *each* location where the business of the mortgage is transacted. All licenses expire on December 31st of each year.

Application for licensure must include:

A fully executed mortgage broker application

Proof of proper business filing with the state

Copies of business organizational documents

A general plan and character of business

Evidence of completion of educational requirements

Investigation fee of $100 and initial license fee of $500

Financial statements prepared within 90 days of the filing of the application (to verify net worth requirements)

Surety bond

Three letters of reference concerning the applicant's good name and reputation in the community

Four letters of reference from individuals or companies in the lending industry concerning the applicant's experience and expertise

Bond

$25,000

Net worth

$25,000

Company registration

Registration with the Alabama Secretary of State is required. You may reach them at www.sos.state.al.us.

Additional requirements

Alabama requires each mortgage applicant to be disclosed with an Alabama Broker Disclosure form in accordance with the Alabama Code Section 5-25-12.

Audits and reports

Examination of records is conducted by the supervisor anytime, but will be conducted at least once every 24 months. The licensee shall pay the supervisor an examination fee. If records are kept out of state, then the broker must either make them available in state or pay for travel expenses for the supervisor to examine them at the place where they are maintained.

Each licensee is required to file a written report annually, by May 1st, reporting his or her prior years in business and operation, including a financial statement.

Alaska

Regulatory agency: Alaska Department of Community Economic Development

Contact info: www.dced.state.ak.us or call (907) 465-2530

The state of Alaska does not regulate mortgage brokering regardless of lien position. Therefore, there is no application process or specific license to be issued to conduct these types of activities.

Many foreign mortgage lenders and brokers choose to register as a foreign corporation with the corporations section of the Alaska Department of Community and Economic Development. You may obtain the necessary forms at www.dced.state.ak.us/bsc/corps.htm.

Arizona

Regulatory agency: Arizona Banking Department

Contact info: www.azbanking.com. or call (602) 255-4421

Requirements

An applicant must have no less than three years' experience as a mortgage broker or equivalent lending experience in a related business during the five years immediately preceding the time of application.

If the applicant is an entity rather than a natural person, the superintendent may require information as to the honesty, truthfulness, integrity, and competency of any officer, director, shareholder, or other interested party of the association, corporation, or group.

An applicant must appoint a "responsible individual" who shall be a resident of this state, shall be in active management of the activities of the licensee, and shall meet the qualifications set forth by the State Banking Department.

A licensee shall not employ any person unless the licensee:

Conducts a reasonable investigation of the background, honesty, truthfulness, integrity, and competency of the employee before hiring

Keeps a record of the investigation for no less than two years after termination.

Education

Each applicant to qualify for the exam must complete and pass a course from an approved Mortgage Broker school. A list of approved course providers is provided with the mortgage broker application. In order to take the exam, the applicant will need to provide a "Certificate of Completion" form.

Exam

$50

The exam is given under the supervision of the Department of Banking of Arizona. The applicant will be tested on his or her knowledge of:

The obligations between principal and agent, the applicable canons of business ethics, and the requirements and rules of article 6-908

The arithmetical computations common to mortgage brokerage, principles of real estate lending, and general purposes and legal effect of mortgages

Licensing fee

> $800 Initial application fee for principal office
>
> $250 Initial application fee for branch location
>
> $29 Processing fee for fingerprints

Actual license fee is prorated and is not due until application is approved. License fee varies and depends on whether any loans were funded in the previous year (license fee ranges between $250 and $500). License is valid for one year; renewal date is September 30th.

Every licensed mortgage broker shall designate and maintain a principal place of business in the state of Arizona for the transaction of business. If a licensee wishes to maintain one or more locations in addition to a principal place of business, he or she shall first obtain a branch office license from the superintendent and designate a person for each branch office to oversee the operations of that office.

Application for licensure must include:

> A fully executed mortgage broker application
>
> Proof of proper business filing with the state (see details listed below)
>
> Copies of business organizational documents
>
> Proof of identity of qualified Arizona resident for Arizona business location
>
> Signed and notarized License Surrender Agreement
>
> W9 Form/Request for Taxpayer Identification
>
> Surety bond
>
> Financial statements
>
> Personal history statements and fingerprint cards
>
> Verification of state exam results (for responsible individual)
>
> Verification of work experience (for responsible individual)
>
> Initial application fee of $800 and fingerprint fee of $29

Bond

$10,000 to $15,000 (maintain a surety bond of either $10,000 or $15,000)

Net worth

$100,000

$50,000 for each additional location

Company registration required

If the applicant is applying as a corporation, he or she must submit an approved copy of articles of incorporation. Arizona State Corporation Commission is available at Tel: (602) 542-3135 or www.cc.state.az.us.

If applying as a foreign corporation, the applicant must submit a copy of an approved application for authority. Arizona Secretary of State is available at Tel: (602) 542-6187 or www.sosaz.com.

If applying as a limited liability company, the applicant must submit an approved copy of articles of organization (for domestic companies) or a copy of the approved registration (for foreign companies).

If applying as a Limited Partnership or Foreign Limited Partnership, then the applicant must provide an *approved copy* of his or her partnership agreement.

A sole proprietorship or individual *must* use his or her name when filing as an individual; otherwise, he or she will need to register a dba or trade name.

A dba or trade name must be registered with the Arizona Secretary of State (Tel: (602) 542-6187 or www.sosaz.com) and the applicant must submit an approved copy of his or her certificate of trade name registration.

Audits/reports

Every mortgage broker must keep at all times correct and complete records in state. If a mortgage broker's principal place of business is out of state, he or she may keep records out of state only when authorization has been obtained from the superintendent. If records are kept out of state, the mortgage broker is responsible for providing records to the superintendent no later than 3 days after demand.

Additional disclosure requirements
Arizona requires each mortgage applicant be disclosed of any up-front fees with an Arizona Application Disclosure Form.

Arkansas

> *Regulatory agency*: Arkansas Securities Department

> *Contact info*: www.arkansas.gov/arsec or call (501) 324-9260

Requirements

Experience
If the applicant is the sole proprietor, the applicant will need to have at least three years of experience in mortgage lending or other experience or proficiency requirements as the commissioner may adopt by rule or order.

If the applicant is a corporation or general or limited partnership, then at least one of its principal officers or general partners shall have the experience. If the applicant is a limited liability company, then at least one of its managers must fulfill the experience requirement.

Each licensee must appoint a managing principal (who must fulfill the educational requirements) and is responsible for the operations of the licensee. If a sole proprietor, he or she may serve as the managing principal.

Licensing fee
> $750 Initial fee

> $100 Fee per branch office

> $350 Annual renewal fee (license expires annually 120 days from business fiscal year-end)

Application for licensure must include:

> FMLA Form 001—A fully executed mortgage broker application

FMLA Form 002—Parents, Subsidiaries, and Affiliates (complete form)

FMLA Form 003—Information on all Principals, Officers, Directors, and Managers

FMLA Form 004—Information on Managing Principal

FMLA Form 005—List all other states in which business is licensed

FMLA Form 006—Branch offices (if applicable)

FMLA Form 007—List all loan officers who will conduct business under licensee

FMLA Form 008—Surety Bond

FMLA Form 009—Assignment of Escrow Agreement

FMLA Form 010—An executed "Consent to Service of Process" by President, CEO, or managing principal

Proof of proper business filing with the state

Financial statements

Identification of proposed business activities in Arkansas

Location of records

Bond
$50,000

Net worth
$25,000

References
The applicant will need three letters of recommendation, including one from his or her banker.

Company registration
Registration with the Arkansas Secretary of State is required. You may contact them at www.sosweb.state.ar.us/ or call (501) 682-1010.

California

Regulatory agency: California Department of Real Estate

Contact: www.dre.ca.gov/brkrlic.htm or call (916) 227-0904

Requirements

Must be 18 years of age or older

Must provide proof of legal residence in the United States

Must be honest and truthful; conviction of a crime may also be cause for denial

Must have a minimum of two years' full-time licensed salesperson experience within the last five years or the equivalent

Must qualify for and pass a written exam

Education and exam

Applicants for a real estate broker license examination must have successfully completed the following eight statutorily required college-level courses:

Real Estate Practice

Legal Aspects of Real Estate

Real Estate Finance

Real Estate Appraisal

Real Estate Economics or Accounting

(If both Real Estate Economics and Accounting are taken, then only two courses from the following group are needed.)

Otherwise, in addition to the above, three courses from the following group are required:

Real Estate Principles

Business Law

Property Management

Escrows

Real Estate Office Administration

Mortgage Loan Brokering and Lending

Advanced Legal Aspects of Real Estate

Advanced Real Estate Finance

Advanced Real Estate Appraisal

Computer Applications in Real Estate

Applicants who have completed the above statutorily required college-level courses are eligible to take the broker examination without providing further evidence of education or experience. Continuing education offerings do not satisfy the college-level course requirements for this exam.

Each college-level course must be a minimum of three semester units or four quarter units. The courses must be completed prior to being scheduled for the examination. Copies of official transcripts are generally acceptable evidence of completed courses. Transcripts of other courses, submitted as an equivalent course of study in lieu of the statutory courses, must be accompanied by an official course or catalog description in order to be evaluated.

Broker qualification courses must be completed at an institution of higher learning accredited by the Western Association of Schools and Colleges or by a comparable regional accrediting agency recognized by the U.S. Department of Education, or by a private real estate school which has had its courses approved by the California Real Estate Commissioner.

Courses completed through foreign institutions of higher learning must be evaluated by a foreign credentials evaluation service approved by the Department of Real Estate. Refer to Examination Applicant Foreign Education Information.

For an evaluation of *previous* college courses, degree, or experience the applicant must submit:

Examination Application form

Required $50 exam fee

Transcripts of applicant's college courses and/or degree. Because of the delays in obtaining college transcripts, a student applicant should make arrangements with the college well in advance.

Copy(s) of catalog description (for the year[s] of attendance) of any courses that the applicant wishes to substitute for the statutorily required courses.

Employment Verification form

Equivalent Experience Verification form

If the applicant is not qualified to take an exam at the time of application, notification will be sent in writing allowing two years from the date of receipt of the application to complete the qualifications and take the examination. If the applicant does not qualify for and pass the examination during the two-year period, the application expires and a new application, qualifying material, and fee will be necessary.

An application for an exam is made only upon the fulfillment of all educational requirements. An application must include: license fee, verification of educational requirements, and Form RE 226 to verify employment. Examinations are conducted in the following areas:

Fresno

San Diego

Los Angeles

Oakland

Sacramento

Those who pass the examination are provided a license application, which must be submitted to and approved by the DRE.

For a list of approved educational vendors, go to www.dre.ca. gov/precours.htm and press Approved statutory/prelicense courses.

Licensing fee

$165

License is valid for four years. To renew a broker's license, applicant must provide proof of meeting continuing education requirements. To renew a broker's license the first time, the applicant must complete 45 DRE-approved continuing education clock hours as follows:

12 clock hours divided up as four separate three-hour courses in the following subjects: Ethics, Agency, Trust Fund Handling, and Fair Housing

A minimum of 18 clock hours of consumer protection courses

The remaining 15 clock hours related to either consumer service or consumer protection.

Fingerprint fee

There is a $56 fingerprint processing fee and also a live scan service fee which should be paid directly to the live scan provider (not the DRE).

For any real estate license, one set of classifiable fingerprints must be submitted and must be acceptable to the State Department of Justice (DOJ), unless the applicant is currently licensed by DRE or has held a real estate license that expired less than two years ago.

All fingerprints must be submitted through DOJ's Live Scan Program, which takes and transmits fingerprints to DOJ electronically. A Live Scan Service Request form (RE 237) will be sent to all applicants who successfully complete the real estate examination. An actual license will not be issued until a report from DOJ is received stating that there is no criminal history or disclosing criminal history information, which then must be reviewed and evaluated.

When an applicant is ready for fingerprints, he or she will take the RE 237 to a participating live scan service provider. After the live scan service provider takes the fingerprints, the applicant must submit to DRE a copy of the RE 237 with Part 3 completed, along with the applicant's completed original license application and the appropriate fee.

A list of live scan service providers is available at http://caag.state.ca.us/fingerprints/publications/contact.pdf.

Registered agent
    Required

Company registration
Registration with the California Secretary of State, Department of Corporations, is required. You may reach them at http://www. corp.ca.gov/.

Additional disclosure requirement
California requires each mortgage applicant to be disclosed with:

A California Broker Agreement

A Hazard Insurance Disclosure

A Credit Score Disclosure

An Equal Credit Opportunity Act Disclosure

A Fair Lending Notice Disclosure

A Right to Receive a Copy of Appraisal Disclosure

Colorado

Regulatory agency: Colorado Division of Securities, Department of Regulatory Agencies

Contact: www.dora.state.co.us/securities/mb(i).htm or call (303) 894-2320

Requirements
Many Colorado mortgage brokers are exempt from Colorado licensing requirements. A mortgage broker whose business is not limited *exclusively* to placing mortgage loans with institutional investors is subject to the mortgage licensing requirements. A mortgage broker who raises money from individual investors to fund mortgage loans *would* need to be licensed. For more information on who needs to be licensed, go to www.dora.state.co. us/securities/mb(i).htm.

Connecticut

Regulatory agency: Connecticut Department of Banking, Consumer Credit Division

Contact: www.state.ct.us/dob or call (860) 240-8209

Requirements

Experience

Each location requires that each licensee or supervisory individual have three years' experience in mortgage lending or brokering within the five years immediately preceding the application.

Licensing fee

$400

Each location conducting business must be licensed. License is valid for two years; e.g., licenses issued 10/1/08 will expire 9/30/10.

Registration and licensing are required for each loan originator under a licensee. Loan originator licensing fee is $100 for each loan originator. Upon termination of an originator from employment, a licensee is required to notify the Department of Banking.

Application for licensure must include:

A fully executed mortgage broker application

Proof of proper business filing with the state

Application for registration of loan originators

Financial statements reflecting net worth as of no later than six months prior to license application

A chronological listing of experience for the supervising authority for location seeking licensure

Surety bond

Licensing fee

Bond

$40,000 (a surety bond of $40,000 must be maintained)

Net worth

$25,000 (audited financials or notarized balance sheet prepared by a CPA is required)

Company registration

Registration with the Connecticut Secretary of State is required. You may contact them at http://www.sots.state.ct.us/ or call (860) 590-6000.

If the applicant is applying for a first mortgage broker license in the state of Connecticut and intends to advertise in the state of Connecticut in print or through the mail, he or she must abide by specific advertisement laws in accordance with Connecticut Section 36a-497.

Delaware

Regulatory agency: Delaware, Office of State Bank Commissioner

Contact: www.state.de.us/bank/services/applicense/mbintro. shtml or call (302) 739-4235

Requirements

Education

None required for brokers; however, experience is reviewed.

Licensing fee

$250 Investigation/application fee

$250 Annual license fee (per location)

License expires annually on December 31st. Application for licensure must include:

A fully executed mortgage broker application.

Investigation fee.

Proof of proper business filing with the state.

If a corporation or LLC/LLP, attach a personal history for principal or senior officers, or any persons with ownership interest.

Resume for owner and principals.

Financial statement dated no more than six months from date of license application. (If a corporation, need personal financials for each principal officer or director.) LLC/LLP needs personal financials for all senior management and for all individual members/partners.

A list of other states in which applicant is doing business.

Three business reference letters.

Surety bond.

A copy of the Broker's Agreement (in compliance with Regulation 2014).

Notarized Authorization and Release Form and Certification of Agent.

Mortgage Loan Broker Fact Sheet.

References
Three business references are required. These references can be from a CPA, attorney, etc. Each letter of reference must be sent directly to the Office of the State Bank Commissioner's office. The applicant is not allowed to include a copy of the reference letter with his or her application. The reference letter must be provided directly from the source.

Bond
$25,000 (maintain a surety bond of $25,000)

Registered agent
Required

Company registration
Registration with the Delaware Secretary of State is required; you may contact them at http://www.state.de.us/sos/default. shtml.

Additional disclosure requirement
Delaware requires an Itemization of Schedule Charges to be both posted prominently and easily visible in the office of the licensee and to be given to each mortgage applicant. A Mortgage Broker Agreement is required in compliance with Regulation 2014.

Audits and reports
Each licensed office must maintain books and records of all-mortgage loans originated in the State of Delaware, on a current basis, either at the office of the licensed broker or a suitable

location available within a reasonable time period, upon request. There is a fee involved with the examination of the applicant's records. This fee includes direct salary for the examiner(s) and charges and fees for filing, copying, inspecting, and other services rendered; it is calculated based on the applicant's volume and assets. In addition, there is a Supervisory Assessment of approximately $500 to $1,000, which is calculated by the examiner assigned and the location of the applicant's records.

Delaware requires that all licensees submit a volume report to the Office of the State Bank Commissioner twice each year. The first report is due on or before July 31st and must contain figures from January 1st through June 30th of the current year. The second report is due on or before January 31st and must contain figures from January 1st through December 31st of the previous year.

In addition, Delaware requires all licensees to submit an assets report to the Office of the State Bank Commissioner once yearly, no later than April 1st of each year.

District of Columbia

Regulatory agency: District of Columbia, Office of Banking and Financial Institutions

Contact: http://www.dbfi.dc.gov/dbfi/cwp or call (202) 727-1563

Requirements

Education
None required

Experience
None required

Licensing fee
$1,100

Breakdown of fees:
$500 Initial application fee

$100 Initial investigation fee

$500 Licensing fee

License expires annually (one year) from effective approval date.

Application for licensure must include:

A fully executed mortgage broker application

Attachment A—Clean Hands Act Certification form

Attachment B—Bond for appropriate amount (see requirements listed below)

Attachment C—General Information form

Attachment D—Signature of Oath of Applicants

Attachment F—Background Check Authorization

Attachment G—Personal Financial Report

Verification of Net Worth Requirement

Financial Report (dated at least 90 days from application date)

Current audited statement if an operating entity (beginning balance sheet and pro forma balance sheet and income statement for the first year if applicant is a newly formed entity)

Certificate of Good Standing

$1,100 total license fee

Bond
Surety bond requirements are based on volume of loans:

For total loan volume $1 million or less = $12,500

For total volume over $1 million to $2 million = $17,500

For total volume over $2 million to $3 million = $25,000

For total volume over $3 million = $50,000

Net worth
An application for a mortgage broker license must have at least $10,000 on deposit or in an established line of credit from a

depository institution. Neither letters of credit nor lines of credit from sources other than a bank or other depository institution will satisfy this requirement.

A current financial report for each individual owning directly or indirectly 10 percent of the entity is required. Current audited financials if the applicant is an operating entity. A beginning balance sheet and pro forma balance sheet and income statement are required for the first year of operation if the applicant is a newly organized entity.

Company registration

A Certificate of Good Standing from the District of Columbia is required for each corporation, limited liability company, or limited partnership doing business in D.C. You may contact the Department of Consumer and Regulatory Affairs, Corporation Division, at (202) 442-4400.

Florida

> *Regulatory agency*: Florida Department of Financial Services, Office of Financial Regulation (OFR), Division of Securities and Finance

> *Contact*: http://www.flofr.com/licensing/ or call (850) 410-9805

Requirements

In Florida a loan originator is referred to as a mortgage broker. Loan originators must be licensed as mortgage brokers, and a mortgage broker is referred to as a mortgage broker business.

Education

Must be licensed as a mortgage broker. Licensing requirements for a mortgage broker individual are to

> Complete 24 hours of classroom education

> Pass state exam

Licensing requirement can only be met by attending the mandatory 24-hour mortgage broker training course offered by an approved Mortgage Business School. When an application is made and a background check is conducted, a deficiency letter is sent to the applicant notifying him or her of any outstanding requirements for the issuance of a license. The deficiency letter will also inform the applicant of the test date and should be received at least seven days in advance of the test date. Testing days are usually the fourth Tuesday and Wednesday of each month. There are six testing sites for the exam spread around the state. The three-hour exam consists of 100 multiple-choice questions, and a test score of 75 or higher is necessary to pass the exam.

For a list of approved prelicensing schools, visit http://www.flofr.com/licensing/MB-Businesses.htm and press 24-hour prelicensing schools.

Experience

Must have a minimum of one year of experience in the mortgage industry

Licensing fee

$425 Initial license/application fee

$375 Renewal fee for main office

$225 Branch office

$225 Renewal fee for a branch office

License expires August 31st of each even-numbered year.

When submitting an application, be aware that Florida does not allow for the word "Federal," "National," or "United States" to be part of a mortgage broker business name.

Each mortgage brokerage business shall designate a licensed mortgage broker as the principal broker. Upon any change of principal broker, the licensee must designate a new principal broker and thus complete a new Form OFR-MB-PB, which must be maintained at the principal office with a copy mailed to the Department of Banking and Finance.

Application for licensure must include:

A fully executed mortgage broker business application

Proof of proper business filing with the state

Copies of organizational business documents

Exhibit A identifying each person who owns 10 percent or more of business

Biographical summary and fingerprint card

Complete Principal Broker Designation Form OFR-MB-PB

Licensing fee

All mortgage broker business licensees are required to have and maintain a physical office location, but it does not have to be a Florida address.

Fingerprint fee
$23

$15 processing fee

The fingerprint card must be completed and returned with the application for licensure.

Registered agent
Required

Company registration
Proof of corporate registration with the Florida Secretary of State (www.dos.state.fl.us) or a copy of the approval letter from the Office of Financial Institutions and Securities Regulation must be provided with the applicant's mortgage broker business license application.

Additional disclosure requirement
Florida requires each mortgage applicant to be disclosed with:

Anti-Coercion Insurance Notice

Mortgage Brokerage Contract

Application Fee Disclosure Form (for any up-front fees)

Reports
Florida requires a Mortgage Broker Business to file a quarterly report to the Department of Financial Services as noted below.

The report requires all employees and associates to be tracked on a quarterly basis. The report requires the person's name, office employment address, date of birth, social security number, branch number (if applicable) and MB audit number.

Georgia

Regulatory agency: Georgia Department of Banking and Finance

Contact: www.gadbf.org or call (770) 986-1269

Requirements

Education

An applicant must demonstrate successful completion of 40 hours of education from an approved provider of mortgage education courses in the areas of:

Basic understanding of technical terms

Licensing requirements

Principles of the mortgage broker process

Mortgage applications and required documentation

Georgia law, rules, and regulations and required books and records

A minimum of four hours of education must be in a course or courses covering the Georgia Residential Mortgage Act and Rules and Regulations of the Department. A copy of the certificate of completion or diploma to demonstrate completion will be required.

For a list of approved educational providers, visit gadbf.org. Press Forms and applications, and then Mortgage related.

Experience

Applicant must demonstrate a minimum of two years of full-time prior experience and employment in the mortgage industry directly originating mortgage loans.

The Department will consider compensation received during this two-year period as an indicator of full-time employment status. A person who earned minimal income or closed only a few loans during the two-year period will likely not meet the full-time employment standard.

> The applicant must provide a letter on letterhead from previous employer(s) certifying completion of two years of work experience directly originating mortgage loans. A current telephone number for such employer(s) should be provided.

> The applicant must submit copies of IRS W2 form(s) for the tax years covering the experience requirement. Income reflected should indicate that the individual earned at least a minimum-wage level of annual income in order for the Department to favorably determine that the work performed qualifies the individual as having experience in the industry.

Applicants for a broker's license relying on experience, whose principal place of business is not in Georgia, must still complete the four hours of education covering the Georgia Residential Mortgage Act.

Applicant must submit an original, signed IRS Form 4506 for each year covering the experience requirement. This enables the Department to verify applicant's W2.

Applicants may be required to submit additional information if required by the Department or it is necessary to verify completion of the experience requirement. The Department will verify compliance with the experience requirement directly with the previous employer and tax authorities.

Licensing fee

$500 Annual license fee

$250 Investigation fee

Note that one branch location, in addition to the main office location, is included in the fee for the initial application for licensing. Any branches in addition to the one included in the initial application, or any branch applications submitted subsequent to license approval, require a $350 application fee per branch.

If applying for a license and the applicant's home state is other than Georgia, a physical presence in Georgia is required *only* if the applicant's home state *also* does not require a physical address to become licensed in that state.

Renewal for a license is April 1st; therefore, if applying prior to March 1st in any given year the applicant will be subject to the renewal process on the following April 1st. If the applicant applies after February 1st a request can be made to hold the application for an April 1st approval date.

Each office is required to have an office or branch manager, who must also submit a background and credit check.

In addition, Georgia code requires that each employer obtain a background check on all employees who work for them in the state of Georgia, who has the authority to enter, delete, or verify any information on any mortgage loan application. A public records check is available online allowing employers to make sure a potential employee is not on this list prior to employment.

In the state of Georgia, a mortgage broker must pay their loan officers with a W2. An independent contractor (1099) must be a "licensed" mortgage broker or processor.

Application for licensure must include:

A fully executed mortgage broker application

Proof of proper business filing with the state

Copies of organizational business documents

Signature of Oath of Applicant

Complete set of fingerprint cards

Background check authorization form (for all appropriate individuals)

Financial report and biographical reports (include photo of applicant[s])

Personal credit report on all required individuals

Audited financials or surety bond

Copy of most recent income tax return

Policy and procedures for grievances and inquiries

Verification of two years' recent work experience (to include a signed 4506T)

Investigation and licensing fee

Fingerprint fee
$30 per set per individual
Fingerprint cards must be submitted in duplicate (both) originals, for all individuals in the application. The fingerprint cards must be obtained from the department and processed at local law enforcement agencies.

Processing of background checks and fingerprint cards through the law enforcement agencies may extend processing time 10 to 12 weeks.

Bond
$50,000 (maintain a surety bond of $50,000)

Net worth
$100,000

Registered agent
Required

Company registration
Registration with the Georgia Secretary of State is required. You may contact them at http://www.sos.state.ga.us.

Additional disclosure requirement
Georgia requires each mortgage applicant to be disclosed with:

1. An Application Disclosure Form (for any up-front fees).

2. A Right to Choose Attorney. The state of Georgia requires all closings to be conducted by an attorney.

In addition, be aware that Georgia charges a per loan fee of $6.50.

Hawaii

Regulatory agency: Hawaii Department of Commerce and Consumer Affairs

Contact: www.hawaii.gov/dcca/pvl or call (808) 586-3000

Requirements

Education

None required

Experience

A licensee in the state of Hawaii must appoint a "Designated Principal Mortgage Solicitor" whose experience must reflect a background in primary or subordinate mortgage financing.

Two years of experience is required for a Designated Principal Mortgage Solicitor.

Licensing fee

$185

The state of Hawaii has a biennial license renewal policy with renewal dates on every even-numbered year. If applying for licensure between January 1st of an even-numbered year to December 31st of an even-numbered year, your license fee is $185. However, if you are applying for licensure between January 1st of an odd-numbered year to December 31st of an odd-numbered year, your license fee will be $320.00.

Breakdown

$50 Application fee

$100 License fee

$35 Credit Report Fee (CRF)

License renewals are biennial, e.g., 12/31/2008 and every even-numbered year thereafter.

An applicant must have a principal place of business in Hawaii. Application for licensure must include:

A fully executed mortgage broker application

Proof of proper business filing with the state

Copies of organizational business documents

Identification of designated principal with verification of at least two years' work experience

Current financial statement

Surety bond

Identification of place of business in Hawaii (must conform to zoning code of county government)

Licensing fee

In a corporation, an officer or employee shall be the designated principal through the "Designated Principal Mortgage Solicitor" form. An application fee, releasing/employing letter and a $10 reissuance fee are required if solicitor is currently licensed through another licensee.

$25 Fee for Designated Mortgage Solicitor

Loan originators in Hawaii are registered as mortgage solicitors. A licensee must ensure that all mortgage solicitors are properly registered with the Hawaii Department of Commerce and Consumer Affairs.

Bond
$15,000 (maintain a surety bond of $15,000)

Company registration
For a corporation, partnership, or LLC, proof of registration is required with the Business Registration (BREG) Division at the following address:

Department of Commerce and Consumer Affairs
State of Hawaii
P.O. Box 40
Honolulu, HI 96810

Request for proper forms must be in writing and applicants will receive one of the certificates mentioned below.

Certificate of Good Standing

Certificate of Qualification

If a trade name will be used, submit a file-stamped copy of the current trade name registration approved by the Business Registration Division of the Department of Commerce and Consumer Affairs.

Idaho

Regulatory agency: Idaho, Department of Finance

Contact: http://finance.state.id.us/industry/Licenses.asp or call (208) 332-8002

Requirements

Education

None required

Experience

A licensee must appoint "A Qualified Person in Charge" who must have a minimum of three years' experience in residential mortgage lending/brokering (does not have to be an owner, officer, partner, or director).

Licensing fee

$350 Initial application fee for each location

$150 Renewal fee

Licenses expire annually on August 31st. Application for licensure must include:

A fully executed mortgage broker application

Proof of proper business filing with the state

Copies of organizational business documents

Identification of person in charge (who meets experience requirements) and complete attachment B, C, and D for person in charge

Samples of all origination (disclosure) forms

Application fee

Surety bond

Notarized application affidavit and certificate of resolution

Attachment B—Notarized Authority to obtain information from outside resources

Attachment C & D—Employment history and residential address form

Bond
$25,000 for the home or main office and $10,000 increased increments for each additional location. The applicant may provide a Certificate of Deposit in lieu of a surety bond. A CD must be payable to the Idaho Department of Finance and must remain in place for three years after cessation of Idaho licensure.

Registered agent
Required

Company registration
Required

Evidence of filing with the Idaho Secretary of State's office is required with the submission of application for a license. This may be a file-stamped (accepted) copy of the appropriate application or a copy of the actual certificate. Contact the Secretary of State at (208) 334-2300 or go on the Web site at www. idsos.state. id.us.

Additional disclosure requirement
Idaho requires that each mortgage applicant be disclosed with the following disclosures:

Mortgage Broker Application Disclosure Form in accordance with Idaho Code 26-3101

Idaho Prepayment Penalty Disclosure

Interest Rate Lock/float Information

Interest Rate Lock-in Confirmation Agreement

Illinois

Regulatory agency: Illinois, Division of Banks and Real Estate

Contact: www.obre.state.il.us/resfin/MBHowTo.htm or call (312) 793-1409

Requirements
Education
None required. However, all licensees who employ persons to take residential mortgage applications from consumers are required to have *those persons* complete a minimum of three hours of education in Real Estate Finance each calendar year.

Experience
Any person holding 10 percent or more interest in the company is required to have at least three years of experience as a loan officer/originator.

Licensing fee
$1,500 Investigation fee

$1,200 License fee due within 10 days of application approval

$250 Each additional location

Licenses are valid for two years. Renewal fee is $2,700. Upon receiving a new license, an audit or examination will be conducted within 12 months of licensure and the second examination within the following 12 months.

A residential mortgage licensee headquartered out-of-state is *not* required to maintain an office in Illinois, if $100,000 of net worth, a $100,000 fidelity bond, and a $20,000 surety bond are maintained.

It is the licensee's (mortgage broker's) responsibility for ensuring that their loan originators be licensed and registered with the Division of Banks and Real Estate. There is a $125 registration fee for each loan originator.

Application for licensure must include:

A fully executed residential mortgage license application.

Proof of proper business filing with the state.

Copies of business organizational documents.

License fee.

Audited financial statements performed within 90 days of application date (must meet financial net worth requirement as listed below).

Surety bond.

Fidelity bond (if applicable, see requirements listed below).

Resume for all individuals with 10 percent or more ownership in business.

A Notice of Intent to Establish an Additional Full Service Office Form, a copy of executed lease agreement, and copy of firm's employment agreement with office manager/loan officer. (This does not have to be submitted with the application but must be received by the regulating department prior to issuance of the license.)

Signed State Police Form.

Signed Access to Credit form.

Signed Release of Audit Workpapers form.

Proof of proper business filing with the state.

Background Check

Any persons with more than 10 percent ownership of the company applying for licensure must submit both a State Police Form *and* an Access to Credit Form.

Bond
$20,000

Net worth
$50,000

Registered agent
Required

Company registration
If the entity is incorporated in the state of Illinois, then a Certificate of Good Standing is required. If the entity is incorporated in a state other than Illinois, then a Certificate of Authority is required. You can obtain either certificate from the Illinois Secretary of State at (312) 793-3380.

Additional disclosure requirement
Illinois requires each mortgage applicant be disclosed with:

A Broker Agreement

A Broker Disclosure Form

Indiana

Regulatory agency: Indiana, Secretary of State, Securities Division

Contact: http://www.in.gov/sos/securities/ or call (317) 232-6681

Requirements
Education
An applicant must provide evidence that during the 24-month period immediately preceding the application, the applicant has completed at least 24 hours of academic instruction, acceptable to the commissioner, related to the loan brokerage business. Additionally, at renewal stage, the licensee must provide proof of 12 hours of continuing academic education.

For a list of approved course providers, visit http://www.in. gov/sos/securities/ and press Approved education programs.

Licensing fee

$200 Application fee.

Initial fee is valid for one year. Renewal license (fee of $200) is valid for two years.

At broker license application stage, broker must register all originators (with proof of completed educational requirements) and submit the information to the Secretary of State Securities Division.

Application for licensure must include:

A fully executed loan broker application

Proof of proper business filing with the state

Copies of business organizational documents

Properly complete registration form for each originator (to include verification of completion of educational requirements)

Application fee

Original signed surety bond

Bond
$50,000

To obtain a mortgage broker license in Indiana, the applicant must register all loan originators with the Indiana Secretary of State. A registration form for each originator will be required at time of application. To register any loan originator, the applicant will need to provide proof that the registrant has completed Indiana's educational requirements for loan originators. For a complete list of educational requirements for loan originators in all states from Alabama to Wyoming you may refer to my book *The Mortgage Originator Success Kit*, published by McGraw-Hill.

Registered agent
Required

Company registration
Proof of proper business filing in Indiana is required with the applicant's mortgage broker license application. You can contact the Secretary of State's Business Services Division at www.sos.IN.gov/business or by telephone at (317) 232-6576.

Additional disclosure requirement

Indiana requires each mortgage applicant to be disclosed with:

A Mortgage Broker Agreement in accordance with Indiana Code 23-2-5-9

An Anti-Coercion Insurance Disclosure in accordance with Indiana Code 27-4-1-4

Iowa

Regulatory agency: Iowa, Division of Banking

Contact: www.idob.state.ia.us or call (515) 281-4014

Requirements

Education

None required

Experience

None required

Licensing fee

$500 Initial license and/or application fee

$200 Renewal fee

Licenses expire annually on June 1st. Application for licensure must include:

A fully executed mortgage broker application

Proof of proper business filing with the state

Copies of business organizational documents

List of any branch locations in Iowa if applicable

Most current audited financial statements

Biographical list of each owner, partner, manager, director, or principal officer

Surety bond

Application fee of $500

Bond
   $15,000

Registered agent
   Required

Company registration
   Required

If a business entity, a Certificate of Good Standing is required to accompany the application for a mortgage broker's license. Registration with the Iowa Secretary of State is required. You may reach them at http://www.sos.ia.us.

Additional disclosure requirement
Iowa requires each mortgage applicant to be disclosed with an Iowa Broker Agreement Disclosure in accordance with Iowa Code Section 535C.7.

Kansas

   Regulatory agency: Kansas, Office of the State Bank Commissioner

   Contact: www.osbckansas.org or call (785) 296-2266

Requirements
To become a mortgage broker in Kansas, an applicant must apply for a mortgage company license.

Education
   None required

Experience
   None required

Licensing fee
   $600 Initial application fee for principal place of business

   $200 Initial application fee for any branch locations

   $400 Renewal fee for principal place of business

   $200 Renewal fee for any branch locations

The mortgage broker license is renewed every odd-numbered year. For example, if the original application is approved in an even-numbered year, it must be renewed the following odd-numbered year.

A physical location in Kansas is not required. However, for licensing purposes, requirements differ depending on office location. A "bona fide" office must meet the following criteria:

The office is located in the state of Kansas.

The office is not a personal residence.

The office has regular hours of operation.

The office is accessible to the public.

The office is leased or owned by the licensee.

The office is separate from any office of another registrant.

All of the licensee's books, records, and documents are accessible through that office.

A licensee is responsible for proper registration of loan originators. Registration fee for loan originators is $75. All loan originators are required to have at least eight hours of continuing professional education (CPE).

Application for licensure must include:

A fully executed mortgage company license application

Surety bond (see bond requirements for "bona fide" or "No Bona Fide" office)

Application fee

Signed and notarized Signature and Oath of Applicant

Form A—Signed and notarized Confidential Background Information Consent form

Form B—Notarized Surety Bond

Form C—State Regulator Questionnaire on Applicant

Form D—Mortgage Company Branch Application (if applicable)

Form G—Loan Originator Registration form

Bond

> $50,000 for a "Bona Fide" office

> $100,000 for a "No Bona Fide" office and must provide proof of $50,000 net worth requirement

Registered agent
> Required

Company registration
It is the opinion of the Kansas Secretary of State that companies exclusively engaged in the mortgage business are exempt from registering with the Kansas Secretary of State as foreign corporations.

Additional disclosure requirement
Kansas requires each mortgage applicant to be disclosed with:

> Kansas Borrower Acknowledgement Disclosure to include specific terminology in accordance with Kansas Code 17-24-1

> Kansas Loan Broker Disclosure

Kentucky

> *Regulatory agency*: Kentucky, Department of Financial Institutions

> *Contact*: www.dfi.ky.gov or call (800) 223-2579

Requirements

Education
An applicant must complete a 30-hour educational course. If applicant is a corporate entity, then applicant must appoint a "Designated Manager" who must complete this course.

   For a list of prelicensing education/continuing education courses, visit www.dfi.ky.gov.

Licensing fee
> If submitted between January 1st and June 30th

> $300 Initial application fee

> $150 Branch location

If submitted between July 1st and December 31st

$450 Initial application fee

$250 Branch location

A licensed mortgage broker in Kentucky is required to maintain a physical location in the state.

Employees of mortgage loan brokers must be registered as loan brokers, with the Kentucky Department of Financial Institutions, along with verification of 12 hours of educational mortgage courses and a criminal background check.

Application for licensure must include:

A fully executed mortgage loan broker application

Proof of proper business filing with the state

If licensed in any other states, completion of State License Confirmation form

Financial statement prepared by CPA or accountant

Personal financials for any individual with 10 percent or more ownership in business

Resume for the owners and managers

Surety bond

List of affiliates

License fee

Proof of educational requirement

Copy of executed lease and three photos of proposed business location

Executive or "Shared" office space is permitted.

If the licensed location is a residence, it must be the main residence of one of the owners of 20 percent or more of the business. This application shall include a signed and notarized letter from the owner of the residence stating that this is their main residence, a copy of the deed or lease, and a letter from the local zoning board stating that the requirements for an in-home office have been met.

Sign and Notarize Consent to Request Credit Report

State License Confirmation Form

All Kentucky loans must be maintained at the licensed location(s).

Criminal Background Check

All Mortgage Loan Brokers must submit proof of an FBI criminal background check, along with licensee application. This record must indicate no felony convictions within the previous five-year period or no misdemeanor convictions involving fraud at any time. Other felonies are subject to investigation on a case-by-case basis.

Fingerprint cards must be submitted to the FBI office below for a personal review; cost is $18.

Federal Bureau of Investigation
Criminal Justice Information Services Division
SCU MOD D2
1000 Custer Hollow Rd.
Clarksburg, WV 26306
Tel: 304-625-3878

Bond
$50,000

Company registration
Required

If the applicant is currently licensed and operating in another state, then a "State License Confirmation Form" must accompany the application for a mortgage broker license. Registration with the Kentucky Secretary of State at (502) 564-2848 is required.

Louisiana

Regulatory agency: Louisiana, Office of Financial Institutions

Contact: www.ofi.state.la.us or call (225) 925-3828

Requirements

Education

Brokers as well as all loan originators are required to have 10 hours of education and pass an exam. A list of approved courses and facilitators is provided along with a loan originator application.

Licensing fee

$400 initial fee

Initial application is only valid for the year in which the applicant applies. For example, if applying in March 2007, then the license expires the same year on December 31st. If applying in June 2008, the license expires December 31, 2008.

Annual renewal fee is $300. Application for licensure must include:

A fully executed Uniform Application for Licensure/ Registration

Proof of proper business filing with the state

Attachment A—Signed and notarized Certificate of Resolution

Attachment B—Signed and Notarized Authority to Obtain Information from Outside Sources

Attachment C—Employment/Experience and Residence History for the last 10 years

License fee

A sample of the applicant's Mortgage Loan Origination Agreement and Promissory Note

Verification of financial requirements as listed below

A Loan Originator Application for each originator to be employed under licensee: $100 application fee for new originators or $50 transfer fee (must include a current resume, picture ID, proof of completion of education requirements, and copy of W4 Employee's Withholding Allowance Certificate, with each Loan Originator Application)

Agent for Service of Process and Acknowledgement Form

A licensee is responsible for ensuring that all loan originators are properly licensed. My book; *The Mortgage Originator Success Kit*, has detailed licensing requirements for loan originators in all states from Alabama to Wyoming.

Financial requirement
    $50,000

May be fulfilled by *one* of the items listed below:

    Audited Financials

    A Certificate of Deposit—Irrevocably to the commissioner

    Securities of type approved by the commissioner, including but not limited to bonds of the state or any political subdivision or bonds of the U.S. government

    A surety bond for $50,000

Registered agent
    Required

Company registration
Registration with the Louisiana Secretary of State is required. You may contact them at www.sec.state.la.us.

Additional disclosure requirement
Louisiana requires each mortgage applicant to be disclosed with:

    A Loan Brokerage Disclosure Statement

    Mortgage Loan Origination Agreement

Maine

   Regulatory agency: Maine, Office of Consumer Credit Regulation

   Contact: http://www.state.me.us/pfr/ccp/ccp_index.htm or call (207) 624-8527

Requirements
To become a loan broker in Maine, an applicant must apply for a supervised lender license.

Education
> None required

Experience
> None required

Licensing fee
> $500 Initial application/license fee for principal place of business
>
> $200 Initial application/license fee for a branch location
>
> $200 Renewal fee for principal place of business
>
> $200 Renewal fee for branch location
>
> Licenses are granted for a two-year period and expire on September 30th.

Application for licensure must include:

> A fully executed supervised lender license application
>
> Proof of proper business filing with the state
>
> Application fee
>
> A list of officers of the corporation (to include history and background)
>
> Resume on principals and the person who will manage daily operations
>
> A set of loan forms (to include choice of title attorney form, and credit denial form)
>
> A written agreement and disclosure to be used with each consumer must be submitted with the application

Net worth
> $25,000 (must maintain verifiable net assets of $25,000)

Bond
> $10,000

Registered agent
> Required

Company registration
Registration with the Maine Secretary of State is required. You may contact that office at http://www.state.me.us/sos.

Additional disclosure requirement
Maine requires each mortgage applicant to be disclosed with:

Right to Receive a Copy of Appraisal

Anti-Coercion Insurance Disclosure

Maine Disclosure to Consumer

Mortgage Broker Agreement

Maryland

Regulatory agency: Maryland, The Commissioner of Financial Regulation

Contact: www.dllr.state.md.us/finance/mortgagel.htm or call (410) 230-6100

Requirements
To become a mortgage broker in Maryland, an applicant must apply for a mortgage lender license.

Education
None required

Experience
One of the principals owning a minimum of 10 percent or more of the company must have at least three years of business experience.

Licensing fee
$1,000 Principal location

$100 Investigation principal location

$1,000 Branch office

$100 Investigation branch location

License fee listed above is for a standard two-year license.

Loan originators must be W2 employees. Each loan originator must be set up as a branch location if they work from an independent location outside of the principal office or they are paid by 1099.

Application for licensure must include:

A fully executed mortgage broker application

Proof of proper business filing with the state

List experience background for all individuals with 10 percent or more ownership in the business

Copies of business organizational documents

Surety bond

Business credit report or personal credit report for all individuals with 10 percent or more ownership in the business

A current (within the last 12 months) audited financial statement

License fee

Bond
The bond requirements are based on activity levels.

Loan Activity Level	Bond Amount
No Activity	$15,000
$3 million or less	$25,000
Over $3 million to $10 million	$50,000
Over $10 million	$75,000
Five or more applications at the same time	$375,000

Company registration
A Certificate of Good Standing is required to accompany the application for a Mortgage Broker/Lender license. For Maryland-chartered entities, the applicant can obtain this from the Maryland Department of Assessment and Taxation at (410) 767-1340.

Additional disclosure requirement
Maryland requires each mortgage applicant to be disclosed with a Financing Agreement Form in accordance with Maryland Law Ann. Code Section 12-125.

Massachusetts

> *Regulatory agency*: Massachusetts, Division of Banks
>
> *Contact*: www.state.ma.us/dob. or call (617) 956-1500

Requirements

Education

> None required

Experience

> One year experience working for a licensed mortgage broker, lender, or financial institution exempt from licensing
>
> If less than one year but more than six months, applicant must complete formal training which covers, at minimum, Massachusetts laws covering the mortgage lending transaction, as well as processing issues.

An applicant who will oversee other individuals that engage in brokering activities must have no less than two years' experience.

Licensing fee

> $115 Investigation fee
>
> $600 License fee due upon approval from the Division
>
> $ 50 Additional branch location fee

License fee is valid for one year. Licenses expire annually on 5/31. The Division of Banks has a waiting period for approval of six to eight months.

> Application for licensure must include:
>
> A fully executed mortgage broker application
>
> Proof of proper business filing with the state
>
> Copies of business organizational documents
>
> Addendum listing all individuals with 10 percent or more ownership in the business
>
> Summarization of professional and educational experience for applicant and/or its principals to verify experience requirements as listed above

Credit report dated within 30 days for all individuals with 10 percent or more ownership in the business

Signed Financial Statement for all principals (if a corporation or LLC/LLP need audited financials and last two years of financial statements)

Addendum with loan disclosures

Addendum with a list of lenders that broker will use to close loans

Three letters of professional reference with at least one from a bank

CORI Request Forms

A completed Record Keeping Plan (for applicants intending to maintain their books and records outside of Massachusetts)

A completed Privacy Awareness Survey

$115 investigation fee

Annual reports

Each licensee must file an annual report with the Commissioner by March 1st, for the preceding calendar year.

Company registration

If the entity is a corporation or limited liability company, evidence of registration with the Massachusetts Office of the Secretary of State is required. You may contact them at www.state.ma.us/sec.

Additional disclosure requirement

Massachusetts requires each mortgage applicant to be disclosed with:

Addendum to the Uniform Residential Loan Application (in accordance with Mass Gen Law Ch 184, Section 17B)

Mortgage Broker Disclosure (to include specific language in accordance with Mass regulations 209 CMR 42.16). Must be provided at time of commitment (signed and dated at that time)

Michigan

Regulatory agency: Michigan, Labor and Economic Growth

Contact: www.michigan.gov or call (517) 373-3460

Requirements

Education

None required

Experience

Must provide W2 for one year of experience working for a licensed mortgage broker or lender.

Licensing fee

For First Mortgage Only

$450 License application fee

$450 Investigation fee

Licenses are valid for one year. Annual renewal date is on June 30th, and renewal fee is based upon productivity from the previous year.

For First and Second Mortgage

$225 License application fee

$450 Investigation fee

If the applicant wishes to do both first and second mortgages, he or she must file a separate registration to engage in second mortgage activities.

Application for licensure must include:

A fully executed mortgage broker application (Form 1018 for licensing)

Proof of proper business filing with the state

Copies of business organizational documents

A Personal Disclosure Statement

Signed Confidential Background Information Consent Forms

Certificate of Resolution (if applicable)

Financial statements to fulfill net worth requirements

Surety bond

Licensing and investigating fee

Net worth
$25,000

Required if broker receives any fees from a prospective borrower prior to the closing of a mortgage loan.

Bond
$25,000

Required if broker receives any fees from a prospective borrower prior to the closing of a mortgage loan. (Applicant will need a bond for first mortgages and another for second mortgages.)

If mortgage broker will not receive any funds from a prospective borrower prior to the closing of a mortgage loan, then a "Statement of Exemption of Proof of Financial Responsibility Deposit" form must be filed with application.

Company registration
If the applicant is doing business under an assumed name or the entity is a partnership, the applicant must provide a certificate from the County Clerk's office.

Additional disclosure requirement
Michigan requires each mortgage applicant to be disclosed with:

Borrowers Bill of Rights

Minnesota

Regulatory agency: Minnesota, Department of Commerce

Contact: www.commerce.state.mn.us or call (651) 282-9855

Requirements

To become a mortgage broker in Minnesota, an applicant must apply for a residential mortgage originator license.

Education
> None required

Experience
> None required

Licensing fee
> $850

License is valid through July 31st of each odd-numbered year. If applying in second year of license term, the fee is

> $425

> $450 Renewal fee

Application for licensure must include:

> Fully executed Residential Mortgage Originator application

> Proof of proper business filing with the state

> Copies of business organizational documents

> Description of the business activities that applicant will conduct in the state of Minnesota

> Resume for owner or principals

> List of any other states in which applicant is currently licensed and conducting business

> If applicant will have any Minnesota employees, must provide evidence of current worker's compensation coverage

> Surety bond

> Notarized Affirmation Under Oath

> BCA (Bureau of Criminal Apprehension Form)

> Licensing fee

Bond
    $50,000

Company registration
If the applicant is an out-of-state originator wanting to do business in Minnesota, then he or she must register as a foreign corporation. Registration with the Minnesota Secretary of State is required. You may contact them at (651) 296-2803.

Additional disclosure requirement
Minnesota requires each mortgage applicant to be disclosed with:

> Originator Non-Agency Disclosure (in accordance with MN Statutes Ch 58.15)
>
> Residential Mortgage Originator Contract (in accordance with MN Statutes Ch 58.16)
>
> Minnesota Prepayment Disclosure

Mississippi

> *Regulatory agency*: Mississippi, Department of Banking and Consumer Finance
>
> *Contact*:   http://www.dbcf.state.ms.us/mortgage_lending_synopsis.htm or call (601) 359-1031

Requirements
To become a mortgage broker in Mississippi, an applicant must apply for a Mortgage Company License.

Education
    None required

Experience/exam
Two years' experience directly in mortgage lending is required. There is an exam (approved by the Department of Banking and Consumer Finance) that can be taken in lieu of the experience.
    There are four approved testing administrators; they are

> Capstone Institute of Mortgage Finance: (770) 956-8252 or www.capinst.com

Mississippi Association of Mortgage Brokers: (601) 924-4006 or www.msamb.org

Residential Mortgage Lending School: (228) 467-9797 or www.nambef.org

Mortgage Research, Inc.: (888) 557-6770 or www.mortgage-education.com

Licensing fee

$750 Initial fee

$100 Initial fee for each additional office location

$475 Renewal fee

$ 25 Annual renewal fee for additional office location

License expires annually on September 30th.

An applicant will be denied for licensure if he or she or any person who is the director, officer, partner, or principal of the applicant has been convicted of a felony in any jurisdiction or has been convicted of a misdemeanor involving fraud, within the last 10 years of the application date.

A mortgage broker is responsible for ensuring that all loan originators are properly registered with the Banking and Consumer Finance Department of Mississippi.

Application for licensure must include:

Fully executed Mortgage Company License Registration Certificate application

Appropriate registration of business organization

Copies of business organizational documents

Contact list

Surety bond

Branch application (if applicable)

Loan Originator Registration Form for all loan originators (must include fingerprint cards)

Licensing fee

Bond
$25,000

Additional disclosure requirement
Mississippi Mortgage Consumer Protection Act, Section 81-18.1 et al., requires each mortgage applicant to be disclosed with:

Mortgage Origination Agreement

Fee Disclosure Agreement

Missouri

Regulatory agency: Missouri, Division of Finance

Contact: www.ded.mo.gov/regulatorylicensing/divisionoffinance or call (573) 751-3242

Requirements
Education
None required

Experience
None required

Licensing fee
$300 Investigation (includes a criminal record check)

$300 Upon approval

$ 10 Any additional branch offices in Missouri

License is valid for one year. Renewal fee is $300 and renewed license is valid for two years.

A licensed mortgage broker in Missouri is required to maintain a physical office in the state.

Application for licensure must include:

A fully executed Residential Mortgage Broker application

Proof of proper business filing in the state

Copies of business organizational documents

$300 investigation fee

Signed Request for Criminal Record Check

Surety bond

Authorization for Release of Confidential Information

Business financial statement (if applicable)

Personal financial statement

Resume

Bond
$20,000

Net worth
$25,000

Company registration
Registration with the Missouri Secretary of State is required. You may contact them at www.sos.state.mo.us.

Annual reports
Reports are mailed out each year by January 1st, and are due back no later than March 1st for business conducted the prior year.

Additional disclosure requirement
Missouri requires each mortgage applicant to be disclosed with the following additional disclosures:

Anti-coercion Insurance Disclosure

Application Disclosure (if any up-front fees are collected)

Loan Brokerage Disclosure and Agreement

Montana

Regulatory agency: Montana, Department of Administration Banking and Financial Institutions Division

Contact: www.discoveringmontana.com or call (406) 841-2930

Requirements
Education
All mortgage brokers are required to be licensed. At the time of application, the applicant is required to take and pass an exam.

The exam is designed to test the applicant's competency to originate loans. Therefore, the applicant will be tested on the following:

Loan origination

Proper disclosures

State and federal laws

Ability to read appraisals and title commitments

Ability to evaluate credit and calculate ratios

In addition 12 hours of continuing education is required.

Experience
Applicant must have a minimum of three years of experience working as a loan originator or in a related field.

Exam
Currently there are only two approved examination and education providers. They are

Mortgage-education.com

Montana Association of Mortgage Brokers

Licensing fee
$500
License is valid for one year and expires on June 30th.

A mortgage broker is required to maintain at least one physical office located in Montana.

It is the mortgage broker's responsibility to ensure their loan originators are licensed and registered with the state. In addition, the mortgage broker is responsible for holding and displaying employed loan originators' licenses at the location where business is principally conducted. Upon termination of employment of any loan originator, the mortgage broker must return the loan originator's license to the regulating agency listed above within five business days of termination.

Application for licensure must include:

A fully executed Mortgage Broker application.

The proposed location of business along with a photograph of proposed location. (A mortgage broker can conduct business from a residence, but verification of zoning laws and regulations is required.)

Irrevocable letter of credit or surety bond.

Verification that the designated manager meets the educational and work experience requirements for licensure (a mortgage broker that is not a sole proprietor requires a designated manager for each location).

Fingerprint cards for each individual applicant, which includes any individuals with more than 5 percent ownership in the company.

Verification of work experience.

Proof of passing exam.

Proof of proper business filing with the state.

Licensing fee.

Fingerprint fee
$32 Processing fee

With the application for a mortgage broker license, the applicant will need to provide a fingerprint card for each individual applicant, and fingerprints must be taken by a law enforcement agency.

Bond
$25,000 (maintain a $25,000 surety bond)

Additional disclosure requirement
Montana requires each mortgage applicant to be disclosed with the following additional disclosures:

Anti-coercion Insurance Disclosure

Loan Origination Agreement

Nebraska

Regulatory agency: Nebraska, Department of Banking and Finance, Financial Institutions Division

Contact: www.ndbf.org. or call (402) 471-2171

Requirements

To become a mortgage broker in Nebraska, an applicant must apply for a mortgage banker license.

Education
> None required

Experience
> None required

Licensing fee
> $300

> $100 Renewal fee

No additional fees for any additional locations. License is valid for one year. License expires annually on March 1st.
Application for licensure must include:

> A fully executed Mortgage Banker License application

> Proof of proper business filing with the state

> An original surety bond

> The address and original written consent of an authorized registered agent located in Nebraska

> $300 licensing fee

Bond
> $50,000

Registered agent
> Required

Company registration
Trade name must be registered with the Nebraska Secretary of State's Office; www.sos.state.ne.us/ or call (402) 471-4079.

Additional disclosure requirement
Nebraska requires each mortgage applicant to be disclosed with:

> Loan Brokerage Agreement in accordance with Nebraska law 45-191.01

Nevada

Regulatory agency: Nevada, Department of Banking and Finance, Financial Institutions Division

Contact: www.mld.nv.gov or call (775) 684-7060

Requirements

Education

None required

Experience

Two years of verifiable experience in the mortgage business. In the state of Nevada a qualified employee must be designated (if other than a sole proprietorship) and must have two years of verifiable experience in the mortgage business.

Licensing fee

$1,500 Nonrefundable investigation fee

$1,000 Initial license fee due upon approval

$500 Annual renewal fee

$60 Initial branch license fee

$100 Annual renewal branch license fee.

To apply for licensure the applicant must include:

A fully executed mortgage broker's license

A Non Personal History Form (for a commercial applicant that is not a natural person)

A copy of partnership, joint venture, or limited liability company agreement or articles of incorporation

For all applicants, a current financial statement dated within three months of this application and the two most recent fiscal year-end financial statements

A Personal History Record (for anyone owning more than 25 percent of the company)

A Personal Financial Questionnaire (for anyone owning more than 25 percent of company)

A Child Support Statement

Fingerprint card

A Qualified Employee Designation Form (each qualified employee must provide a Personal History Record, a Child Support Statement, a fingerprint card, and verification of two years' mortgage business experience)

$1,500 nonrefundable investigation fee

If the licensee is to be a subsidiary of a nationwide or parent organization, the applicant must disclose the percentage of ownership by the parent company and the following information: The last two fiscal year-end reports of the parent company

A *detailed* description of the general plan of the proposed business venture in Nevada (to include company policies for loan approval process, frequency of head office review, how appraisals are handled, escrow accounts, etc.)

Additional branch licenses must be applied for separately. However, a branch license will not be issued until the principal Nevada office has been licensed for at least six months, and has received a "satisfactory" rating upon examination. *All* proposed advertisements must be submitted to the commissioner for approval. This is to include all television, radio, and Internet advertising. Proposed advertisements may be faxed to (702) 486-0785, e-mailed to seckhardt@mld.nv.gov, or mailed to Nevada Financial Institutions Division; 2501 E. Sahara Ave., #300; Las Vegas, Nevada 89104; Tel: (702) 486-4120.

A mortgage broker must maintain at least one physical office in the state of Nevada. The mortgage broker must obtain a license for all additional branch locations. A mortgage broker must do business in the state of Nevada from a licensed office in Nevada.

Net worth
Only required when a trust fund is present. These guidelines would apply based on the trust account's balance.

Average Monthly Balance	Minimum Net Worth Required
$100,000 or less	$25,000
More than $100,000 but not more than $250,000	$50,000
More than $250,000 but not more than $500,000	$100,000
More than $500,000 but not more than $1,000,000	$200,000
More than $1,000,000	$250,000

Company registration

Once the above documentation is submitted and reviewed, the commissioner will issue a *conditional approval letter*. Thereafter, the applicant must submit the following information.

A copy of an appropriate municipal business license for the company, if applicable, or an application for such business license with proof it has been filed with the municipality.

A copy of recorded Certificate of Fictitious Name.

A copy of the State Business License (issued by the Nevada Department of Taxation) or an exemption from such a license. All businesses, Nevada corporations, foreign corporations, and partnerships operating in Nevada are required to have a State Business License issued by the Department of Taxation. A sole proprietorship with one or more employees is also required to have the State Business License. Statute imposes a tax based on the number of employees working in Nevada or entering Nevada to work or conduct a business activity (NRS 364A).

Secretary of State Certificate of Good Standing.

$1,000 licensing fee.

To request filing with the Secretary of State, the applicant must have a copy of the conditional approval letter. Then he or she may write or fax it to:

Mortgage Lending Division
Attn: Sheila Walther
400 W. King St., #406
Carson City, NV 89703
Fax no: (775) 684-7061

The applicant may reserve a name with the Secretary of State, Commercial Filings Division, on the Web at www.soscommerce.state.nv.us.

New Hampshire

Regulatory agency: New Hampshire, Banking Department

Contact: www.state.nh.us/banking or call (603) 271-3561

Requirements

Education
None required

Experience
None required

Licensing fee

First Mortgage Broker

$250 Annual fee

$250 for any additional locations

Second Mortgage Home Lender

$250 Annual fee

$250 For any additional locations

License expires annually on December 1st.

Registration of all loan originators, regardless of where they are located, is required. Registration of loan originators can be done electronically at the following Web address: www.state.gov.us/banking.

If a mortgage broker licensee is to employ loan originators as independent contractors (1099), then a written contract of employment is required. An independent contractor in New Hampshire is required to be exclusive with the licensee.

Application for licensure must include:

A fully executed first (or second or both) mortgage broker application(s).

Surety bond.

Name and address of New Hampshire business agent, if applicable. (An applicant whose principal place of business is outside of New Hampshire must appoint a New Hampshire agent with a NH business address. This is where examination of applicant's books and records will be held.)

Proof of registration of proper business filing.

Copies of business organizational documents.

Financial statement and most recent tax return. (If a corporation, then only business financials and most recent federal business income tax return must be included.)

Personal, financial, background, and criminal investigation authorization forms for all individuals with 10 percent or more ownership in the business and for the New Hampshire agent, if applicable. (A $15 investigation fee for each person on the list is required. A separate check for the total investigation fee is payable to State of New Hampshire—Criminal Records.)

Copies of resume of senior management personnel and New Hampshire branch managers.

If applicant will be providing rate lock commitments, please enclose GNMA, FNMA, and FHLMS approval letters.

Notarized Uniform Consent to Service of Process.

Licensing fee.

Bond

First Mortgage Broker—$20,000

Second Mortgage Home Lender—N/A

Independent contractor requirements

A mortgage broker licensee is required to provide the names and addresses of all independent contractors that are hired or that are on staff. *Independent contractor* is defined as an employee who is paid by 1099.

> Each licensee who has exclusive contracts with 10 or more independent agents for purposes of originating first mortgage loans in the state of New Hampshire shall file a copy of the language of the form contract he or she uses and copies of any subsequent amendments made to the form contract. In addition, each licensee who contracts with 10 or more independent agents shall file with the department on a monthly basis a list of independent agents with whom he or she has exclusive contracts, which shall include the names of the independent agents, business addresses, and the independent agents' tax identification numbers. Failure of the licensee or license applicant to file the form contract or list of independent agents without good cause shall result in license revocation or denial.

> Each licensee who contracts with fewer than 10 independent agents shall file with the department copies of the executed contracts that he or she currently holds and within 30 days of the effective date copies of each new exclusive contract with an independent agent entered into by the licensee. In addition, each licensee shall notify the department in writing within 30 days of the termination of any such exclusive contracts. Failure of the licensee or license applicant to file the exclusive contract or notice of termination of such an exclusive contract without good cause shall result in license revocation or denial.

Company registration

For filing of trade name and registration of foreign corporation, LLC/LLP, contact the New Hampshire Secretary of State at (603) 271-3244.

New Jersey

Regulatory agency: New Jersey, Department of Banking and Insurance

Contact: www.state.nj.us/dobi/index.shtml or call (609) 292-5340

Requirements

To become a mortgage broker in New Jersey, an applicant must apply for a licensed lender license.

Education

There are no educational requirements. There are no required courses to be taken in connection with the examination.

Experience

No experience required

Exam

The individual licensee will be required to take and successfully pass a written exam administered by the department for the authority requested, *prior* to the submission of an application for licensure.

The exam is administered by Promissor. Contact info: www.promissor.com or call (888) 204-6231. The exam consists of 80 scored questions and will include the testing of:

Federal mortgage-related laws

General mortgage knowledge

Mortgage loan process

New Jersey statutes and regulations

Licensing

Licenses are issued for a prescribed biennial period beginning on July 1st of an odd-numbered year through June 30th of the next odd-numbered year, e.g., 7/1/07–6/30/09.

Fee

$1,400 License fee

$300 Nonrefundable application fee

If an applicant applies anytime during the first 12 months of the two-year licensing period (e.g., in July 2007), then he or she will pay the full licensing amount.

If an applicant applies anytime within the second year of the biennial licensing period (e.g., in July 2008), then the fee is pro-rated down to a one-year ($700) fee.

When applying for a mortgage broker license and the legal structure is anything other than a sole proprietorship, an individual license is required in conjunction with the entity. The person to be the licensed individual of record (who must be a corporate officer or a member of a partnership) must reside within commuting distance of the location to be licensed. An individual application must be included with the licensee packet.

A licensed mortgage broker in New Jersey is required to maintain a physical office in that state.

Loan originators in the state of New Jersey are considered mortgage solicitors and they must be registered with the state. The registration fee per loan originator is $100.

Application for licensure must include:

Fully executed licensed lender application.

Proof of proper business filing with the state.

The original Pass Notice of exam, signed and attached to application.

A copy of deed, lease, or rental agreement for the licensed location.

A letter of intent to occupy the premises may be provided with the actual deed, lease, or rental agreement within 60 days of receipt of the application for licensure. An "executive suite" is *not* acceptable.

Copies of business organization documents.

Audited financial statement to demonstrate net worth requirements.

Surety bond.

Certified Consent Certificate for each officer, director, or substantial stockholders (10 percent or more ownership of partners and owner[s]).

Complete out-of-state or in-state agreement (whichever applies) for information on record retention.

Licensing fee.

Bond
    $100,000

Net worth
    $50,000

Company registration
If a corporation, LLC, or partnership, applicant must register with the New Jersey Treasurer. If a sole proprietorship, then trade name must be registered with the County Clerk's Office.

Additional disclosure requirement
New Jersey requires each mortgage applicant to be disclosed with the following additional disclosures:

    Anti-coercion disclosure or Choice of Insurer Notice

    Mortgage Broker Service Agreement Disclosure

    Loan Origination Agreement

    Non-affiliate Certification

    Cash-out Certification, if applicable

New Mexico

Regulatory agency: New Mexico, Financial Institutions Division

Contact: www.rld.state.nm.us/fid or call (505) 476-4885

Requirements
Education
    None required

Experience
    None required

Licensing fee

$400 Initial registration cost

$300 Annual renewal fee

License is renewable on the anniversary date of the original licensure date. Application for licensure must include:

A fully executed loan broker application

Proof of proper business filing with the state

Copies of business organizational documents

Exhibit 4—Biographical information on any individual with ownership interest in the company

Exhibit 5—Current (within six months) signed financial statement

Exhibit 6—List of business experience

Exhibit 7—Disclosure of any criminal conduct for any individuals with ownership interest in the company (if applicable)

Exhibit 8—Surety bond

Registration fee of $400

Bond

$25,000

Company registration

There are legal determinations for company registration with the state of New Mexico. For more information, contact the Public Regulation Commission at (505) 827-4500 or http://www.nmprc. state.nm.us/.

New York

Regulatory agency: New York, Banking Department

Contact: www.banking.state.ny.us/iambb.htm or call (212) 709-5543

Requirements

Education

> None required

Experience

> *Real Estate Brokers* licensed in the state of New York qualify to apply for a mortgage broker license. A copy of the license or pocket card issued by the Department of State must be supplied. The license must be current and in good standing. In addition, an applicant must provide the department with a letter stating that the applicant will be actively involved in the daily operations of the mortgage broker and that he or she has read and will comply with the dual disclosure requirements.

> *Attorneys* licensed in New York qualify to apply for a mortgage broker application. An applicant must include an original Certificate of Good Standing issued by the appropriate New York State court within two months of the filing date of the application. In addition, an applicant must also provide a letter stating that he or she will be actively engaged in the daily operations of the mortgage broker.

> *All others* must have a minimum of two years' verifiable experience in the mortgage field, as an originator, processor, or similar position. Experience in credit analysis or loan underwriting will also be accepted. A sworn, notarized affidavit, verified under penalty or perjury, detailing the applicant's:

> Duties and responsibilities

> Term of employment

> Name, address, and telephone number of a business reference, or current or former supervisor

The applicant may be asked to substantiate employment with copies of W2s or 1099s. In addition, other verification sources may be required such as a list of lenders, attorneys, or consumers that the applicant did or does business with, in order to verify his or her experience.

If an applicant has relevant business experience or relevant educational background, then he or she must demonstrate *how* the experience or education qualifies the applicant to be a registered mortgage broker. To do so, attach a statement to the application, verified under penalty or perjury, indicating:

The specific duties and responsibilities of employment

The term of employment

Name, address, and phone number of business reference or current or former supervisor

Educational experience
The specific courses taken and dates of completion

Licensing fee
$500 Initial application fee

$500 Upon approval of licensing fee. (If applying after June 30th, then license fee is $250.)

Licenses expire annually on December 30th. Application for licensure must include:

Fully executed application.

Proof of proper business filing with the state.

Copies of business organizational documents.

A notarized statement detailing qualifying experience.

Recent original credit reports for all owners, directors, or executive officers.

Personal Financial Statement to be completed by each principal and/or owner of 10 percent or more of the business.

Taxpayer Identification Information form.

New York State Banking Questionnaire for each individual with 10 percent or more ownership in the business, also included are executive officers and directors.

A Certificate of Discharge plus schedule of debts (if a bankruptcy has been declared).

A satisfaction of judgment (if applicable).

Litigation Affidavit.

Web site questionnaire.

Evidence of appropriate worker's compensation and disability insurance coverage.

Fingerprint cards.

Authority to Release Information.

Dual Agency Certification.

If applicant is currently working for a mortgage broker, a letter addressed to the New York State Banking Department must be included, to state the applicant's intent to resign from current position upon notification of the approval of mortgage broker registration.

Surety bond.

Application and fingerprint fees.

In regard to branch locations, the state of New York identifies a "full service branch" as a location where the processing of a mortgage loan takes place (regardless of whether loan solicitations are conducted there). For a "full service branch," enclose a biographical summary, including a resume, and form of payment (salary or commission) for the branch manager. Must also enclose a signed finalized lease agreement for the branch location.

A "loan solicitation branch" is a location where *only* loan solicitation is conducted.

Licensing fee for branch locations

$750 For a "full service branch"

$500 For a "loan solicitation branch"

Subsequent filing before June 30th has the following fees:

$500 For a "full service branch"

$375 For a "loan solicitation branch"

Fingerprint fee
> $99 for each set of cards

Fingerprint fee must be in a separate check. Two blue fingerprint cards are to be submitted on each owner, director, and executive officers. These cards must be obtained from the Banking Department.

Bond
> $10,000

Upon approval of mortgage broker registration, the applicant must submit an original surety bond for a minimum of $10,000.

Company registration
Corporations, LLPs, and LLCs need to register with the New York Secretary of State. You may contact them at (518) 473-2492.

Sole proprietorship using a trade name must register with the New York State County Clerk's office. A copy of the business certificate must be submitted along with the application.

Additional disclosure requirements
New York requires each mortgage applicant to be disclosed with the following additional disclosures:

> Fair Credit Reporting Act Disclosure (in accordance with New York Fair Credit Reporting Act)
>
> Hazard Insurance Disclosure
>
> Pre Application Disclosure (in accordance with NYCRR 82-6)

North Carolina

> *Regulatory agency*: North Carolina, Office of the Commissioner of Banks
>
> *Contact*: http://www.nccob.org/NCCOB or call (919) 733-0589

Requirements
Education
A sole proprietor must be licensed as a Mortgage Broker and a Loan Officer. For corporations or partnerships, a managing

principal must be designated and that individual must be licensed as a loan officer.

Loan officers must complete educational requirements that include an eight-hour mortgage lending fundamentals course. Applicants must successfully complete this course within three years preceding the date of application.

For a list of approved educational providers, visit http://www.nccob.org/NCCOB/Mortgage/Education/mledprovider.htm.

Experience

Applicant must have a minimum of three years' experience in mortgage lending.

Licensing fee for a Loan Officer

$100

A sole proprietor must also pass the NC Mortgage Loan Officer test. PSI is contracted by the Commissioner of Banks to conduct the test. You can contact PSI at (800) 733-9267 or www.psiexams.com. PSI provides examinations through seven computer examination centers in North Carolina. The tests are available daily.

Licensing fee for a Mortgage Broker

$1,000 Initial application and license fee

$100 For each branch office

$500 Renewal fee

License expires annually on June 30th.

Each branch office must have a designated Branch Manager, who must have a minimum of three years' experience in mortgage lending and must have a North Carolina Loan Officer License.

Each mortgage broker licensee must also designate a Managing Principal who is responsible for resolving consumer complaints regarding loan officers of the company and is the primary contact for licensing matters. If the Managing Principal is a licensed Loan Officer, then the Managing Principal may serve as the Branch Manager as well.

Licensee is responsible for ensuring all loan officers are properly licensed. Nonlicensing in North Carolina is a felony.

A licensed mortgage broker in North Carolina is required to maintain a physical office in the state.

Application for licensure must include:

Form MLA 001—a fully executed mortgage broker application

Proof of proper business filing

Copies of business organizational documents

Complete Schedule C (which lists all loan originators)

Complete Schedule D (biographical report of all individuals with 10 percent or more ownership in the business)

Notarized Schedule D1 (information and release form for all noted on Schedule D)

Complete Schedule E (list of subsidiaries or affiliates, if applicable)

Complete Schedule F (financial info)

Surety bond

A fingerprint card for each individual with 10 percent or more ownership in the business

Authority for Release of Information (state and federal record check)

Nonrefundable application fee

Fingerprint fees

$55 (required for each individual listed on Schedule D of the mortgage broker application)

Bond

$50,000

Additional disclosure requirement

North Carolina requires each mortgage applicant to be disclosed with the following additional disclosures:

Anti-coercion insurance disclosure

Application Disclosure (in accordance with NC Admin Code Section T04:031.0702(b)(1) and (2))

North Dakota

Regulatory agency: North Dakota, Department of Banking and Financial Institutions

Contact: www.state.nd.us/dfi. or call (701) 328-9933

Requirements

To become a mortgage broker in North Dakota, an applicant must apply for a money broker license.

Education

None required

Experience

None required

Licensing fee

$400 Investigation fee

$400 Annual license fee

License expires annually on June 30th. Application for licensure must include:

Fully executed money broker license.

Investigation and license fee

Proof of proper business filing with the state

Copies of business organizational documents

Surety bond

Financial statement to include a balance and income sheet

Personal financials for any individual with 25 percent or more ownership in the business

Organizational chart, if the applicant is a parent company, subsidiary corporation, or LLC

Resume of the proposed manager

Form SFN 50716—Names of Brokers (a list of all the applicant's loan originators)

Copy of disclosure—"Money Broker Contract"

List with names and addresses of all proposed sources of credit and supporting documentation specifying the credit limits

Schedule of commissions proposed

Bond
$25,000

Independent contractor requirement
If a money broker intends to staff independent contractors, a request must be made in writing to the Department for proper licensure. The decision is made on a case-by-case basis.

Additional disclosure requirement
North Dakota requires each mortgage applicant to be disclosed with the following additional disclosure:

Money Broker Contract (in accordance with ND Code 13-05-01 and 13-05-01-09)

Ohio

Regulatory agency: Ohio, Department of Commerce, Financial Institutions Division

Contact: www.com.state.oh.us/dfi/or call (614) 728-8400

Requirements
Education
None required

Experience
Each registered mortgage broker must designate an operations manager. Each designated operations manager must possess at least three years' experience in the mortgage-lending field. This may include:

Employment with a mortgage broker or financial institution, mortgage lending institution, or other lending institution

Three years of other experience related specifically to the business of mortgage loans

Exam fee
   $65

Mortgage Broker Operations Managers are required to pass the 100 multiple-choice item test. The test will cover:

   The Ohio Mortgage Broker Act

   Mortgage Loan Processes

   Mortgage Loan Programs

   Mortgage terminology

   Federal Mortgage Lending Legislation

   The exam is conducted by an outside contractor—Experior. Contact Experior at (800) 741-0934 or www.experioronline.com.

Licensing/registration fee
   $350 Nonrefundable application fee

   $350 Nonrefundable application fee for each branch location

Annual renewal fee varies and is based on mortgage activity.
   A licensed mortgage broker in Ohio is required to maintain at least one physical office in the state.
   Each licensed mortgage broker is responsible for ensuring that their loan originators are properly licensed.
   Application for licensure must include:

   A fully executed Main Office Certificate of Registration Application

   Photo of main office location and copy of lease agreement

   Mortgage Broker Operations Manager Profile (resume and verification of work experience and fingerprint background check)

   Statutory Agent Authorization

   Registration fee

   Ohio Mortgage Broker Surety Bond

Schedule A—Disclosure Form (biographical report on all individuals with 5 percent or more ownership in the business)

Proof of proper business filing with the state

Copies of business organizational documents

Criminal History Attestation

The licensure address in the state of Ohio *may* be a place of residence. If the licensure address is residential, the applicant must provide a certified copy of a zoning permit authorizing the use of the residence for commercial purposes.

Fingerprint/background check
In the processing of applications, the Division of Financial Institutions conducts background checks. Therefore, background checks are required of individual applicants, operations managers, all partners of a partnership, all members of a limited liability company, and the top four officers of a corporation.

In-state applicants have two options:

Option 1 is the electronic fingerprinting and scanning system "WebCheck," which is available at:

National Background Check, Inc. (NBCI)
Tel: (877) 932-2435
www.nationalbackgroundcheck.com

Secure Check
Columbus: Tel: (614) 222-8100
Akron: Tel: (330) 253-7410
www.securecheckinc.com

The Pre-check Company
Tel: (216) 226-7700
www.pre-check.com

Option 2 is a "Civilian Identification Card," which is available by calling the Division of Financial Institutions at (614) 728-8400, or by writing the Division at:

Ohio Department of Commerce
Division of Financial Institutions
77 South High St., 21st Floor
Columbus, OH 43215-6120

Out-of-state applicants must furnish a statewide criminal history report from their state's law enforcement department. The records check must be verified on the law enforcement agency's stationery or on a computer printout. The reporting agency *must* send the report *directly* to the Division of Financial Institutions.

Bond
$50,000

Additional disclosure requirement
Ohio requires each mortgage applicant to be disclosed with the following additional disclosures:

Right to Receive a Copy of Appraisal

Loan Brokerage Agreement (in accordance with Ohio Statute section 1233.062(A))

Oklahoma

Regulatory agency: Oklahoma, Department of Consumer Credit

Contact: www.okdocc.state.ok.us or call (800) 448-4904

Requirements
Education
None required

Experience
A licensee is required to provide proof of three years' continuous experience in the residential mortgage loan industry, real estate sales, *or* lending industry in the immediate five years preceding the license application.

A licensee must designate a responsible individual who is a resident of Oklahoma and is an employee active in the management activities of the licensee. The designated individual must meet the qualifications of a licensed mortgage broker.

Exam fee

$150 for Mortgage Broker Test (to be paid with application)

Testing is daily and must be scheduled 24 hours in advance. Testing times are 9:00 a.m. and 10:00 a.m. Tests are conducted at 4545 N. Lincoln Blvd, #104; Oklahoma City, OK 73105. Call: (405) 522-3736 to schedule an appointment.

Licensing fee

$750 Application fee

$100 Initial and renewal fee

$ 50 Branch office annual license fee

License is valid for three years.

A licensed mortgage broker in Oklahoma is required to maintain a physical location in the state.

All mortgage brokers are responsible for ensuring that *all* loan originators employed are licensed. A mortgage broker is responsible for conducting a reasonable investigation of their loan originators' background and must keep these records for a minimum of two years. In addition, mortgage brokers must notify and return the loan originator license to the Department of Consumer Credit Office, upon termination of any such loan originator.

Application for licensure must include:

Fully executed mortgage broker application

Proof of proper business filing with the state

Copies of business organizational documents

Notarized personal Affidavit

Appointment of Resident Agent

Financial Statement (no more than 30 days old from date of application)

Identities of Stockholders or Partners

Copies of mortgage loan disclosure forms that will be used

Evidence of Trust Account

Application, license, and test fee

Other state's License Inquiry Form (if applicable)

Copy of Brokerage Agreement

Proof of three years' work experience of officer or owner taking the test

Trust account
A trust account in a federally insured bank in Oklahoma will be required.

Additional disclosure requirement
Oklahoma requires each mortgage applicant to be disclosed with the following additional disclosures:

Mortgage Broker Agreement (in accordance with OK Statutes Title 59 Section 2086)

Company registration
Trade names must be registered with the Secretary of State. Foreign corporations will need a Certificate of Authority; LLC will need a Certificate of Organization; and for general partnerships applicant will need a Certificate of Fictitious Name.

Oklahoma Secretary of State
101 State Capitol Building
Oklahoma City, OK 73105
Tel: (405) 521-3911

Registered agent
Required

Oregon

Regulatory agency: Oregon, Division of Finance and Corporate Securities

Contact: www.cbs.state.or.us or call (503) 378-4140

Requirements

To become a mortgage broker in Oregon, an applicant must apply for a mortgage lender license. A mortgage lender license in Oregon permits a company to act as a mortgage banker, mortgage broker, or both.

Education

None required

Experience

A licensee must appoint the company's experience person. This experience person must be a full-time W2 employee or an owner with mortgage lending experience in three of the past five years.

All mortgage brokers and/or lenders are required to conduct a criminal records check of any loan originators the licensee intends to employ. A loan originator applicant may not be hired if the criminal records check discloses a disqualifying conviction.

Licensee must ensure that any loan originators hired meet the educational requirements for loan originators in the state of Oregon.

Licensing fee

$825 Initial license fee for the principal office

$165 Initial license fee per branch office (if submitted with initial application)

Initial license is valid for one year; thereafter, a two-year license is issued. Renewal fees are the same as initial licensing fee.

Application for licensure must include:

A fully executed Mortgage Lender License application

Financial statement that is less than six months old (to include a balance sheet and profit and loss statement)

Proof of proper business filing

Copies of business organizational forms

Loan Originator Information Form

License fee

Signed original surety bond

Form 440-2776 (executed affidavit if applicant does not take client funds prior to closing a loan *or* Form 440-2777 for trust account information)

Bond
$25,000

$5,000 for each additional location

$50,000 maximum

Trust account
If licensee accepts client funds (for third-party fees or other refundable purposes) prior to closing, then licensee must maintain a clients' trust account. With the initial application, an applicant must submit a completed copy of Notice of Clients' Trust Account and the Authorization to Examine Clients' Trust Account. The clients' trust account must be physically located in the state of Oregon.

If a mortgage broker does not intend to accept client funds, then a completed Affidavit and Undertaking must be submitted with the initial application.

Registered agent
Required

DFCS provides a partial list of registered agents for Oregon. They are

CT Corp. System: (800) 227-4734

Corp Service Co.: (800) 222-2122

Data Research, Inc.: (800) 992-1983

Charles F. Mathias: (888) 375-6188

National Registered Agents, Inc.: (800) 554-3113

Company registration

If the applicant is a corporation in Oregon or has a physical location in Oregon, registration is required with the Oregon Secretary of State at (503) 986-2200. If the applicant is a corporation formed in a state other than Oregon, then registration is required as a foreign corporation. If the applicant will be conducting business under an assumed business name, then registration is required with the Oregon Secretary of State.

Pennsylvania

Regulatory agency: Pennsylvania, Department of Banking

Contact: www.banking.state.pa.us and click on financial institutions or call (717) 787-3717

Requirements

Education

There are no initial educational requirements; however, there are six credit hours of continuing education required.

In the case of a mortgage broker, the licensee must maintain at least one separate mortgage professional at each licensed office who has successfully completed the continuing educational requirements.

For a list of approved educational providers, visit www.banking.state.pa.us and click on financial institutions, then mortgage lenders/brokers, then continuing education requirements.

Experience

None required

Licensing fee

First Mortgage Broker

$500 Initial license fee

$200 Annual renewal fee

$ 50 Each branch location

$ 25 Annual renewal fee for branch locations

A first mortgage broker licensee is required to maintain a principal office in the state of Pennsylvania with at least one W2 employee.

Second Mortgage Broker

$500 Initial license fee

$50 for each branch location

License expires annually on July 1st.
Application for licensure must include:

Fully executed first (or second) mortgage broker license

Copies of proper business filing in the state

Copies of organizational documents

Proof from the telephone service provider that *all* telephone numbers are in the designated company name

Company Web address (must be registered with the Department of State *if* it is significantly different from the company name or not prominently displayed in the opening page)

Surety bond (if applicable)

Copies of forms and documents used in the loan origination process, excluding the loan application and other standard federal forms and documents licensing fee

Criminal record check

The Department of Banking requires all applicants to provide *both* a National Criminal History Record Information (Fingerprint Cards) *and* a Pennsylvania Criminal Record Check. The fingerprint cards will be mailed to the applicant by the Department of Banking upon receipt of a completed application.

Pennsylvania criminal record check is required by all sole proprietors, office managers, partners, and officers of corporations (President, Vice President, Secretary, and Treasurer). Form SP 4-164 (available online at www.banking.state.pa.us) must be submitted to the Pennsylvania State Police at time of application, along with a certified check or money order for $10 made payable to Commonwealth of Pennsylvania. Each request must be sent to:

> Pennsylvania State Police
> Central Repository-164
> 1800 Elmerton Ave.
> Harrisburg, PA 17110-9758
> Tel: (717) 783-9973

The criminal record check will go to the Department of Banking directly from the Pennsylvania State Police.

Bond

$100,000

A bond is required for a first mortgage broker licensee who collects fees prior to a loan closing. Up-front fees excluded are fees that an applicant pays *directly* to a credit agency reporting company, title company, or real estate appraiser. If a first mortgage broker licensee can demonstrate that he or she does not collect any advanced fees *in his or her own name*, then an exemption from bonding may be exercised.

Net worth

$25,000

An applicant for a second mortgage broker license is not allowed to collect any advanced fees, unless the applicant maintains $25,000 in capital as required by Section 4(b) of the Secondary Mortgage Act of Pennsylvania.

Company registration

Registration is required with the Pennsylvania Department of State. You may contact them at (717) 787-1057 or www.dos.state.pa.us.

Additional disclosure requirement

Pennsylvania requires each mortgage applicant to be disclosed with the following additional disclosure:

  Anti-coercion disclosure

Audits/reports

Licensees are required to file an annual report with the Department of Banking before May 1st of each year. The report requests information about business conducted during the preceding calendar year.

Rhode Island

> *Regulatory agency*: Rhode Island, Department of Business Regulation
>
> *Contact*: www.dbr.state.ri.us or call (401) 222-2405

Requirements

Education
> None required

Experience
Each licensee must have a manager of record. This person must have five years of experience in the industry and must have a criminal background check.

Licensing fee

> $275 Application fee
>
> $550 Annual license fee, due upon approval of application
>
> $ 25 Power of Attorney Form filing fee

License expires annually on March 31st. Application for licensure must include:

> A fully executed mortgage broker license
>
> Evidence of proper business filing in the state
>
> Copies of organizational documents
>
> Zoning certificate, if place of residence is to be licensed
>
> A biographical report, *signed*, and completed background check, and *signed* personal financial statement for each individual with 10 percent or more ownership in the company
>
> A certified copy of corporation bylaws or operating agreement for an LLC

A description of business structure (identification of any parent or subsidiary company, if applicable)

Certified copy of resolution of board of directors

A description of past activities conducted by applicant and a history of operations (if a new business, will need a three-year business plan to include statements of income and expenses)

A description of business activities that applicant seeks to be engaged in, in the state of Rhode Island

A statement describing how the community will be served by the applicant and a marketing plan

A Power of Attorney Form

Authorization for Background Check (for each officer, director, and manager)

Surety bond

Application fee

Bond
$10,000

Net worth
$10,000

Registered agent
Required

Company registration
If a corporation or LLC, a Certificate of Good Standing or Certificate of Registration (for LLC) is required from the Rhode Island Secretary of State. Limited Partnerships must provide a Certificate of Limited Partnership, and General Partnerships must provide a Certificate of General Partnership from the Rhode Island Secretary of State.

Contact info: www3.sec.state.ri.us/divs/corps/index.html

Additional disclosure requirement

Rhode Island requires each mortgage applicant to be disclosed with the following additional disclosures:

Anti-coercion Disclosure

Notice of Nonrefundable Loan Fees (in accordance with RI Gen Law Section 34-23-6)

Notice to Buyer of Withholding Tax Requirement (for purchases only and in accordance with RI Gen Law 44-30-71.3)

Prepayment Disclosure (for loans with prepayments only)

Right to Choose Title Agent or Attorney (in accordance with RI Gen Law Chapters 19-9-5 and 19-9-6)

Appraisal Fee Disclosure (in accordance with RI Gen Law Chapter 19-9-3)

South Carolina

Regulatory agency: South Carolina, Department of Consumer Affairs

Contact: www.state.sc.us/consumer/ or call (803) 734-4200 or (800) 922-1594

Requirements

Education

Although no initial educational requirements are necessary, all licensed mortgage brokers must complete at least eight hours of professional education annually.

Experience

Each owner, member, manager, and/or partner must have at least two years' experience working as an originator and have a criminal records check.

In lieu of one of the required years of experience, applicant may show proof of the equivalent of six or more semester hours of satisfactorily completed course work in real estate finance, real estate law, or similar; counting toward the successful completion of a degree that is baccalaureate level or more advanced with a major or minor in finance, accounting, business administration, real estate finance economics, or similar baccalaureate or more advanced degree approved by the administrator or the administrator's designee from an accredited college or university.

Licensing fee

$200 Processing fee

$550 Upon approval

$150 For each branch location

$550 Renewal fee

License expires annually on September 30th.

Originators must be licensed with the state of South Carolina Department of Consumer Affairs. Loan originators are required to have eight hours of continuing education.

A licensed mortgage broker is required to maintain a physical location in the state of South Carolina.

Application for licensure must include:

A fully executed mortgage broker license.

Proof of proper business filing in the state.

Copies of organizational documents.

Supplemental Form A—Owner/Employee Information, for each owner, partner, member, corporate officer, shareholder, and employee other than originators.

Supplemental Form B1—Location.

Supplemental Form B2 (if any branch locations).

Most recent financials (no later than 180 days prior to date of application) to reflect net worth requirements. (Personal financials may be used if applicant is a new company.)

Sample of disclosure Mortgage Broker Fee Agreement.

$200 processing fee.

Upon approval, application fee of $550 (certified or cashiers check) *and* surety bond are required.

Criminal records check
> $25 is payable to the S.C. Department of Consumer Affairs.

Bond
> $10,000 (maintain a $10,000 bond or $10,000 in cash or securities)

Registered agent
>   Required

Company registration
>   Secretary of State, contact info: www.scsos.com

Additional disclosure requirement
South Carolina requires each mortgage applicant to be disclosed with the following additional disclosure:

>   Loan Broker Agreement (in accordance with SC Code Law Title 40, Chapter 58, Section 40-58-78)

South Dakota

>   *Regulatory agency*: South Dakota, Division of Banking Department

>   *Contact*: www.state.sd.us/banking or call (605) 773-3421

Requirements
Education
>   None required

Experience
>   None required

Licensing fee
> $300 Annual license fee

License expires annually on June 30th. Application for licensure must include:

>   A fully executed mortgage broker application

>   Proof of proper business filing in the state

Copies of business organizational documents

Resume for responsible person

Strategic business plan

License fee

Registered agent
The law requires that an applicant designate a registered agent to accept service of process. A written acceptance of the appointment by the agent must be attached to the applicant's application for licensure.

Company registration
South Dakota requires fictitious name filings to be registered in the county where the business is located. A corporation filed in the state of South Dakota requires a Certificate of Authority.

Tennessee

Regulatory agency: Tennessee, Department of Financial Institutions

Contact: www.state.tn.us/financialinst. or call (615) 741-3186

Requirements
Education
None required

Experience
None required

Licensing fee
$500 Annual license fee

$100 Nonrefundable investigation fee

License expires annually on December 31st.
A mortgage broker licensee will be responsible for the yearly registration of all loan originators employed under said license.

The registration fee for a loan originator is $100. The law also requires a mortgage broker licensee to designate a Managing Principal to assume overall responsibility for a Tennessee-based office, *and* a Branch Manager for any branch locations (if any in the state of Tennessee). These individuals must have sufficient experience for said duties; however, no specific experience requirements are specified.

Application for licensure must include:

A fully executed mortgage broker license

Proof of proper business filing in the state

Copies of business organizational documents

Surety bond along with a Power of Attorney

Financial statement

Complete Affidavit of Official Signing of Registration and Certificate of Resolution, if a corporation or LLC

Confidential Background Information Consent Form

License and investigation fees

Bond

$90,000 or Letter of Credit payable to the People of the State of Tennessee

Bond must run the calendar year from January 1st to December 31st, renewable each year and must remain in effect for two years after close of business for any reason. The Letter of Credit must be for three years initially, renewable, and must remain in effect for two years after close of business for any reason.

Net worth

$25,000

Registered agent

Required for a corporation

Company registration
If a corporation or LLC, the applicant will need a Certificate of Authority. Please contact the Tennessee Secretary of State at www.state.tn.us/sos.

Annual report/financial statement
The commissioner will determine the filing date for an annual report and an annual statement that shall include the names of any individuals with 25 percent or more ownership in the business.

Additional disclosure requirement
In the state of Tennessee if an applicant collects any fees up front, then he or she must disclose appropriately in accordance with TN Code Section 45-13-109c.

Texas

Regulatory agency: Texas, Finance Commission of Texas, Savings and Loan Department

Contact: www.sml.state.tx.us. or call (512) 475-1350 or toll free at (877) 276-5550

Requirements
Education
None required

Experience
An applicant must have 18 months of experience in the mortgage or lending field and must have graduated with a four-year degree from an "accredited college or university" in Finance, Banking, Business Administration, or a related field
or
Hold an active license in Texas as a real estate broker, attorney, a local recording agent or insurance solicitor, or agent for a legal reserve life insurance company
or
Have three years of experience in the mortgage-lending field.

Exam fee

    $42

The exam is conducted by an outside contractor: Promissor at (800) 275-8246 or www.promissor.com. The exam will consist of 75 multiple-choice questions, and applicants are permitted two hours to complete the exam. The exam will cover the following:

    Equal Credit Opportunity Act (ECOA) & Regulation B

    Real Estate Settlement Procedures Act (RESPA) & Regulation X

    Truth-in-Lending Act (TILA)

    Texas Mortgage Broker License Act

    Texas Mortgage Broker Regulations

    General Knowledge, Terms, and Concepts and Math

For full exam details, visit http://www.sml.state.tx.us/mblolicensing.htm and press prelicensing exam.

Licensing fee

    $375 Annual license

    $20 Mortgage broker recovery fund

    $39 FBI background check

License is valid for a two-year period and expires two years from original date of approval.

A licensee must ensure that all loan originators are licensed ($155 licensing fee). In addition, a loan originator must be an employee (W2) of a licensee. If applicant has any independent contractors (Form 1099), they must be licensed as a mortgage broker in order to originate any loans in the state of Texas.

When advertising, the applicant must comply with The Mortgage Broker License Act, to include but not be limited to the following: disclose in said advertisement that a mortgage broker or loan originator is running the advertisement and include the applicant's license number.

All licensed mortgage brokers in Texas are required to maintain a physical address in that state.

An application for licensure must include:

A fully executed mortgage broker application

Proof of proper business filing with the state

Copies of business organizational documents

Evidence of previous industry experience

Signed and dated current personal financial statement

Signed and dated current company financial statement (to include profit and loss)

Surety bond (if applicable)

Completed and signed FBI fingerprint card

Verification/Confirmation Authorization form

Copy of prelicensing exam certificate issued by Promissor, Inc.

License fee of $300 plus $39 for FBI check

Bond
$50,000 (only required if net worth is not met)

Net worth
$25,000 (personal net worth requirement)

Company registration
Registration is required with the Texas Secretary of State. You may contact them at www.sos.state.tx.us.

Additional disclosure requirement
Texas requires each mortgage applicant to be disclosed with the following additional disclosure:

Mortgage Broker/Loan Officer Disclosure (must include information on how to file a complaint and information regarding the mortgage broker recovery fund in accordance with the Texas Mortgage Broker Act)

In addition the consumer complaint and mortgage broker recovery fund information must be prominently posted in registered office, and if a Web site is used, it must be posted on the Web site.

Whenever a mortgage broker or loan officer provides a loan applicant with a confirmation of the status of a mortgage loan that has *not yet* been approved, the licensee shall use the Texas Conditional Qualification Letter. (If loan has been approved, then licensee will issue the Texas Conditional Approval Letter.)

Notice Concerning Extensions of Credit Defined by Section 50(a)(6), Article XVI, Texas Constitution (for cash out refinances).

Annual reports

Annual reports are required to be filed with the regulating department. The applicant will need to provide information about the total loans and loan amounts produced for the previous year. Annual reports can be faxed in to (512) 475-1360. Nonfiling of an annual report can lead to a revoked license.

Utah

Regulatory agency: Utah, Division of Real Estate

Contact: www.commerce.state.ut.us/dre or call (801) 530-6747

Requirements

To become a mortgage broker (referred to as an entity) in Utah, an applicant must apply for a Residential Mortgage Lender license.

Education

A mortgage broker (referred to as an entity) must appoint a Control Person who must have 20 hours of an approved educational course. In addition, the Control Person (a licensed individual) must have 14 hours of continuing education in order to renew his or her license.

For a list of approved prelicensing educational providers, visit http://www.commerce.state.ut.us/dre/education.html.

Experience

None required

However, to qualify for licensure an applicant must:

Have good moral character and the competency to transact the business of residential loans

Not have been convicted of a felony or misdemeanor involving moral turpitude in the 10 years preceding the date the individual applies for a license

Not have had a license or registration suspended, revoked, surrendered, canceled, or denied in the 5 years preceding the date the individual applies for a license.

Exam

$75

A mortgage broker (referred to as an entity) must appoint a Control Person (referred to as an individual) who is required to take and pass a test as required by the commissioner in the state of Utah. Promissor, a national test administrator company, administers the Utah mortgage lender exam. You can reach Promissor toll free at (800) 274-7292 or on the Web at www.promissor.com. The exam consists of two parts: general and state law. An "individual license application" form will be generated by Promissor upon successful completion of the mortgage lender exam.

Licensing fee

$200 Entity application fee

$50 Education and recovery fund fee

$39 Control person background/fingerprint processing fee

A license is valid for two years. Renewal fee for an entity is $200 + a $50 education and recovery fund fee. Renewal for an individual is $136.

A mortgage broker (referred to as an entity) must appoint a Control Person as an individual that directly manages or controls the entity's transaction of the business of residential mortgage loans. The entity application form should include information for all Control Persons. Each Control Person must be licensed as an individual ($200 individual fee plus $36 education and recovery fee) and must pass the mortgage lender exam.

All loan originators must be licensed and registered with the state, as an individual.

Application for licensure must include:

> A fully executed Residential Mortgage Lender application form containing information on the Control Person and signed by the Control Person.

Fingerprint fee
> $39

Two fingerprint cards are required for each named Control Person. In addition a fingerprint letter of waiver must accompany the application. Fingerprint cards are available through the Division of Real Estate.

Bond
> $25,000

Company registration
Registration for an entity is required. A Certificate of Existence or evidence of registration is required from the Utah Division of Corporations.

Vermont

> *Regulatory agency*: Vermont, Department of Banking, Insurance, Securities and Healthcare Administration

> *Contact*: www.bishca.state.vt.us or call (802) 828-3307

Requirements
Education
> None required

Experience
> None required

Licensing fee

> $250 Annual license fee
>
> $250 Investigation fee

License is valid for one year and expires December 31st. Applications for licensure received after September 30th are prorated.

Application for licensure must include:

A fully executed mortgage broker application

Proof of proper business registration with the state

Copies of business organizational documents

Attachment B (biographical report for all individuals with 10 percent or more ownership in the business)

Attachment C—Authority to Release Information

Attachment D—Certification by Licensing Agency/ Supervisory Board, if licensed in any other state

Attachment E—Mortgage Broker Addendum (list all partners, officers, managers, and designated employees who will act under licensee)

A business plan (to include any promotional literature)

A copy of the Broker/Prospective Borrower Agreement (as required by Regulation B-96-1)

Current and prior two-year financials

License and investigation fees

Bond

> $10,000

Company registration

Required is a Certificate of Authority or a Certificate of Good Standing issued by the Vermont Secretary of State dated no more than six months. For sole proprietors, a Certificate of Trade Name Registration will be required. You may contact the Vermont Secretary of State at www.sec.state.vt.us.

Additional disclosure requirement

Vermont requires each mortgage applicant to be disclosed with the following additional disclosures:

Addendum to Uniform Residential Loan Application

Mortgage Broker Agreement (in accordance with VT Banking Regulation B-96-1)

Virginia

Regulatory agency: Virginia, State Corporation Commissions Bureau of Financial Institutions

Contact: www.state.va.us/scc/division/banking/index.htm or call (804) 371-9657

Requirements

Education

None required

Experience

None required

Licensing fee

$500 Application fee for *each* location

In the state of Virginia there is no expiration of license. A licensee will incur a yearly assessment fee based on the annual report (productivity for previous year).

Application for licensure must include:

A fully executed mortgage broker application

Proof of proper business filing with the state

Copies of business organizational documents

Original surety bond

A current (less than 90 days old) personal financial report and biographical information on any individual with 10 percent or more ownership in the business

Audited financials (if sole proprietor, then only complete CCB-1123)

Application fee of $500

Bond
$25,000

Company registration
If applicant is a corporation, LLC, or LLP, prior registration with the Clerk of the State Corporation Commission at (804) 371-9733 is required. A sole proprietor must register the trade name with the commission.

Additional disclosure requirement
Virginia requires each mortgage applicant to be disclosed with the following additional disclosures:

Mortgage Broker Agreement (in accordance with VA Code Section 6.1-422 (B) (5))

Choice of Settlement Agent Notice (in accordance with VA Code Section 6.1-2.22)

Washington

Regulatory agency: Washington, Department of Financial Institutions, Division of Consumer Services

Contact: www.wa.gov/cs/mortgage.htm or call (360) 902-8756

Requirements
Education
None required

Experience
A licensee must appoint a Designated Broker. The Designated Broker must have:

At least two years' experience in the mortgage loan industry *or*

Completed the educational requirements established by rule of the director, *and*

Passed a written examination given by the Financial Division of Institutions of Washington

Exam

For the exam, the Designated Broker will need to be familiar with:

Truth in Lending Act, Fair Lending, and RESPA

Mortgage Broker Practice Act

Consumer Protection Act

The exam consists of 100 multiple-choice questions. Registration for the exam is through the Financial Division in Washington (www.dfi.wa.gov/csmbtestschd3.pdf). The test must be passed, with at least a score of 70, prior to submitting the mortgage broker license application. Test results are given after the Designated Broker has completed the exam.

Licensing fee

$371.60 Application fee

$185.80 For each additional office

In the state of Washington there are no renewals of licensure; instead, the applicant will incur a yearly assessment of $530.86.

The application for licensure must include:

A fully executed mortgage broker application

Proof of proper business filing in the state

Copies of business organizational documents

Addendum A, consists of ownership information

Addendum B, requires a list of all personnel by location

Addendum C, required if employing any loan originators on a 1099 (as independent contractors)

Addendum D (requires a registered agent if the applicant's office is outside of the state of Washington)

Addendum F (requires a list of wholesale lenders)

Addendum G (requires a list of all third-party service providers)

Addendum H (requires a master business license)

Addendum K (requires a Designated Broker)

Addendum M (Trust Account). If applicant never intends to accept monies from borrowers for the payment of third-party providers, then he or she should complete "The Alternative Certificate of Compliance."

Addendum N—Prior Disciplinary Action form, if applicable

Addendum O—Civil Litigation information form, if applicable

Addendum P (if licensed in other states—requires references)

Addendum Q (application deposit)

Addendum R (Individual Information Background form, also a personal credit report)

Addendum S (Surety bond)

Addendum T (Records location)

Background check
An Individual Background Check form must be submitted along with two FBI format fingerprint cards.

Bond
The bond amount in Washington is determined by how many loan originators will be originating loans in Washington. The bond forms differ if employing independent contractors or employees. See table below.

Monthly Average Loan Originators	Minimum Surety Bond
Three or fewer	$20,000
Four to six	$30,000
Seven to nine	$40,000
Ten to fifteen	$50,000
Sixteen plus	$60,000

A Letter of Credit or Certificate of Deposit can be used as alternative methods to the Surety bond.

Registered agent
If applicant's office will be located outside of the state of Washington, then a Registered Agent is required.

Company registration
Master Business License Application

In order for a company to conduct business in the state of Washington, an application needs to be submitted to the Department of Licensing at Tel: (302) 902-3600. This license will issue a Unified Business Identifier (UBI) number. This license must be in the applicant's possession prior to submitting a mortgage broker application.

In addition, registration with the Washington Secretary of State, Division of Corporations, is required. You may contact them at (360) 753-7115.

Additional disclosure requirement
Washington requires each mortgage applicant to be disclosed with the following additional disclosures:

Anti-coercion Disclosure

Loan Brokerage Agreement (in accordance with WA Code 19.146.040)

Broker Application Disclosure (in accordance with WA State Mortgage Broker Practices Act, Chapter 19.146)

West Virginia

Regulatory agency: West Virginia, Division of Banking

Contact: www.wvdob.org or call (304) 558-2294

Requirements

Education

   None required

Experience

   None required

Licensing fee

   $350 Annual license fee for each location

Licenses expire annually on December 31st.

All loan originators working for a mortgage broker must be licensed. A mortgage broker licensee is responsible for ensuring their loan originators are licensed appropriately. In addition mortgage brokers must ensure that their loan originators meet continuing education requirements, as verification will be required upon mortgage broker's license renewal.

Application for licensure must include:

   A fully executed mortgage broker application

   Proof of proper business registration with the state

   Copies of business organizational documents

   An Authorization for Release of Individual's Personal Background, Credit Report Information, Credit History Release Form, and two completed FBI fingerprint cards for *all* (principals/individuals) with 10 percent or more ownership in the business

   A list of all other states licensed in (if applicable)

   Current financial statement to include a detailed balance sheet and income statement

   Audited financials (if applicable)

   Surety bond

   A current resume for all principals and managers

   Licensing fee of $350 for each location

Fingerprints/background investigation
> $44 Fee

Two completed FBI fingerprint cards are required for each principal of applicant. Fingerprint cards must be submitted on the forms provided by the West Virginia Division of Banking.

Bond
> $50,000

Net worth
> $10,000

Company registration
An LLC, LLP, and corporation must register with the West Virginia Secretary of State. You may contact them at (304) 558-8000. A Certificate of Authority or Certificate of Good Standing will be required.

A sole proprietor or general partnership must register with the West Virginia Department of Tax and Revenue, in which case a Current Business Registration form will be required.

In addition *all* mortgage broker license applicants will need to provide a copy of the West Virginia Credit Service Organization Registration Statement as filed with the West Virginia Secretary of State.

Record keeping requirement
Examiners for West Virginia will be checking for compliance of the new record keeping requirements pursuant to an Order entered by the Circuit Court of Kanawha County. Specific details can be found online at: www.wvdob.org/professionals/n_mortgage.htm.

Additional disclosure requirement
West Virginia requires each mortgage applicant to be disclosed with the following additional disclosures:

> Anti-coercion Disclosure

> Collateral Protection Insurance Disclosure (to be given at closing in accordance with WV Code Section 46A-3-109a)

Wisconsin

Regulatory agency: Wisconsin, Department of Financial Institutions

Contact: www.wdfi.org. or call (608) 261-7578

Requirements
Education

None required

Experience

None required

Licensing fee

$750 (license is valid for two years)

Wisconsin does not require an office in the state of Wisconsin, but there are different financial responsibilities to fulfill if there is no bona fide office.

A Bona Fide office

Is located in the state of Wisconsin

Has regular hours of operation

Is accessible to the public

Serves as an office for the transaction of a business

Has a licensed employee and is not shared with another business

Is separate from the offices of other entities

Contains the books and records of the mortgage broker

A Bona Fide office can be in the applicant's home if he or she can meet all of the above requirements, and only one business is being conducted from the home.

A mortgage broker is responsible for the registration of all employed loan originators under their license with the Department of Financial Institutions with the State of Wisconsin. The loan originator licensing/registration fee is $250.

An application for licensure must include:

A fully executed mortgage broker application

Proof of proper business registration with the state

Copies of organizational business documents

Audited financials (to satisfy net worth requirements)

Surety bond

Licensing fee of $750

Bond

A mortgage broker with a Bona Fide office must have:

A $10,000 surety bond, *or*

A personal bond or third-party guarantee for $10,000 (such as a CD), *or*

Audited financials with a net worth requirement of $100,000

A mortgage broker without a Bona Fide office must have:

A $120,000 surety bond, *and*

Audited financials with a net worth requirement of $250,000

Company registration

If a corporation, partnership, or LLC and the company was formed outside of Wisconsin, then a Certificate of Authority will be required. One may be obtained by contacting the Department of Financial Institutions at (608) 261-7577.

Additional disclosure requirement

Wisconsin requires each mortgage applicant to be disclosed with the following additional disclosure:

Application Disclosure (must cover specific requirements as required by WI Revised Stat Section 138.052(7e)(b))

Mortgage Broker Agreement (in accordance with Wisconsin Admin Code 43.04(5 m))

Anti-coercion Disclosure

Annual reports

Mortgage broker applicants that meet their financial responsibility with net worth requirements are required to submit a copy of an annual audit of their operations within six months after the close of their fiscal year. The annual audit is required to be conducted by an independent CPA.

If the mortgage broker applicant has met their financial responsibility with a surety or personal bond, then an (internally prepared) balance sheet, income statement, and retained earnings statement is required within six months after the close of their fiscal year.

Wyoming

> *Regulatory agency*: Wyoming, Department of Audit, Division of Banking

> *Contact*: http://audit.state.wy.us or call (307) 777-7797

Requirements

Education

> None required

Experience

> None required

Licensing fee

> $150 Application fee

> $ 25 Initial license fee due upon approval for each location

> $ 25 Renewal fee for each location

Licenses expire annually on July 1st. Application for licensure must include:

> A fully executed Supervised Lender License application

> Proof of proper business registration with the state

> Copies of business organizational documents

> One Bank Reference Form

Two State Regulator Reference Forms (if applicant is licensed in additional states)

Two Professional Reference Forms (if applicant is *not* licensed in any other states)

Current financials (within 30 days)

Application fee of $150

Company registration

Registration with the Wyoming Secretary of State for a Certificate of Authority is required. You may contact them at (307) 777-5334 or email: jsawye@missc.state.wy.us.

Sample State Disclosures for Mortgage Brokers

SAMPLE BROKER AGREEMENT

Date: Loan Number:

Lender:

Borrower(s):

Property Address:

This agreement is provided pursuant to Section _____

This agreement shall remain in effect for _____ days before return of the fees for nonperformance can be required by the consumer.

1. Unless the Broker specifically tells you otherwise in writing, once fees and charges have been collected they are not refundable unless otherwise required by law.

2. The services the Broker shall perform for Borrower include (*check all that apply*):

❑ Take information from you and fill out an application.

❑ Analyze your income and debt to determine the maximum mortgage you can afford.

❑ Collect financial information and other related documents from you that are part of the application process.

❑ Initiate and order verifications of employment and verifications of deposit.

❑ Initiate and order requests for mortgage and other loan verifications.

❑ Educate you in the home buying and/or financing process, advise you about the different types of loan products available, and demonstrate how closing costs and monthly payments could vary under each product.

❑ Assist you in understanding and clearing any credit problems.

❑ Initiate and order appraisal(s).

❑ Initiate and order any inspections or engineering reports.

❑ Maintain regular contact with you, any realtors, and lender between application and closing to apprise you and them of the status of the application and gather any additional information as needed.

❑ Order legal documents.

❑ Determine whether the Property is located in a flood zone or order a service to determine the same.

❑ Participate in the loan closing.

❑ Other:

3. The terms and conditions of payment are:

4. The total of payments to be made by you for the service is: $_____.

I/We hereby acknowledge receipt of this Broker Agreement.
NOTICE TO CONSUMER: Do not sign this agreement before you read it. You are entitled to a copy of this agreement.

_____   _____
Borrower   Date   Borrower   Date

SAMPLE MORTGAGE BROKERAGE
BUSINESS CONTRACT

(hereinafter called Borrower), employs_____(hereinafter
called Business) to obtain a mortgage loan commitment (hereinafter called Commitment) within days from the date hereof and
acknowledges that Business cannot make loans or commitments or guarantee acceptance into specific programs, terms or conditions of any loan. However, Business may issue a rate lock-in or commitment on behalf of a lender to the Borrower.

I. PROPERTY:
Address:
Borrower's estimates of fair market value:
Borrower's estimates of the balances on any existing mortgage loan: $

II. TERMS OF LOAN APPLICATION:
Loan Amount: $ Interest Rate: %   Loan Term/Due In: months   months
Monthly Payment: $
Loan Type: _____First Mortgage_____   Second/Junior Mortgage

III. MORTGAGE BROKERAGE FEE
Business, in consideration of the Borrower's agreement to pay a mortgage brokerage fee along with actual costs incurred in connection with this loan, agrees to exert its best efforts to obtain a bona fide mortgage loan commitment in accordance with the
terms (or better terms) and conditions set forth herein. The Business and its associates or employees shall be held harmless from
any liability resulting from failure to obtain said loan commitment. Borrower hereby agrees to pay the actual costs as estimated
herein and Borrower agrees to pay Business a mortgage brokerage fee of $ _____ for obtaining the commitment. Additionally,
Borrower acknowledges that Business may receive additional compensation from Lender based on the mortgage program and
terms Borrower has engaged Business to obtain in securing the commitment and that Business will receive a sum in the range
of ___% to ___% of the total loan amount. This additional compensation, the exact amount of which will be disclosed at the
time of closing, is part of the total brokerage fee due Business. In no event will the brokerage fee, additional compensation
included, exceed the maximum fee permitted by the applicable state law.

IV. APPLICATION FEE
An application fee is charged for the initial cost of processing, verifying, and preparing your loan package to submit to a lender
for commitment, and will be credited against the amount the Borrower owes if closing occurs. This fee is ____Refundable
____Nonrefundable ____ Applicable to your closing costs at the time of the settlement of your loan. Business acknowledges the
receipt of $____ as an Application Fee.

V. DEPOSIT
Business acknowledges the deposit of $___ will be used toward the costs incurred by the Business, or by third party, on behalf of
Borrower, to pay expenses necessary to secure the mortgage loan commitment. Actual costs incurred by the Business for items listed
on Good Faith Estimate are nonrefundable, even if the mortgage loan commitment is not received. In the event of default by the
Borrower, Business is authorized to immediately disburse from the deposit all sums then due Business or any third party. The disbursement is not a waiver of any other sums due Business by Borrower, as more fully enumerated herein. Money retained by Business
as the deposit shall be returned to the Borrower, within 60 days of disposition of the loan, in accordance with the following:

  (a) the services for which the money is expended are not performed,
  (b) the services for which the money is expended are performed, but there is an excess amount that would be paid as bro-
      kerage fee but this commitment is not obtained.

VI. SERVICES TO BE PROVIDED BY MORTGAGE BROKERAGE BUSINESS
In consideration for Business earning its fee, the services to be provided by Business are: assembling information, compiling files and
completing credit application for borrower(s), processing the application file including verifying of information received and ordering
vendor reports, preparing and submitting the completed file for conditional loan commitment between borrower(s) and lender, and
any incidental services necessary to obtain commitment including courier, express mail, photographs, and telephone toll charges.

_____   _____

Applicant   Date   Mortgage Broker Business   License #

_____   _____

Applicant   Date   By   License #

STANDARDS AND DISCLOSURES

COMMITMENT: Brokerage Business hereby agrees to act on behalf of Borrower to secure a mortgage loan commitment. Brokerage Business cannot guarantee acceptance into any particular loan program or promise that any specific loan terms or conditions will be obtained. Receipt of a mortgage loan commitment by Brokerage Business satisfies Brokerage Business's obligation under the Mortgage Brokerage Business Contract and Good Faith Estimate of Borrower's Costs and the terms of this contract are deemed fulfilled upon receipt of the mortgage loan commitment. Brokerage Business cannot make a mortgage loan or a Mortgage Loan Commitment. A Commitment may, however, be passed through to the Borrower if received from a lender. The term "Commitment" shall mean a written or oral Commitment received by the Brokerage Business, unless otherwise agreed in writing between Brokerage Business and Borrower. Upon demand by the Borrower, the Brokerage Business shall produce for the Borrower's inspection evidence of the mortgage loan commitment.

AGENCY; NONLIABILITY FOR LENDER'S ACTS: Borrower acknowledges that Brokerage Business is acting as an "agent" on behalf of the Borrower in securing a mortgage commitment pursuant to this Agreement. Borrower acknowledges that Brokerage Business shall not be responsible for any errors of the Lender or Investor nor for any term or condition of the loan documentation that may be contrary to any federal law. Brokerage Business shall not be responsible for any nonperformance of a commitment or mortgage by any Lender or Investor.

LITIGATION: In the event of any litigation arising out of this Agreement, Brokerage Business shall be entitled to all costs incurred, including attorney's fees, whether before trial, at trial, on appeal, or in any other administrative or quasi-judicial proceedings.

ADDITIONAL CLAUSES: If not precluded by the provisions of this Agreement, any loan commitment and loan obtained by Brokerage Business may contain such additional clauses or provisions as the Lender may request including but not limited to, nonassumable clauses, late fee clauses and prepayment penalties.

TIME FOR PAYMENT: Unless otherwise agreed between Brokerage Business and Borrower, the mortgage brokerage fee shall be due and payable in full upon delivery to the Borrower of mortgage loan commitment from the Lender or Investor, or may be paid at closing, if agreed to by Brokerage Business.

DECISION: In applying for this loan, Borrower acknowledges that Borrower has reviewed his or her personal and financial situation and that it is in Borrower's best interest to proceed with the loan. Borrower further acknowledges that Borrower has not relied on the advice of the Mortgage Brokerage Business or its colleagues as to wisdom of doing so.

GOOD FAITH ESTIMATE OF COSTS: The estimated costs stated may be expressed as a range of possible costs and can be charged only when such costs have actually been incurred in connection with securing the loan or loan commitment. Actual costs incurred for items which include, but are not limited to, express mail fees, long distance calls, and photographs will be paid by Borrower unless otherwise stated herein.

TITLE: Borrower represents and warrants that he or she is the fee simple titleholder to the property described in this Agreement and there are no liens, judgments, unpaid taxes, or mortgages, which will affect title to the property except Borrower agrees to pay all costs necessary to clear any defect if status of the title differs from the representation made herein

DEFAULT: If commitment is secured and title is not found to be good, marketable and insurable by the attorney or title company acting for the lender, or the Borrower refuses to execute and deliver the documents required by the lender, or in any other way fails to comply with this Agreement, or if for any reason the loan referenced to herein cannot be closed through no fault of the Brokerage Business, Borrower acknowledges that the full brokerage fee has been earned by Brokerage Business and agrees to immediately pay same plus any and all costs incurred on Borrower's behalf.

DISCLOSURE: Borrower acknowledges that Brokerage Business has advised him or her of any existing business relationship Brokerage Business has with any vendor. Borrower also acknowledges that Lender may require that certain preapproved vendors be used exclusively for services required by this agreement. Brokerage Business has no business relationship with any vendor except as may be listed on attached Provider Relationship form.

SEVERABILITY OF CLAUSES CONTAINED HEREIN: In the event that any part or portion of this Agreement is held invalid or unlawful through any administrative, quasi-judicial, or judicial proceeding, the invalidity or illegality thereof shall not affect the validity of this Agreement as a whole and the other provisions and terms contained herein shall remain in full force and effect as if the illegal or invalid provision had been eliminated.

_____		_____	
Applicant	Date	Applicant	Date

SAMPLE APPLICATION DISCLOSURE

Date: Loan Number:

Lender:

Borrower(s):

Property Address:

ADVANCE UP-FRONT FEES

The following fees are being charged in connection with the processing of your loan application. Other fees not shown here may be payable later and are shown on the RESPA Good Faith Estimate. Nonrefundable fees are subject to applicable limitations of state and/or federal law.

Name of Fee	Amount	Important Information
Application Fee	_____	The application fee will be applied toward the cost of processing of the loan. The fee is nonrefundable.
Appraisal Fee	_____	The deposit will be applied toward the total cost of the appraisal, which may exceed the amount of the deposit. The deposit is refundable only if the loan is denied or withdrawn prior to the Lender ordering the appraisal.
Credit Report Fee	_____	The deposit will be applied toward the total cost of the credit report, which may exceed the amount of the deposit. The deposit is refundable only if the loan is denied or withdrawn prior to the Lender ordering the credit report.

This agreement will remain in effect for _____days, at which time you can require a refund of the monies paid by you to the Lender for nonperformance.

Unless prohibited by law, you are entitled to the return of all documents provided by you or at your expense to the Lender, upon your request, if your application for a mortgage loan is declined by or on behalf of the Lender or canceled by you.

[Enter state law regulation]

By signing below, you acknowledge receipt of this disclosure.

BY:_____

Lender Representative

_____   _____

Borrower   Date   Borrower   Date

SAMPLE ANTI-COERCION INSURANCE DISCLOSURE

Date: Loan Number:

Lender:

Borrower(s):

Property Address:

The lender **shall not require** that you, upon financing the purchase of real property or lending money on the security of real property, as a condition precedent, concurrent, or subsequent to financing the purchase of such property or renewal or extension to lending money upon the security of a mortgage thereon, **negotiate any policy of insurance, or renewal thereof through a particular insurer, agent, solicitor, or broker**. The lender may, for reasonable cause, refuse to accept the insurance provided by you based on the financial ratings and strength of the insurer.

{Enter state law regulation}

By signing below, you acknowledge receipt of this disclosure.

_____   _____

Borrower   Date   Borrower   Date

_____   _____

Borrower   Date   Borrower   Date

Watch your thoughts; they become words.
Watch your words; they become actions.
Watch your actions; they become habits.
Watch your habits; they become character.
Watch your character; it becomes your destiny.

INDEX

ABOUT THE AUTHOR

 Originally from New York City, **Darrin J. Seppinni** went to California in 1982 and began his mortgage career. One of America's leading authorities on becoming a loan officer and mortgage broker, Darrin has more than two decades of experience as a top-producing loan officer, manager, and trainer, helping both new loan officers and mortgage brokers reach their goals by providing the most up-to-date resources, training, and employment opportunities. He is a licensed real estate broker in the state of California and a member of the California Association of Mortgage Brokers and the National Association of Mortgage Brokers.

Darrin is founder of Mortgage Smarts, LLC, an education and training company, which focuses on career and business development strategies that deliver results in one of the most financially rewarding businesses today. He is also the author of *The Mortgage Originator Success Kit*. He lives in Newport Beach, California.

For more information, visit: www.mortgage-smarts.com; telephone: 800-442-5028 (toll free); e-mail: darrin@mortgage-smarts.com.